Testing Student Learning, Evaluating Teaching Effectiveness

*The Hoover Institution gratefully acknowledges
the following individuals and foundations for their
significant support of the*

**Initiative
on**
American Public Education

KORET FOUNDATION
TAD AND DIANNE TAUBE
TAUBE FAMILY FOUNDATION
LYNDE AND HARRY BRADLEY FOUNDATION
BOYD AND JILL SMITH
JACK AND MARY LOIS WHEATLEY
FRANKLIN AND CATHERINE JOHNSON
JERRY AND PATTI HUME
BERNARD LEE SCHWARTZ FOUNDATION
S.D. BECHTEL, JR. FOUNDATION

Testing Student Learning, Evaluating Teaching Effectiveness

Edited by
Williamson M. Evers and Herbert J. Walberg

HOOVER INSTITUTION PRESS
STANFORD UNIVERSITY
STANFORD, CALIFORNIA

www.hoover.org

Hoover Institution Press Publication No. 521

First printing 2004
11 10 09 08 07 06 05 04   9 8 7 6 5 4 3 2 1

Manufactured in the United States of America

The paper used in this publication meets the minimum requirements
of the American National Standard for Information Sciences—
Permanence of Paper for Printed Library Materials, ANSI Z39.48–1992.

Library of Congress Cataloging-in-Publication Data

Testing student learning, evaluating teaching effectiveness /
Williamson M. Evers and Herbert J. Walberg, editors.
     p. cm.
  Includes bibliographical references and index.
  ISBN 0-8179-2982-7 (pbk. : alk. paper)
  1. Educational tests and measurements—United States.
  2. Educational accountability—United States.   3. Teacher
  effectiveness—United States. I. Evers, Williamson M., 1948–
  II. Walberg, Herbert J., 1937–
  LB3051.T4425 2004
  371.14'4—dc22
                                2004001558

Contents

Introduction and Overview

Williamson M. Evers and Herbert J. Walberg

Schooling is one of the top domestic policy issues of the day, and testing and the effectiveness of teaching, broadly considered, are among the top issues in education. Nearly all states have developed standards and have begun state testing programs in the last several years. The 2002 federal No Child Left Behind act makes testing and accountability policies even more crucial because poorly performing schools may be closed; already many failing schools must allow and pay for their students to attend successful schools.

More than ever, parents want to know how their children are achieving and how their children's school ranks compared with others or with standards. Testing and evaluating districts', schools', and staff members' teaching results are enduring concerns. Today they are particularly timely and are the reasons for this book.

Purposes of Testing and Public Policy

Of course, tests can serve a variety of purposes. For example, educators can use them to pinpoint students' strengths and weaknesses to plan curricula and adopt teaching practices tailored to their needs, both as individuals and groups. State legislators increasingly want to know how schools rank, and local school boards should be studying the results of their programs, curriculum offerings, and staff efforts. Parents can contribute more to their children's learning if they understand their progress, and, increasingly, they can choose their children's school partly on the basis of publicly available school report cards, which reveal, to a greater or lesser degree, the quality or effectiveness of teaching.

Achievement test scores certainly do not reveal all the important outcomes of schooling nor can they form a comprehensive index of the quality of teaching. Nonetheless, well-designed commercial and state-developed tests usually provide reliable indications of the academic knowledge and skills children acquire largely in school, and no one has shown that these reasonable goals require sacrificing other objectives, such as character development. Even though some education experts and even some testing experts may disagree, Congress, state legislators, and citizens are increasingly insistent on such objective testing and accountability for measuring the results of teaching.

Such priorities are matters of public policy to be decided by citizens and their representatives rather than only by educators and testing experts on professional and technical grounds—since their interests may not be identical. The authors of the chapters in this book unabashedly and critically examine controversial professional, technical, and public policy issues that may divide educators and experts from citizens and their representatives.

Setting the Stage

Herbert Walberg begins by showing why citizens and legislators have become increasingly concerned about American student achievement and why they increasingly maintain that tests and standards are necessary. Though the achievement of American students is comparable with that of students in other countries when American students begin school, they fall increasingly behind as they progress through the grades. By the end of high school, their achievement is near the bottom of advanced countries, despite American schools' being close to the top in per-student spending among economically advanced countries. Walberg attributes this productivity problem to a lack of school board and staff accountability—which, in turn, requires systematic testing and standards. Among the other problems he identifies are defective tests and standards and the proclivity of educators to promote and graduate students even when they have not met proficiency standards. Ending on a positive note, he identifies ways that tests can be used to help solve America's achievement crisis.

Oddly, in this period of national crisis, some prominent testing experts have objected to testing's having an enlarged role when it comes to making "high-stakes" decisions about student promotion and graduation and to evaluate the teaching provided by districts, schools, and individual staff members. Richard Phelps describes eight common objections and shows why they are false. Among the myths he debunks are that learning is narrowed because teachers concentrate solely on what is tested; that standardized tests measure only facts; that standardized test are biased against minorities; and that standardized tests are too expensive.

Constructive Uses of Tests

This section presents several constructive uses for tests including (1) diagnosis of children's learning difficulties and evidence-based procedures for solving them, (2) the study of curriculum impacts on specific aspects of achievement, and (3) assessment of teachers' strengths and weaknesses. First, Barbara Foorman, Jack Fletcher, and David Francis cite research revealing that a weak start in reading usually prevents children from catching up with their peers, then they show how tests can help even in the child's earliest years of learning to read. They are careful to point out, however, that their own research shows assessment of early reading skills is useful only to the extent that teachers understand and act upon the results. Such assessment can help teachers, parents, administrators, and policy makers in judging the effectiveness of programs as children move forward in school.

Though agreeing that testing of students is critical for educational reform, Stan Metzenberg takes issue with the validity of the NAEP Science and Mathematics tests, finding it suspicious that student performance should correlate strongly with Reading test scores. He suggests that the learning of mathematics and science may depend upon foundational reading skills that are not supported by hands-on activities and that mathematics and science tests that are largely based on constructed-response questions may fail to serve their intended purposes. Metzenberg also finds that previous interpreters of TIMSS data are mistaken in their suggesting that too many topics are covered in the U.S. curricula. Overall, Metzenberg calls for exercising great caution in interpreting the results of NAEP Science and Mathematics tests and in drawing causal conclusions from sloppy educational research.

Alan Siegel, on the other hand, finds much value in the TIMSS filming of teaching practices. As part of the TIMSS achievement survey, researchers filmed eighth-grade mathematics lessons in Germany, Japan, and the United States. Siegel's detailed analyses of the films suggest the reasons for the outstanding performance of Japanese teachers. Like Metzenberg, Siegel finds previous assertions about TIMSS mistaken. He concludes, for example, that Japanese teachers actively teach students rather than letting them discover mathematical ideas on their own. In fact, Japanese teachers engage in more lecturing and demonstration than even the most traditional American teachers. In short, Siegel's analyses refute the claim of many education theorists that student discovery rather than expert teaching primarily determines outstanding performance of Japanese students on the mathematics tests.

Constructive Tests for Accountability

Essay examinations, live performances, and portfolios of students' work can provide insights for classroom teachers about what their students have learned. But should they be used, as many contend, for purposes of large-scale accountability? The chapters in this section refute this common contention.

Brian Stecher reviews California, Kentucky, Pittsburgh, Pennsylvania, and Vermont "portfolio assessments," that is, ratings of collections of students' work products. He finds the poor reliability of the ratings severely limits their validity in measuring student progress and the teaching effectiveness of districts, schools, and teachers. Portfolio assessments, moreover, are expensive to score compared with multiple-choice tests, and they require large amounts of teacher and student time without adding to the validity of accountability programs. Portfolios are, however, effective tools for changing instructional practices, and their greatest potential may lie in their use as classroom assessment tools rather than large-scale accountability measures.

William Mehrens similarly concludes that "performance assessments" are problematic in providing useful information for holding educators accountable. Performance assessments require students to "construct" answers rather than to choose the best answers, as on multiple-choice tests. Performance assessments usually do not meet technical standards of reliability, validity, and objectivity and are subject to legal challenge when used for purposes of accountability. They are more expensive and more subject to bias and breaches of security than multiple-choice tests, which have a long record of measuring student knowledge and skills effectively, efficiently, and objectively.

State Testing Policies

State legislatures have largely initiated testing initiatives to hold school boards and educators accountable for student achievement. Even the new federal No Child Left Behind act gives states considerable latitude in determining the nature and content of accountability tests. For these reasons, the last section of this book presents case studies of successful and unsuccessful state testing initiatives and concludes with recommendations for improved policies.

In a case study of Kentucky's state testing and accountability program, George Cunningham describes the lessons that can be drawn from a state's failure to carefully plan and execute education policies. In his view, these lessons include (1) avoiding the claim that all students can learn at the same high level, (2) delineating the content to be covered by the curriculum and tests, (3) employing normative rather than absolute standards, and (4) preferring multiple-choice tests. Cunningham provides a number of other insights that should be considered by policy makers.

Darvin Winick and Sandy Kress offer a counterexample. State testing policy, they show, has worked well in Texas. They identify four factors as most important: leadership, accountability, decentralization, and external pressure for achievement results. Their extensive consideration of accountability is highly pertinent to this volume. In Texas, the state's successful accountability system included clear curriculum standards, objectives for each grade and campus, widely distributed reports on student achievement, and substantial consequences for accomplishments and failures. Several of the elements of the Texas accountability system form the basis of the recent federal No Child Left Behind act, which is intended, among other things, to influence state-level testing and teaching accountability in other states.

Conclusion

Well-educated young people tend to prosper and contribute much to our economic, cultural, and civic life. Yet American educators and students are not living up to their potential, even though taxpayers have generously supported their efforts. The chapters in this book show the ways forward: Tests results can show educators' and students' strengths and weaknesses as a basis for planning. Test results can inform educators and students of their progress or lack thereof and thus serve to reward and sanction their actions. Test results can reveal the degree to which educational products, programs, and practices are working and thus inform state and local school boards about choices they face. In these and other ways described in the subsequent chapters, tests can play a vital role in improving American schools.

This book stems from an October 1998 Hoover Institution symposium entitled "Testing America's Schoolchildren." The talks by George Cunningham, Barbara Foorman, Sandy Kress, Stan Metzenberg, Brian Stecher, and Herb Walberg at that conference were based on papers written for this volume. These papers have been revised in the intervening time to bring them up to date. In addition, the editors selected three important articles written in the past decade by Richard Phelps, Alan Siegel, and William Mehrens to round out the book's coverage of testing and teaching practices.[1]

The editors wish to thank all those who contributed their papers or wrote original chapters for this volume. In addition, we thank Marion Joseph and Jerry Hume for inspiration and suggestions on participants for the original symposium. Hoover Institution director John Raisian supported this endeavor as part of the institution's Initiative on American Public Education. Senior associate director Richard Sousa aided in the preparation for the symposium and the publishing of the book. Executive editor Patricia Baker oversaw the production of the book, and Ann Wood and Joan D. Saunders were responsible for the copyediting. Kate Feinstein and Elizabeth Maples provided the editors with research assistance for the preparation of this volume.

Notes

1. Original places of publication: Richard P. Phelps, "Why Testing Experts Hate Testing," Fordham Report (Thomas B. Fordham Foundation) 3, no. 1 (January 1999); Alan R. Siegel, "Effective Teaching and the TIMSS Observational Study," http://www.cs.nyu.edu/cs/faculty/siegel/; William A. Mehrens, "Using Performance Assessment for Accountability Purposes," *Educational Measurement: Issues and Practice* 11, no. 1 (spring 1992), 3–9, 20.

Part One

Setting the Stage

Chapter 1

Examinations for Educational Productivity

Herbert J. Walberg

This chapter addresses three questions: (1) Where do U.S. schools stand on international examinations relative to those in other affluent countries? (2) Why do they do so poorly at such great cost? (3) How can examinations help? I argue that objective examinations, though imperfect, are reasonable measures of important results of schooling. Though they may not tell the whole story, they can be readily employed to discover effective practices, to improve accountability, and to evaluate choice experiments. Other examinations, such as portfolios and laboratory exercises, are appropriate for assessing students' classroom work but have proven costly and impractical for evaluating schools and districts. In any case, it is important to employ value-added measures to assess the contributions of schools, programs, and staff.

Examinations can be keys to improving the productivity of U.S. schools. Educational policy makers can employ them to evaluate educational organizations, policies, and programs to determine which are most effective and efficient. Value-added analyses of examination results offer a way to achieve their policy and accountability purposes.

In a free society, however, consumer choice would seem to offer the ultimate and best accountability. Since private and public scholarships are unlikely to predominate soon, examinations can serve to help evaluate various means and degrees of enlarging choice and competition in the educational systems.

Where Do U.S. Schools Stand?

It is increasingly well-known that our secondary school students score poorly on objective examinations compared with those in other economically advanced countries. By such standards, our high school students have long done poorly in these subjects, although primary school students have scored nearer to the average. These differences suggest that our students make poor progress during the school years. But how much worse is their progress relative to that of students in other countries? My report for the Thomas B. Fordham Foundation took up this question and compiled all recent achievement comparisons.[1]

The report compared advanced countries that are members of the Organization for Economic Cooperation and Development in North America, the Pacific Rim, and Western Europe. Among schools in OECD countries, those in the United States made the smallest achievement gains. The longer U.S. students were in school, the further they fell behind students in the other countries. Yet per-student expenditures on U.S. schools are among the very highest. More specifically:

1. In reading, science, and mathematics through eighth grade, U.S. schools ranked last in four of five comparisons of achievement progress. In the fifth case, they ranked second to last.

2. Between eighth grade and the final year of secondary school, U.S. schools slipped further behind those in other countries.

3. Because they made the least progress, U.S. secondary schools ranked last in mathematics attainment and second to last in science—far from the goal to be first in the world by the year 2000, set by the fifty governors and endorsed by Congress and the 1996 presidential candidates.

4. U.S. per-student spending (adjusted for purchasing power) on primary and secondary schools was third-highest among more than twenty advanced countries.

5. Unlike in the past, more secondary school students remain in school on average in comparable countries than in the United States. Thus, their superior gains do not depend merely on student selectivity or higher dropout rates.

6. Because they made the poorest progress and ranked in the highest category of expenditures, U.S. schools, by internationally agreed-upon standards, are the least productive among those in comparable economically advanced countries.

Value-Added Comparisons

These conclusions are based on the most recent, largest, and most rigorous international achievement surveys. Unlike other reports, the conclusions concern the value added largely by schools as indexed by progress made by students during the school years.

Value-added scores are particularly important in evaluating schools. Consider the case of reading. Until children start school at about age six, families, media, and other agencies—rather than schools—are the chief sources of influence on vocabulary and comprehension. For this reason, children start school with widely varying degrees of preparation. Some parents but not others, for example, teach their children to read before first grade. The big education question is: How much progress do students make after they start school?

Static comparisons of schools (employed in the past) are less useful for this purpose because students' tests scores are partly determined by their experiences before they begin school, attributable to parental efforts, socioeconomic status, and related factors. Thus, gains in achievement during the school years are better indexes of schools' contributions to learning than scores at a single point in time.

Gains, progress, and value added—terms used synonymously here—are particularly important for policy. They allow predictions of eventual attainments. Policies that do not add satisfactory value may be revised. Units of the system, such as primary and secondary schools, may be separately evaluated by measuring students' progress while under their responsibility. In addition, many economists, psychologists, and others believe incentives influence performance. For this reason, principals should give merit raises for recent progress rather than for degrees and years of experience, for which most teachers are paid. If carrots and sticks were employed in education, value-added progress would be one reasonable indicator of teaching merit.

Educational policy makers increasingly recognize the usefulness of value-added indicators. Internationally, the OECD pioneered the use of value-added indicators in the 1995 edition of *Education at a Glance*[2] and has employed them in subsequent reports. Similarly, Dallas, Texas, and Tennessee are employing value-added indicators and incentives to increase school productivity. Other cities and states, such as Chicago and Virginia, employ static indicators to assign schools to probation and, in cases of failure to progress, eventual extinction. Such systems identify schools that serve poor children but that are not ineffective. A fairer and more efficient evaluation system would employ value-added indicators as at least one consideration in evaluating schools.

Why Do U.S. Schools Do So Poorly?

Several problems appear to account for poor productivity of U.S. public schools. After reviewing these, we can consider how effective practices, better accountability, and enlarged choice together with objective examinations may help solve them.

Lack of State Standards

Unlike many other countries, the U.S. education system has no education ministry nor well-defined national goals, curriculum, or testing system. The U.S. system leaves states largely responsible for providing schools, but states leave varying amounts of discretion to local boards. What is taught in classrooms, in turn, is highly variable even within the same school and district. For these reasons, a teacher in any grade cannot depend on what the teacher in the previous grade has taught. The lack of coordination across grades and subjects is especially harmful to children who move, particularly if they also are poor.[3]

Lack of standards means that state and local boards can hardly assess progress made by districts, schools, and teachers. To the extent that curriculum and goals vary, it is difficult to compare schools, which makes accountability for results nearly impossible.

Centralized Finance and Control

Despite the lack of uniform standards and accountability, the governance and funding of public schools have become more centralized in the last half-century, leading to other kinds of inefficiency. States have increasingly assumed responsibility for educational finance, goals, and operations. They paid ever-larger shares of school costs, but the higher the state's share, the worse the state's achievement, despite vast increases in inflation-adjusted per-student spending. Higher state shares make local school boards and administrators less accountable to local citizens since they need not justify expenditures as carefully.[4] California's tie for last place in recent national reading assessments may be attributable to whole-language teaching and highly centralized state funding rather than the greater local control and accountability afforded by local funding.

Larger state shares also entail increased regulation, reporting, bureaucracy, and distraction from learning. Much energy goes into the question of who governs—the federal government, the state, the local district, the school, or the teacher. It is nearly impossible to affix responsibility for results.

Schools and school districts, moreover, have increasingly con-
solidated into larger units that achieve less. Over the course of a
recent fifty-year period, average school enrollments in the United
States multiplied by a factor of five, even though large schools
tend to be more bureaucratic, impersonal, and less humane. Large
middle and junior high schools tend to departmentalize and
employ specialized teachers and ancillary staff who confine themselves to their specialties rather than imparting a broad view of
knowledge. The teachers in large, departmentalized schools tend
to know their students much less well than teachers who have the
same students for most subjects for nearly the whole day.

About a half-century ago, there were 115,000 U.S. school districts; now there are about 15,000, the largest of which tend to be
least effective. The reasons for their inefficiency are best seen in
New York and other large cities that have up to 900 schools. In
such huge districts, school board members can hardly name the
schools let alone hold them accountable.[5]

On the other hand, small adjacent public school districts and
private schools within districts give rise to incentives that cause
all schools to compete and raise their productivity, that is, raise
achievement and student retention while lowering costs. Choice
plans that allow students to cross school and district boundaries
may also prove to increase competition and productivity. Choice
among schools, nonetheless, is severely constrained, which helps
account for poor U.S. productivity.

Lack of Board Accountability

School boards frequently split into factions. And few members
have extensive board, business, or education experience. Often
serving limited terms, they seem more interested in personnel
and ideological issues than in whether the schools are achieving
results. Assessing learning progress, moreover, requires some
mastery of educational productivity research, psychometrics, and
statistics, just as assessing businesses' progress requires accounting
and other skills. Few board members or educational administrators have mastered such skills. Instead, they take up such fads as

Ebonics, whole language, authentic tests, and bilingual education—the success of which remain undemonstrated in randomized experiments or statistically controlled research.

Unaccountable Management

Public schools are government-subsidized quasi-monopolies. They are unchallenged by entrepreneurial leadership and the incentives, efficiency, and consumer appeal provided by market competition. With legislators and school boards often under their thumbs, teachers' unions and administrators can exploit forced-choice customers in service of their interests in minimizing workload and maximizing pay and perquisites.

In particular, teachers' unions—few call them professional associations—have actually done well for their members. In college, education majors typically have scored worst or near worst on ability tests among undergraduate majors. Yet as teachers, they have a 180-day school year—the shortest among teachers in industrialized countries (and much less than the 220 or so days most salaried U.S. professionals normally work). In large cities and elsewhere, according to contract, many teachers are in school only about six hours daily. Some grade papers in the evening, but many professionals take work home. In addition, teachers have little accountability, nearly inviolable tenure, and early and generous pensions that increasingly threaten city and state budgets.

Teachers' unions have done better for themselves than for their members. During the last half-century when membership in private-sector unions declined, teachers' unions increased their membership. They contracted for expensive smaller classes, which do little for learning. With fixed budgets, smaller classes actually mean lower teacher salaries because costs must be spread among more teachers. Thus, smaller classes, which increase the number of teachers, indirectly result in an increase in union membership, central coffers, and legislative influence.

Teachers' unions are understandably acting in their own interests of maximizing their benefits while reducing their efforts. It is school boards and state legislators that have been remiss in failing to provide effective management, informed stewardship, and accountability to citizens who pay the bills. School boards have hardly been a match for nationally organized unions that can bring to negotiations strong, narrow self-interests, statistical research, and specialized expertise.

Harvard and University of Chicago economists Caroline Hoxby and Samuel Peltzman showed that teachers' union success was associated with worse results for students. Their analyses showed that the sharp rise in teachers' union membership and militancy for the period 1971–1991 not only increased per-student costs dramatically but also increased dropout rates and adversely affected examination scores in the forty-eight states surveyed. As teachers' unions grew in membership, income, and power, they gained greater influence over state legislatures, which, in turn, increasingly usurped local control and left the schools increasingly ineffective and unaccountable to local taxpayers.[6]

Lack of Incentives

American schools provide little incentive for educators and students to attain higher standards. A 1996 Public Agenda national survey of high school students showed that three-fourths believe stiffer examinations and graduation requirements would make students pay more attention to their studies. Three-fourths also said students who have not mastered English should not graduate, and a similar percentage said schools should promote only students who master the material. Almost two-thirds reported they could do much better in school if they tried. Nearly 80 percent said students would learn more if schools made sure they were on time and did their homework. More than 70 percent said schools should require after-school classes for those earning Ds and Fs.[7]

In these respects, many teacher educators differ sharply from students and the public. A 1997 Public Agenda survey of education professors showed that 64 percent think schools should avoid competition. More favored giving grades for team efforts than for individual accomplishments.

Teacher educators also differ from employers and other professions on preferred ways of measuring standards or even employing such measures at all. Many employers use standardized multiple-choice examinations with job candidates. So do selective colleges and graduate and professional schools with candidates for admission. Such examinations are required in law, medicine, and other fields for licensing because they are objective and reliable. In the case of teachers, academic mastery (as indicated by objective examination results and completion of rigorous courses) influences their students' achievement. Yet, 78 percent of teacher educators wanted less reliance on objective examinations.[8]

Because of such views, schools—the very institutions that should academically prepare youth for doing well in adult life—make little use of high-stakes examinations and effective incentives for accomplishments. School boards and administrators, for example, rarely measure and reward teachers' individual performance. Unions prevail in contracts that require paying public school teachers according to their degrees and years of experience, neither of which affects how much their students learn. After decades of declining union membership in other sectors, schools remain one of the few institutions that provide no merit incentives for their workforce.

The Social Promotion Disincentive

Examinations can allow educators to employ sticks as well as carrots. Consider the case of social promotion. Perhaps because the U.S. school system lacks accountability and incentives, students are usually promoted from one grade to the next whether they have or have not mastered the subject matter. Promoting failed students, however, does many harms. It wrongly informs them that they have learned what they need to know. It robs them of motivation. Why study if you know you will be promoted and graduate?

Such social promotion mixes failed students and successful students, which reduces teachers' effectiveness. They must teach things either that the successful students already know or that the failed students are yet incapable of learning. In the long run, social promotion is unfair because the same high school diploma goes to all students whether they have earned it or not. This debases the value of diplomas—employers cannot depend on graduates' knowing what they should—and colleges and universities are forced to offer expensive programs and remedial courses for students to learn what they should have mastered in high school.

To reverse this common pattern, Chicago and other cities are instituting summer school for failing students. To be promoted, they must make satisfactory progress over the summer months. A longer school year seems appropriate in any case. In *A Nation at Risk,* the National Commission on Excellence in Education pointed out that the United States has the shortest school year in the industrialized world—only 180 days in contrast to about 200 in Europe and 240 in Japan.[9]

Harris Cooper of the University of Missouri, moreover, compiled thirty-nine studies of the "summer slump." The studies show achievement declines over the long summer vacation, especially among low-income, urban students.[10]

The first year of Chicago's summer program showed that the students gained substantially during the summer. Though about a fourth were not promoted to the next grade, they still had time to make up for lost ground.[11] They now also have the advantage of knowing that Chicago schools take standards seriously.

It is hardly a new insight that more study and classroom time increases learning. Indeed, it is one of the most consistent findings in educational and psychological research. Nearly all 130 surveys and experiments I compiled show the positive effect of more learning time.[12] What seems to be lacking are examination standards and incentives to elicit the learning time that would substantially raise achievement.

Defective Assessment Examinations

One of the latest harmful fads in education is "authentic" tests. Those who accept this terminology must subscribe to the view that other tests are "inauthentic." As the term is often used in education circles, authentic tests consist of examinations that require recalled, or constructed, responses, as in essay questions, rather than examinations that offer a choice of correct answers among alternatives, as in standardized multiple-choice tests. Examples of authentic tests are oral examinations, laboratory exercises in science, musical and other performance exhibitions, and art and writing portfolios. Such so-called authentic tests, however, are hardly new; they have worked well in classrooms for decades if not centuries. What is new about them is using them in wide-scale surveys for school comparison, assessment, and accountability purposes.

Though the authentic-testing movement of the last decade is new and good, the new parts are not good, and the good parts are not new. The virtues of multiple-choice tests for large-scale assessment are that they are objective, reliable, valid, cheap, and hard to corrupt. They can widely sample students' knowledge of sixty ideas in as many minutes, whereas an essay examination may sample only one or two ideas. Multiple-choice tests can be made very difficult as in two- and three-step mathematics and science items. For these reasons, multiple-choice tests are most often employed in selection decisions for universities, graduate and professional schools, employment, and professional licensure in law, medicine, and other fields.[13]

In contrast, authentic tests used in large-scale assessments are easily compromised because a few essay questions or laboratory exercises are readily leaked. Even when students have mastered a few prespecified or leaked questions before examinations, they often do poorly on similar problems that are stated slightly differently or pertain to a different context. Also, in a given amount of time, such tests can only sample a limited number of ideas and skills. And finally, zealous parents can construct art, writing, and science portfolios.

These problems have long been known, and common sense would rule against the use of such examinations in large-scale assessments, particularly without small-scale trial assessments.

Nonetheless, it took very expensive, statewide trials of such examinations in California, Kentucky, and Vermont to prove what would seem obvious.

None of this is to say that traditional classroom examinations should be ruled out of large-scale assessments. But because they are far more expensive and rarely meet technical standards, they need to meet a high burden of proof of the additional value they bring to an assessment. Empirical studies of scores on well-designed "constructed-answer" tests show that they tend to rank students similarly to the rankings made by multiple-choice tests.

What "authentic tests" seem to bring to assessment, as demonstrated so far, is seemingly insuperable difficulties and prohibitively high costs. No wonder they are supported by those who wish to evade accountability.

The Governance Problem

The accompanying figure (Figure 1.1) broadly illustrates the governance problems that make U.S. schools unproductive. Ideally, schools should be as quickly and accurately responsive to individual consumer preferences as markets; they should reflect what local citizens and parents desire. But they can exert only indirect, cumbersome, slow-acting influence through elective processes of Congress, state legislators, and local school boards. What these governing agencies deliver might at best be an average preference of their constituents—but education tastes obviously vary.

Notwithstanding individual and local preferences, taxes are determined, collected, funneled, constrained, and filtered through national, state, and local governments. California, Hawaii, and the District of Columbia, for example, severely constrain variations on what local districts spend. States increasingly regulate local districts and induce them to follow what seems best in state capitols, which are often subject to special concentrated interests. So citizens cannot easily suit schools to their own preferences; their influence is indirect, attenuated, and interpreted by others.

FIGURE I.I   Flow of Money and Influence

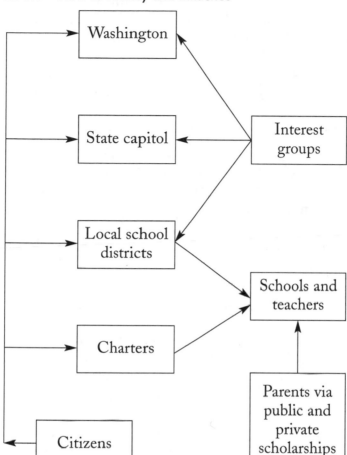

How state tax monies for schools are spent is strongly influenced by special interests, particularly teachers' unions, and the education administrators at the several levels. They have strong, well-defined interests, such as higher salaries, a short school year, an absence of competition, and no accountability—hardly identical with the public's interest or students' interests. Their interests make it worthwhile for status quo providers to follow and influence legislation and policy implementation.[14] In contrast, parents cannot afford the time to study and modify voluminous, complex legislation and rule making that may affect their children.

The federal government pays only about 6 percent of the public school bill. It exerts much more influence, however, through regulations and various financial inducements for states to do things Washington's way. Federal categorical programs such as bilingual and special education grew mightily and created large self-interested bureaucratic units in state departments of education and local school districts, which is a major reason for the United States' having the highest administrative costs among affluent countries.[15] In any case, citizens' and parents' voices are hard to hear, and they are hardly a match for the status quo special interests.

How Can Examinations Help?

Three alternatives promise increased productivity: (1) employing more effective methods, (2) improving accountability, and (3) expanding local control, particularly through citizen and parent choice. Since choice enhances practices and increases accountability, it seems by far the best alternative.[16] Still, statewide public scholarships cannot be expected next month. Under the influence of special interests and the latest fads, Congress, state legislators, and school boards seem likely to increase accountability and regulate local practices by fiats, carrots, or sticks. Whatever combination of practices, accountability schemes, and choice ensues in a given city or state, achievement examinations can serve to evaluate results.

Examinations for Evaluating Education Methods

During the last half-century, scholars have published hundreds of randomized experimental studies of methods of instruction in dozens of journals, largely employing standardized objective examinations to evaluate the comparative results. During the past ten years, much of this was reviewed in edited handbooks of research on instruction in science, mathematics, foreign language, and the other school subjects, some of them running to 900 double-columned pages by dozens of specialized chapter authors.

Synthesizing Research

A project sponsored by twenty-eight professional education organizations further condensed these works to 170 pages.[17] The specialized handbook editors, including my own work on generic methods, described in a page or two each of ten most effective teaching strategies. These include such traditional methods as direct instruction and mastery learning. Some newer methods, such as reciprocal teaching and employing "wait time" for students to answer science questions, are also discussed.

The evidence on the effect of the amount of time for study is particularly voluminous. Of 376 estimates of its effects, 88 percent were positive—one of the most consistent findings in education research. The sizes of the effects are moderate over a week or a semester; so time is hardly a short-term panacea. Over many years, however, student engagement in classes and in homework time yields huge benefits.

In a 1999 article,[18] I compiled the numerical sizes of effects of some 275 educational practices, some generic, others for separate subject matters. Some practices are several times more effective than others. Other things being equal, these should be chosen more often. Yet effective practices are often unemployed or poorly employed. Instead of relying on research, educators have often gone from fad to fad such as whole-language teaching, which had little basis in control-group research employing objective examinations.

Countering Biased Evaluations

Standard national examinations also can help with a growing problem of program self-evaluation. Some federally funded and foundation-funded groups have designed and evaluated their own programs. What would seem an obvious conflict of interest has been generally overlooked. Two of these programs, Success for All and Reading Recovery, have reported superior results and have been widely popular despite their high costs. Their designers, however, carried out evaluations that in several ways biased the results in favor of their own programs.[19] Chief among these built-in biases was comparing their programs with others using tests that directly reflected what they were teaching. Combined with independent evaluations, standard examinations can help protect consumers in giving more objective estimates of program efficacy.

Identifying Promising Technologies

Although some were developed during the last decade, the effective programs discussed above are conventional and make little use of computer, electronic, and other technologies. Some technologies, however, offer the possibility of not only greater effectiveness but also lower costs and student convenience. We may immediately think of the Internet, but we have little solid research on its present or potential effects on learning. Distance learning may be a better example. As I learned in a survey I carried out for World Bank,[20] distance learning can free students from the limitations of space, time, and age and has a record of success in high- and low-income countries. Broadcast media, moreover, can multiply the effects of both books and traditional teaching.

Distance learning can include correspondence texts, books, newspaper supplements, posters, radio and television broadcasts, audio and video cassettes, films, computer-assisted learning, and self-instructional kits, as well as such local activities as supervision, supplementary teaching, tutoring, counseling, and student self-help groups. Scarce resources of scientific, pedagogical, and media expertise concentrated in development centers can be spread widely. The shortage of mathematics and science teachers in the United States and elsewhere are good reasons for employing distance programs.

Distance approaches can be highly cost-effective when large numbers of students follow the same preproduced courses. Far more than a single teacher working alone, distance courses can incorporate validated subject matter and systematic instructional design and spread developmental costs over thousands of students. In rural areas such as Minnesota and Oklahoma, they can provide excellent courses in such subjects as calculus that would otherwise be unavailable. They can build on proven principles of individualized study by including clear learning objectives, self-assessment materials, student activities, and opportunity for feedback periodically or on demand. In high-density areas, the British Open University and the Chicago City Colleges have greatly enlarged opportunities for study, especially for those who cannot attend daytime classes.[21]

Objective examinations should prove helpful in identifying the best and most cost-effective of the old and new methods. Although cost, convenience, philosophical assumptions, and other considerations deserve weight, the consistency and magnitude of learning effects should be primary.

Examinations for Accountability

Since citizens pay for public schools, they should know how well the schools are doing. So also should parents, educators, legislators, and state and local school boards. To know this, they would need to compare the achievement scores of teachers, schools, and districts with one another and with standards of performance. James Coleman argued that if standards were externally set, as they are in many countries, educators could not lower them.[22] Teachers could then concentrate on helping their students meet the standards, as do coaches in competitive sports.

In addition, as Coleman emphasized, student heterogeneity needs to be taken into account if there are to be fair standards and accountability. Therefore, student progress or the value added to learning by the teacher or school during the most recent year or other time period should be the chief criterion.

The value added by a unit at each step can be the basis of accountability. This requires a measure at the end of each step so that the gains made by a student or group of students can be measured. Such value-added gains largely eliminate socioeconomic and other extraneous differences and provide a fairer basis for evaluating progress.

As shown in Figure 1.1, the present cumbersome accountability system leaves the various governing units pressured by special interests without clear responsibilities. Complex regulations at the federal, state, local, and school levels not only slow decision-making but also remove the possibility of such clear accountability and responsibility. Education providers may benefit from the present system, but it might be in their long-term best interests as a profession to increase their productivity. Together with carrots, sticks, and choice, objective examinations, if well designed and used, seem likely to increase their accountability.

Examinations and Surveys for Evaluating Choice[23]

Objective examinations and other indicators of performance are proving useful in evaluating public and private scholarships, charter schools, and other means of choice. Various experiments in privatization and "contracting out" public services to private (including for-profit) firms suggest that they respond swiftly and accurately to citizens' desires. An economist's version of "meta-analysis" (analysis of results of many studies) shows that, other things being equal, private organizations on average perform better at lower costs and that they are more satisfying to their staff and their customers.[24] Requiring performance, satisfaction, and cost indicators, these studies concern airlines, banks, bus services, debt collection, electric utilities, forestry, hospitals, housing, insurance sales and processing, railroads, refuse collection, savings and loans, slaughterhouses, water utilities, and weather forecasting. In the United States and other countries, governments are privatizing prisons, police and fire protection, and public pensions.

Objective examinations and other indicators already suggest that choice works similarly in education. One instance in the United States of a randomized experiment employing publicly funded scholarships for school students is Milwaukee.[25] Minority-children applicants to private schools were admitted at random because there were insufficient spaces to meet demand (even though the costs of the program were about half that of public schools, the state department of education created many uncertainties and difficulties, and various start-up difficulties ensued).

After several years, the selected students did significantly better on standardized tests, sufficiently well that the usual national minority-majority achievement gap could be substantially cut. Perhaps even more important and notwithstanding the start-up difficulties, parents were delighted with the private schools.

Private schools, moreover, improve public education because what public schools lack is competition; most are local monopolies. Recent research supports the value of local private competition in improving public schools. Rather than "creaming off" the best students, the presence of private schools and public schools of choice is associated with better examination performance and lower costs among nearby public schools.

Examinations and Consumer Preferences

Surveys can usefully supplement objective examinations in evaluating choice. They show that citizens increasingly favor choice in education, including private schools. A 1992 Gallup poll showed that of those polled, 70 percent supported publicly funded scholarships that include private school choice. Eighty-five percent of African Americans and 84 percent of Hispanics supported such scholarships.[26] Big-city poor and minorities particularly favor scholarships because government schools available to them are most often dominated by teachers' unions, federal categorical programs, and regulations, which make their schools unresponsive to their preferences. In Milwaukee, for example, which has had the most experience with privatization, 95 percent of African Americans favored private and public school choice, and 70 percent believed that students get a better education from independent and sectarian schools.[27]

This accords well with my recent experience as a board member of the Chicago Charter School Foundation, a publicly funded and privately governed and operated charter school of about

4,700 mostly African American and Hispanic students on seven campuses. Unlike most charters in Chicago and elsewhere, the not-for-profit board contracts with for-profit and other providers[28] of the education program. Despite the usual start-up difficulties of finding, purchasing, and refurbishing buildings and hiring an entirely new staff, the campuses have long waiting lists. Our students comprised 70 percent of the students in Chicago's charter schools. They scored best on standardized examinations among students in the charter schools.

Other behavioral indications of private preference can be cited: Consider the rise in home-schooled children from 300,000 in 1990 to about 1.5 million today. Their parents give attention, time, and money for what they think is a superior education.[29] Though they are mostly amateur teachers, their children's average achievement on standardized tests exceeds 77 percent of regular school children.

Another indication of preference for private over public education is the quiet but meteoric growth of privately funded scholarships, often concentrated on poor, big-city children. Funded by individuals, philanthropies, and firms, their numbers in seventeen cities have grown from 744 to 6,572 in a recent four-year period—further evidence of consumer preference that complements what we can learn from examination performance.[30]

Reconciling Choice and Standards

Those who favor choice should know that most American schools are unlikely to be funded through public and private scholarships today. Powerful special interests—the teachers' unions and other education lobbying groups—adamantly oppose school choice, especially free choice by parents. These groups strongly influence legislators, school boards, and the mass media. They have, for example, severely restricted the number and nature of charter schools.

For choice advocates, it seems reasonable to avoid both incrementalism and radicalism while collecting more evidence. Aside from consumer preference, the best evidentiary criteria are high scores on objective achievement tests in the standard school subjects. These should be employed in experiments to evaluate the many variations on choice that have been proposed. Once these experiments have been completed, there may be less need for evidence. Even so, it seems likely that policy makers and parents would continue to want to know about how well students perform on objective tests.

Vast amounts of research and common experience suggest that markets and competition work well; they increase effectiveness, lower costs, and better satisfy citizens who are free to choose. Providers of public education insist, nonetheless, that education is an exception. They claim to protect the poor and minorities even though these groups most strongly favor and benefit from choice. They oppose trials of choice but insist on more evidence before it is tried.

As citizens of a country that has the near highest per-student costs and the worst value-added achievement gains,[31] Americans have the right to ask where the burden of proof lies. Objective examinations, parent satisfaction surveys, waiting lists for places, and other indicators have important roles in better answering the questions before us.

Notes

1. Herbert J. Walberg, *Spending More While Learning Less* (Washington, D.C.: Thomas B. Fordham Foundation, July 1998).

12. Organisation for Economic and Co-operative Development, "Education at a Glance 1995" (Paris: OECD, 1995).

3. For further examples, details, and documentation for this section, see my "Uncompetitive American Schools: Causes and Cures" in ed. Diane Ravitch, *Brookings Papers on Education Policy* (Washington, D.C.: Brookings Institution, 1998).

4. Herbert J. Walberg and Herbert J. Walberg III, "Losing Local Control: Is Bigger Better?" *Educational Researcher* (June/July 1994) 23–29.

5. Ibid.

6. Caroline Minter Hoxby, "How Teachers' Unions Affect Education Production," *Quarterly Journal of Economics* (August 1996): 1–24; Sam Peltzman, "Political Economy of Public Education: Non-College-Bound Students," *Journal of Law and Economics* 39 (1996): 73–120.

7. For Public Agenda surveys of teacher educators and others cited in this section, visit *http://www.publicagenda.org/aboutpa/aboutpa2p.htm*.

8. Nearly all public school teachers are paid according to their degrees and experience—neither of which influences their students' achievement—rather than academic mastery, the use of effective practices, their students' achievement, or other indicators of merit.

9. National Commission for Excellence in Education, *A Nation at Risk: The Imperative for School Reform* (Washington, D.C.: U.S. Government Printing Office, 1983).

10. Harris Cooper, *Making the Most of Summer School*, Monograph Series of the Society for Research in Child Development (Malden, Mass.: Blackwell, 2000).

11. Julian R. Betts and Robert M. Costrell, "Incentives and Equity Under Standards-Based Reform," in *Brookings Papers on Education Policy 2001*, ed. Diane Ravitch (Washington, D.C.: Brookings Institution, 2001), 9–74.

12. Herbert J. Walberg, "Uncompetitive American Schools: Causes and Cures" in *Brookings Papers on Education Policy*, ed. Diane Ravitch (Washington, D.C.: Brookings Institution, 1998), 173–206.

13. For more detailed information on standardized and traditional tests and on assessment reform issues, see Herbert J. Walberg, Geneva D. Haertel, and Suzanne Gerlach-Downie, *Assessment Reform: Challenges and Opportunities* (Bloomington, Ind.: Phi Delta Kappa, 1994).

14. Myron Lieberman finds the AFT and the NEA are among the most powerful and sophisticated interest groups. They enroll more than three million members whose dues exceed $1 billion annually. Lieberman calculates that they employ more political operatives than the Democratic and Republican parties combined. Their 405 representatives at the 1996 Democratic convention exceeded all states but California. See *The Teacher Unions* (New York: Free Press, 1997), 2–5.

15. Block grants of money for education returned to states might simplify educational administration; such grants would probably reduce costs and special interest influence and increase state and local accountability, control, and productivity. Another administratively simplifying alternative is assigning goal setting and monitoring to states and assigning operations to local districts or schools. In addition, charter schools in principle strengthen direct, local control, but many appear hampered by regulations, union contracts, and initial capital costs. For a variety of reforms, including national standards, charter and for-profit schools, vouchers, New American Schools, and the especially interesting cases of Charlotte-Mecklenburg, Chicago, San Diego, California, Kentucky, and Minnesota, see Chester E. Finn Jr. and Herbert J. Walberg, eds., *Radical Education Reforms* (Berkeley, Calif.: McCutchan Publishing, 1994).

16. See Herbert J. Walberg and Joseph Bast, "School Choice: The Essential Reform," *Cato Journal* (spring/summer 1993): 101–22.

17. Gordon Cawelti, ed., *Handbook of Research on Improving Student Achievement* (Arlington, Va.: Educational Research Service, 1995).

18. Herbert J. Walberg and Jin-Shei Lai, "Meta-Analytic Effects for Policy" in *Handbook of Educational Policy*, ed. Gregory Cizek (San Diego, Calif.: Academic Press, 1999).

19. Herbert J. Walberg and Rebecca C. Greenberg, "The Diogenes Factor: Why It's Hard to Get an Unbiased View of Programs Like 'Success for All,' " *Education Week* 52: 36.

20. Herbert J. Walberg, "Improving School Science in Advanced and Developing Countries," *Review of Educational Research* 61 (1991): 25–69.

21. Because of some causal uncertainties, a few early negative studies, and uncertain cost figures, it would seem advisable to conduct a comprehensive review of all accessible distance-education studies. Such a review would not only estimate over-all comparative effects and costs under varying conditions, but also identify the most effective practices and combinations of media.

22. James S. Coleman, "Achievement Oriented School Design," paper prepared for the Social Organization of Schools Conference held at the Center for Continuing Education at the University of Notre Dame, March 19, 1994.

23. For further examples, details, and documentation for this section, see my "Uncompetitive American Schools: Causes and Cures" in *Brookings Papers on Education Policy*, ed. Diane Ravitch (Washington, D.C.: Brookings Institution, 1998).

24. Charles Wolf, *Markets or Governments: Choosing Between Imperfect Alternatives* (Cambridge, Mass.: MIT Press, 1988), 137–48.

25. Paul Peterson of Harvard University has been analyzing parent satisfaction and examination performance of students given or not given vouchers by lottery in Dayton, Ohio, New York City, and Washington, D.C.

26. Stanley M. Elam, Lowell C. Rose, and A. M. Gallup, *The 24th Annual Gallup/Phi Delta Kappa Poll of the Public's Attitudes Toward the Public Schools* (Bloomington, Ind.: Phi Delta Kappa, 1992).

27. Nina Shokraii, "Free at Last: Black America Signs up for School Choice," *Policy Review* (December 1996):20–26.

28. In my view, for-profit firms offer exciting prospects for improving productivity. They must furnish entrepreneurial talents and energies to satisfy their customers. Unlike public schools, if they fail to please, they go out of business. If they please

parents (and, we could add, meet achievement goals), they deserve their profit in return for invested risk and the ability to serve. If subject to competitive bidding, they would probably reduce costs while improving achievement, satisfaction, and other outcomes.

29. Barbara Kantrowitz and Pat Wingert, "Learning at Home," *Newsweek* (October 5, 1998): 64–71.

30. Terry M. Moe, *Private Vouchers* (Stanford, Calif.: Hoover Institution Press, 1995), 14.

31. Herbert J. Walberg, *Spending More While Learning Less* (Washington, D.C.: Thomas B. Fordham Foundation, July 1998).

Chapter 2

Why Testing Experts Hate Testing

Richard P. Phelps

Introduction

The public has often been asked how it feels about testing. Over several decades and in a variety of contexts, the American people have consistently advocated greater use of standardized student testing, preferably with consequences for failure (that is, high stakes). The margins in favor have typically been huge, on the

The author would like to thank: the Fordham Foundation for its support; Chester E. Finn Jr., Marci Kanstoroom, Diane Ravitch, Steve Ferrara, and Mike Petrilli for their very helpful edits; Scott Oppler, Chris Sager, and Deb Wetzel for advice on certain psychometric concepts; and James Causby, Karen Davis, Kathleen Kennedy Manzo, Vanessa Jeter, and Janet Byrd for supplying important information about North Carolina's testing program. The author retains all responsibility for errors.

This chapter originally appeared as *Fordham Report* 3, no. 1 (January 1999). It has been slightly revised and updated.

order of 70-point spreads between the percentage in favor of more testing and the percentage against.[1]

But the public may not get its way. Many educators and education "experts" oppose standardized testing and high stakes. Although this throng includes some school administrators who fear the fallout from poor test results, it also, and most notably, includes many education school faculty members. In a 1997 survey, a national sample of them voiced substantially less support for high-stakes standardized testing than did other groups. "[O]nly 49 percent believe raising the standards of promotion from grade school to junior high and letting kids move ahead only when they pass a test showing they've reached those standards would do a great deal to improve academic achievement. In sharp contrast, the percentage reaches 70 percent among the general public [and 62 percent among teachers]."[2]

The polling organization Public Agenda found that "while supporting standards in concept, professors of education seem reluctant to put into place concrete, high-stakes tests that would signal when kids are meeting the standards."[3] They are especially opposed to multiple-choice tests. "Fully 78 percent want less reliance on multiple-choice exams in the schools. . . . [E]ducation professors . . . call for more reliance on portfolios and other authentic assessments."[4]

These faculty members don't think standardized tests demonstrate learning. "The fact is that all of the data say standardized tests don't predict what they are intended to. They just don't do it. . . . There is no standardized test that is good," a Boston professor told Public Agenda.[5] The professors recognize that the public has a different view of testing, however. Public Agenda reported that many faculty members expressed "disappointment and some exasperation that so much current educational research seems to be ignored or dismissed by the public."[6]

In June 1991, the American Educational Research Association (AERA), a group consisting primarily of education professors, hosted a press conference on student testing issues in Washington, D.C., as a "public service to build bridges between researchers and policy makers." Five prominent members of the group presented papers, such as "The Teacher, Standardized Testing, and Prospects of Revolution," in unanimous opposition to President George H. W. Bush's then-pending proposal for national tests; high-stakes use of standardized tests; multiple-choice formats; "external" tests (that is, tests not wholly controlled by school staff); and other features of student testing that they disliked.[7]

The reader may be struck by a paradox: It frequently seems that experts on testing have never met an actual test that they like and want to see used. What is it about testing that troubles them so? At the AERA press conference, a now-familiar litany of assertions was offered to explain how "research" shows that standardized testing is bad. The antitesting canon includes allegations that standardized tests, particularly those with high stakes,

- induce "teaching to the test," which, in turn, leads to artificial inflation of scores.

- narrow the curriculum to a small domain of topics.

- tap only "lower-order thinking" and hence discourage innovative curricula and teaching strategies.

- cause student achievement to decline.

- are unfair to minorities and women.

- are costly in terms of money and time.

- are overused in the United States, especially in comparison with other countries.

- are opposed by all who truly care about children.

Not all testing experts dislike testing, however. Hundreds of them work cheerfully for state and local testing agencies and for test developers. The opponents we hear from the most are a relatively small group of "testing policy" researchers, who are on the faculty of education schools or who work at organizations such as the federally funded Center for Research on Evaluation, Standards, and Student Testing (CRESST),[8] the Center for the Study of Testing, Evaluation, and Educational Policy (CSTEEP)[9] at Boston College, and an advocacy group known as the National Center for Fair and Open Testing (FairTest).[10] A brief excerpt from a FairTest publication entitled *Fallout from the Testing Explosion: How 100 Million Standardized Exams Undermine Equity and Excellence in America's Public Schools* sums up the basic position of the organization.[11]

> Standardized tests often produce results that are inaccurate, inconsistent, and biased against minority, female, and low-income students. Such tests shift control and authority into the hands of the unregulated testing industry and can undermine school achievement by narrowing the curriculum, frustrating teachers, and driving students out of school. [12]

In this chapter, the arguments of the testing experts who dislike testing are held up for careful scrutiny. First, four case studies that suggest how these experts deploy their arguments in the real world are examined. Then those arguments are appraised.

Case Study 1: The National Assessment of Educational Progress

The nominal reason for the AERA press conference was to criticize then-President George H. W. Bush's national testing proposal. Proposals for national testing systems, be they from George H. W. Bush or Bill Clinton (George W. Bush has not proposed any additional national test), tend to attract a great deal of attention. To date, however, there has been only one such test—the National Assessment of Educational Progress (NAEP). The NAEP is an assessment based on samples of schools, and no individual student information is made available. It is a no-stakes test.

For decades, NAEP samples were exclusively national and so were NAEP scores. In the 1980s, however, many people pressed for state-representative NAEP samples ("State NAEP"). Almost half the states had instituted their own testing programs, many of them high-stakes "minimum competency" graduation requirements. Some state leaders wanted to gauge their students' levels of achievement or the progress of their states' education reform efforts against an external benchmark, and the scores of state-representative samples of schools and students on the NAEP seemed the perfect candidate to be that benchmark.

But what sounds like an obvious idea drew strong opposition from testing experts. Daniel Koretz, a researcher with CRESST and the RAND Corporation, made three separate arguments against releasing state-by-state NAEP scores. First, he argued that the public cannot be trusted with such information. Koretz wrote that "[S]ome differences among states would be too fragile— too dependent on the specifics of the test—to warrant the simple interpretations that they will receive."[13] Second, Koretz argued, academic success is predicted primarily by the socioeconomic background of students, so state-level NAEP will just show once again that richer states do better:[14] "To infer that a difference between two states on the NAEP reflects specific policies or practices, one needs to be able to reject with reasonable confidence other plausible explanations, such as economic or demographic difference."[15] (Other opponents of State NAEP have made these arguments even more forcefully.[16]) Third, Koretz insisted that because State NAEP provides only cross-sectional data, it cannot show improvements in achievement that may coincide with education reform programs: "NAEP is purely cross-sectional, which eliminates a large number of the designs that could be used to draw causal inferences."[17]

The essence of these objections is that state-level NAEP results would be used to judge states and these judgments would inevitably be unfair. So, because people who don't understand what the scores really mean would use this information to evaluate the states, we shouldn't gather the information at all.

In a counter to Koretz, Gary W. Phillips of the U.S. Education Department's National Center for Education Statistics noted that although a single administration of State NAEP might not allow us to evaluate the impact of reforms, a system needed to be established that could be used to appraise such changes in the future. We had to start somewhere.[18] The National Academy of Education, assigned to review the efficacy of State NAEP, recommended implementation and reiterated that recommendation in a 1996 review.[19]

With several administrations of state-level NAEP now behind us, we have time-series data with which to gauge the progress (or lack thereof) that each state's youngsters are making in mathematics, reading, and science. We can thus begin to see where state education policies are effective, with background factors controlled. The utility of NAEP scores as markers for monitoring state education reforms is seen in the next two case studies, of Texas and North Carolina.

The 1988 legislation establishing state-level NAEP also permitted "standards-based" reporting of scores. Historically, NAEP results were reported only according to abstract "scale scores" that were not anchored to any standards. But the National Assessment Governing Board—to the continuing dismay of many testing experts—judged that NAEP results would be far more useful, particularly in tracking progress toward the national education goals that the President and governors set in 1989, if they showed how U.S. children were doing academically in relation to how well they *ought* to be doing. The Governing Board established three performance levels, which it termed "basic, proficient, and advanced," and accompanied each with descriptions written in English about the specific skills and abilities represented by each level. Like State NAEP, the performance level concept and the method for setting the levels have drawn controversy, with some testing critics favoring the old scale scores' aloof abstractness and many policy makers desiring more useful and understandable measures.[20]

It would appear, however, that the performance levels are here to stay. The National Assessment Governing Board has remained steadfast. And a National Research Council review of NAEP, while agreeing with the critics on a number of specific points, also conceded: "It is clear that Americans want the kind of information about the achievement of the nation's students currently provided by NAEP summary scores and achievement-level results."[21]

Case Study 2: Texas

Perhaps no state testing program has aroused the ire of testing critics more than the Texas Assessment of Academic Skills

(TAAS), since 1990 the backbone of the Lone Star State's education accountability program. In its ratings of all state testing programs, FairTest rated the TAAS at 2 on a scale of 1 to 5, with 1 being the worst score possible.

FairTest explained its dim view of TAAS as follows:

> The Texas assessment system needs many major changes. It relies almost entirely on multiple-choice items, except for a writing prompt, and has a high-stakes graduation test. On most of the other standards, however, the state does very well. It has strong bias review procedures, provides solid public information, accords parents substantial rights, and has a thorough and continuing review system. Professional development appears fairly extensive.[22]

Observe that FairTest gave the state's testing program the second-lowest possible rating for only two reasons: high-stakes and multiple-choice formats. According to Monte Neill of FairTest, "When you have high stakes and then add an exit exam, that jacks up the system so that the test becomes the curriculum. . . . One should not be using scores on tests to make serious educational decisions."[23]

Responding to evidence that pupil achievement in Texas has improved markedly since the TAAS was introduced, Neill "concedes that the improvements are impressive," reports *Education Week*, "but he says that an enriched curriculum, not test preparation, is behind the shifts."[24] There may be a contradiction here. According to Neill, the test has *become* the curriculum in Texas and the improvement in student achievement is the result of an enriched curriculum. Still, he declines to see the improvement as linked to the testing.

In addition to FairTest's criticisms of the TAAS for its high-stakes and multiple-choice formats, the Texas testing program was the subject of two separate lawsuits. The NAACP asserted that it was biased against blacks since they performed worse than whites on the test.[25] The Mexican-American Legal Defense Fund followed with a suit using the same logic.[26] Both cases were heard by the U.S. Education Department's Office for Civil Rights and Texas state courts and were dismissed.[27]

Through the clouds of flack, the citizens of Texas remained on course, retaining and expanding the TAAS. Moreover, the results do appear to be positive. Texas students' average state test scores have shown achievement gains year after year. That Texas students have also made gains well above the national average on the NAEP throughout the past decade would seem to corroborate the improvement.[28]

Other benefits have also followed. Observers of Texas education report

- a greater focus on academic learning.

- a culture of high expectations and enthusiasm toward reaching standards.

- generous and immediate remediation efforts offered to poorly performing students, both because a system is in place to identify their problems early and because, with high stakes, students' problems are not just passed along to the next grade, where they become compounded.

- greater interest among teachers in academic strategies and more cooperation with each other to learn which ones work best, and how.

- that with a regular system of assessment, school staff can get quicker feedback on which instructional systems work best.

- Texas has built a school-specific information system on the World Wide Web for all parents to see, helping them understand their schools better.[29]

Though always intended to match Texas's curriculum and performance standards, the state's student testing program first took aim at basic skills and minimum competency, a focus that may have neglected the more advanced students. It is now being expanded to cover more grades and purposes (statewide high-school-level end-of-course examinations, for example). It has strived to achieve better integration with the curriculum, professional development, and program planning, as well as with student evaluation, and is today a key component of one of the most comprehensive accountability systems in the country.[30]

Texas's accountability system has received strong political support from both parties. Republican and Democratic governors alike have resisted most attempts to soften its requirements, even in the face of sustained criticism. Indeed, gubernatorial opponents in the 1994 election attempted to outdo each other in their support for still higher standards and tougher requirements.[31] In 1998, it was not even an issue.

Case Study 3: North Carolina

A similar story can be told about North Carolina, a state that, like Texas, ranked near the bottom on the NAEP but has improved its student achievement dramatically after instituting a comprehensive, integrated, high-stakes testing program and sticking with it despite serious opposition.[32]

The North Carolina Education Department rates schools based on their results on state tests. It is a value-added rating system in which adjustments are made—for socioeconomic and other background factors—to the expected performance of each school. Teachers at schools rated "exemplary" are rewarded monetarily. But poorly performing schools are not abandoned. The department assembles teams of three to five experts in curriculum and instruction who work with those schools for an entire year. These teams help school staff align their curricula with state academic standards, and they also demonstrate effective teaching techniques and try to locate additional resources for the schools.[33] Fifteen schools designated for "mandatory assistance" at the end of the 1996–1997 school year finished 1997–1998 by achieving "exemplary" ratings for improving their performance by more than 10 percent.[34] In 1998–1999, state "assistance teams" visited forty-six public and seven charter schools, eleven of them under a "mandatory assistance" provision for the worst-performing schools in the state, the rest under voluntary arrangements.[35]

The sixty-odd schools visited by state assistance teams represent less than 3 percent of the state's schools. Most schools either develop their own programs or rely on assistance from their school district. Jeff Moss, the associate school superintendent in

Hoke County, one of the state's poorest districts, describes how his district treats low-performing students there:

> . . . on a Friday the students take a test. If they do not pass the test, they have to come back after school hours the following week, Tuesday, Wednesday, and Thursday. They take another test the next Friday. They'll get the higher of the two grades; we don't penalize them for coming back after school hours.[36]

Students even get a third chance with the help of another round of after-school classes. A Southern Regional Education Board study of the Hoke County schools found that:

> . . . the percentage of students who now meet the state's algebra proficiency standard has doubled. Twenty percent more now meet the history standard. And the high school's overall Scholastic Assessment Test (SAT) scores are up 11 percent over three years. Also . . . employers are more welcoming of graduates now.[37]

The whole process of reform in Hoke County was set in motion by its initial poor showing in the state testing program, which identified the district's academic problems.

Still, holding students, teachers, or schools to fixed standards means that some will do less well than others and may be held back. Johnson County, North Carolina, for example, passed a student-accountability policy of its own in 1996. The policy called for intensive remediation, but also for retention in grade of students who did not score at a proficient level on state exams.[38]

District officials claim the accountability program has boosted student performance. According to Johnson County officials, more than one-third of students performed below grade level on the tests four years ago, yet just 1 percent of students were held back.[39] This year, less than one-fourth of the students performed below grade level and 8.8 percent of students were retained under the policy—and for other reasons, such as absenteeism. The other 16 percent were promoted "based on the grades they earned and other academic factors."[40]

Not everyone liked the new policy. Fourteen parents filed suit against Johnson County on behalf of children who were held back. They argued that the tests were intended by the state to rate districts and schools, not individual students, and thus were "not valid for measuring individual performance."[41]

Walter Haney, a researcher with CSTEEP at Boston College, agreed:

> It is a prime example of a test that was developed for one purpose . . . and applied for a purpose that is totally inappropriate and unintended. . . . The North Carolina end-of-grade tests were designed to hold schools and districts accountable. There is considerable potential for people trying to use [a] national test for similar decisions without stopping to examine whether, in fact, the content parallels the local curriculum.[42]

The North Carolina tests do match state curriculum standards, however, and cover a representative sample of it. Because the state uses the tests to evaluate districts and schools, individual students usually see only one-third of each subject-area exam; by sampling this way, the state can cut testing time and costs. Had Johnson County held students back for poor performance on a test that covered only one-third of the curriculum, that would have been unfair. Instead, the district put the three separate pieces of the exam together to form complete exams that covered the entire curriculum.[43]

A U.S. District Court judge rejected the plaintiffs' request for an injunction to prevent another year of student retention.[44] The plaintiffs later dropped the case.[45]

Richard Jaeger, one of the speakers at the AERA press conference mentioned earlier, who was then a professor at the University of North Carolina, criticized his state's testing program in general, but particularly its high-stakes, minimum-competency, elements; the testing program is geared toward a relatively low level of basic skills and students have several chances to pass, starting in tenth grade. They cannot graduate from high school until they pass it.

Jaeger argued that the costs to society of denying students diplomas might be too high. "As a determinant of a student's life chances in American society, possessing a high school diploma is far more important than scoring well on a basic skills competency test." [46] He cited statistics showing that high school dropouts are more likely to have blighted lives and argued that "the use of such tests jeopardizes the future of those young people denied a high school diploma by limiting their employability, reducing their quality of life, and diminishing their opportunity to contribute to society through the productive applications of their abilities."[47] Jaeger also presented evidence purporting to show that meeting higher standards and passing high-stakes tests do not improve students' economic prospects. He implied that if North Carolina just gave poorly performing students their diplomas with no impediments, the state would enjoy less crime, fewer out-of-wedlock births, and shorter welfare rolls.[48]

Two other presenters at the AERA conference also accused high-stakes tests of increasing the dropout rate.[49] Their evidence, however, was spotty. Most U.S. dropouts leave school when they reach the limit of the compulsory attendance law, not when they fail an exam.[50] When students in the large-scale Indiana Youth Poll explained why some dropped out, either disinterest in school or non-academic-related problems (such as pregnancy or family problems) were cited more than four times more often than academic failure.[51]

A careful examination of the dropout issue by Bryan Griffin and Mark Heidorn, using data from Florida from the early 1990s (when a test similar to the one used in North Carolina was in place), found that:

> . . . failure on a [minimum competency test] provided a statistically significant increase in the likelihood of leaving school, but only for students who were doing well academically. Students with poorer academic records did not appear to be affected by MCT [minimum competency test] failure; similarly, minority students did not demonstrate an increased likelihood of leaving school as a result of failing an MCT.[52]

More recent studies of the relationship between high-stakes tests and the dropout rate have shown that it can move in either direction—the dropout rate can rise if struggling students are ignored or decline if they are given the attention they need when they need it.

Speaking about the same high-stakes exit exam in Florida, psychologist and attorney Barbara Lerner explained:

> On the first few tries, 80 to 90 percent of Florida's students failed the test. But they were not crushed, as the experts predicted, and they did not give up and drop out in droves without diplomas. They kept trying, and their teachers did, too, working hard to help them learn from failure and, ultimately, to master the skills they needed to graduate. By the fifth try, better than 90 percent of them did just that. They left school not just with a piece of paper, but with basic skills that prepared them better for life.[53]

In spite of great advances in student achievement linked to the testing system in North Carolina, however, FairTest gave the state's system its lowest rating of 1 (on a scale of 1 to 5):

> North Carolina's assessment program needs a complete overhaul. It relies far too heavily on multiple-choice tests, tests too often, and has a graduation exam. It should reduce the grades tested, drop the graduation requirement, ensure districts do not rely on the tests for grade promotion decisions, and implement a performance assessment system based on the state standards.[54]

Overall, North Carolina showed the most improvement of any state on the NAEP in the 1990s.[55]

Case Study 4: SAT I (formerly the Scholastic Assessment Test)

The test attracting the loudest and most sustained opprobrium from critics over the years is the SAT I (formerly the Scholastic Assessment Test), used by almost two-thirds of U.S. colleges in making admissions decisions.[56]

One of the primary sustaining causes of FairTest is its crusade to convince colleges to cease using SAT scores in admissions decisions. If one read only FairTest's literature, one might well conclude that the group's campaign against the SAT has been very successful.[57] According to FairTest, hundreds of colleges now have optional or limited SAT requirements.[58]

Those colleges that offer the possibility of admissions sans test scores may, however, require additional proof of ability, such as a graded writing sample or an on-campus interview. Moreover, even if not *required* for admission, the absence of a test score may still bias an application negatively.[59]

Still, the SAT's impact is often overstated. The overwhelming majority of colleges are not selective, so a low SAT score will rarely keep a student out of college. Even at the most selective colleges, the SAT is seldom used alone by college admissions staff to make decisions. Typically, it is one of many factors, which include a student's high school grade point average, extracurricular activities, recommendations, essays, and so on.[60] When surveyed, however, admission counselors rate the SAT score as a more reliable measure than these other indicators.[61]

The primary argument of SAT critics pertains to the test's "predictive validity"; it explains only 15 percent of the variation in first-year college grades, after other predictive factors are accounted for.[62] If that's all the good it does, why bother with it? they ask.[63] As Haney of CSTEEP says:

> Which is more accurate? Does a person's height more accurately predict a person's weight? Or do national college entrance exams more accurately predict a student's success in college?
>
> The answer: Height is a better predictor of weight. And there might be some crude relationship between height and weight. But it ain't real good.[64]

To a college admissions counselor, however, 15 percent is a lot of predictive power, and the SAT costs only about $20.[65] It costs society about $25,000 to educate a high school student. For an incremental cost of 0.08 percent over the cost of a high school education, the SAT score provides a college admissions counselor a 34 percent increase in information. The incremental benefit-cost ratio for the SAT is 425:1 over the high school record.[66] The break-even value of the SAT is more than $8,500 per student; at $20, it's a bargain.

The SAT is a nationally *standardized* measure; a grade point average is not. One student can achieve a high grade point average by working extremely hard in difficult courses in a high school with exacting standards, while another can get by choosing easy courses at a high school with low standards.

Ultimately, the makers of the SAT do not determine its success; its customers do. Those customers are thousands of college admissions officers throughout the United States who are doing their best to select students they believe can handle the level of academic rigor at their institution.

College admissions officers are not ignorant. They hear and read the arguments against use of the SAT. Nor are they elitist conspirators opposed to fair admission policies. Moreover, they are not required to use the SAT (or the ACT). They use such tests because they believe, based on personal experience, that they are valuable—so valuable that they consider test scores to be the second most important criterion in making admissions decisions, higher than grade point averages or class ranks, and second only to grades and test scores from Advanced Placement courses, the only other nationally standardized measure of achievement commonly available to them.[67]

Appraising the Criticisms

The basic argument made by testing critics is that high-stakes standardized tests are counterproductive. Instead of leading to stronger academic achievement, they actually interfere with good teaching and learning. Testing experts embrace a sort of domino theory: Pressure to produce higher scores leads teachers to focus on material that will be covered by the tests and to exclude everything else.[68] The curriculum is thereby narrowed, which means that some subjects are ignored. Within those that are taught, lower-order thinking skills are emphasized because these are what the tests tap. As a result of teachers teaching to the tests, subsequent test scores are inflated while real learning suffers.

In addition to the alleged harms of (1) test score inflation, (2) curriculum narrowing, (3) emphasis on lower-order thinking, and (4) declining achievement, testing experts add a quartet of other arguments against testing: (5) that standardized tests hurt minorities and women, (6) that the tests are too costly, (7) that other countries don't test nearly as much as we do, and (8) that parents, teachers, and students in this country are all opposed to testing. These eight claims are examined in detail in the section that follows and a rebuttal is offered to each.

What testing experts do not like are high-stakes, multiple-choice, external tests. These tests are excoriated with bad-sounding words ("lower-order thinking," "factory model of education," "uncreative," "rote recall," and so on), but such terms are seldom well explained. The root of most objections to testing can be traced to the dominant worldview of testing experts (and many other educators).

The education philosophy driving many of these criticisms is constructivism, the view that every student and teacher constructs his or her own meanings from classroom activities, books, and so on. Hence no construction is wrong or bad. We all know that there is often more than one way to get to a right answer. We all think differently, using different combinations of several different kinds of intelligence. Moreover, we all know that a student can process much of a problem well but still get the "wrong" answer in the end because of a fairly minor error, such as misplacing a decimal point.

As test critic (and constructivist) Mary Lee Smith of CRESST and Arizona State University describes it:

> Constructivist theory assumes that students construct their own knowledge (rather than passively receiving knowledge transmitted by school) out of intentional transactions with materials, teachers, and other pupils. Learning is more likely to happen when students can choose and become actively engaged in the tasks and materials and when they can make their own connections across subject matter on tasks that are authentic and organized around themes. According to this theory, literacy is whole, embodying reading authentic texts and writing as a way of unifying all the subjects. For example, to be literate is to be able to explain the reasoning one uses to discover and solve math problems. Explicit in constructivist theory is the rejection of the pedagogy of worksheets and the exclusive reliance on phonics, spelling out of context, computation, isolated subject matter and the like.[69]

Constructivists oppose school practices that they think "fix" behavior. They see standardizing curricula and instructional practice as restricting teacher behavior and multiple-choice standardized tests as shackling student responses to problems.

For constructivists, the more open-ended the assessment the better, and portfolios are the most open-ended of all. They involve no standardized, mandated preset response and not necessarily even a standardized question to impede any student's unique understanding of the problem, creative solution, and personal construction of the work.[70] This constructivist worldview is seen to underlie most of the arguments marshaled by testing experts against testing.[71]

1. Test Score Inflation

An initial set of harms ascribed to standardized testing fall under the rubric of teaching to the test. A CRESST paper entitled "The Effects of High-Stakes Testing on Achievement," by Daniel Koretz, Lorrie Shepard, and others, purports to demonstrate that high-stakes tests in fact cause teaching to the test.[72] The researchers compared student performance in math and reading from one commercial test given under high-stakes conditions with student performance on a different commercial test with no stakes. Student performance on the high-stakes test improved over time, according to the researchers, as the teachers adapted their instruction to the curriculum implicit in the test. Student performance on the other test, administered solely for the purpose of the study, did not improve over time. The difference in student performance between the two tests is offered by the CRESST researchers as proof that high-stakes tests "narrow the curriculum" and induce "teaching to the test." Test critics would describe the first set of scores as artificially inflated, polluted, or corrupted.

The idea behind score inflation is that as teachers become more familiar with test content, they spend more time teaching that test content and less time teaching other material. So, over time, as familiarity grows, scores climb on the test while real learning suffers.

In the early 1980s, a West Virginia physician named John J. Cannell investigated a statistical anomaly that he had discovered:

Statewide average scores for students on some widely used test batteries were above the national average in every state in which they were given.[73] It was dubbed the Lake Wobegon Effect after the fictional community where "all the children are above average."

Response:

The skeptical reader might see the catch-22. Some of the same critics who argue that tests must be well-aligned to a curriculum in order to be valid will howl "narrowing the curriculum" when scores increase on an aligned test, but not on an unaligned test. There is no justifiable reason why one should expect student test scores on a test not aligned to their curriculum to increase over time. Nor is there anything sacrosanct about the other, unaligned test used in the CRESST researchers' study. One wouldn't expect student scores to increase on a plumbers' test after they had taken an electricians' course, either. But one would be worried if their scores on an electricians' test did not improve.

The Lake Wobegon anomaly might have been caused—observed Cannell and a group of test experts—by a number of factors, including schools' reusing old tests year after year and growing familiar with their specific content and test publishers' waiting years before "renorming" the reference scales. Other factors could have included: the "nonrepresentativeness" of the norming samples;[74] school districts' choosing from among various versions of tests the one most closely aligned with their curriculum and on which their pupils would likely perform best; and the fact that student achievement really was improving throughout the 1980s, as verified by independent testing, such as the scores on SAT, ACT, and NAEP exams. There may also have been some statistical anomalies in Dr. Cannell's calculations.[75]

The Lake Wobegon controversy led to calls for more state control over test content and administration and less local discretion. In most states, those calls were answered. Today most school districts are aware of the problem of test score inflation and do not use tests with exactly the same questions year after year. Many jurisdictions now either use tests that are custom-built to their state standards and curricula or that are adapted from commercial publishers' test-item banks. A simple way of preventing score inflation is to use different tests or test forms from year to year without announcing in advance which one will be used. Indeed, most of the likeliest sources of the Lake Wobegon effect are fairly easily avoided.[76]

The larger argument about teaching to the test has several components.

2. Curriculum Narrowing

We might suppose that preparing youngsters to do well on tests would find favor with testing experts, yet many of them condemn all forms of "teaching to the test." These arguments tend to come in several forms. One is that valuable subjects that are not tested (for example, art and music, maybe even social studies or science) will be ignored or slighted by test-obsessed teachers and school systems. In her talk at the AERA press conference, for example, Lorrie Shepard of CRESST and the University of Colorado asserted: "Although critics may originally have feared that testing would take instructional time away from 'frills,' such as art and citizenship, the evidence now shows that social studies and science are neglected because of the importance of raising test scores in the basic skills."[77]

A variation on this theme holds that even within a subject that is taught, content coverage will be narrowed (or curricular depth made shallow) in order to conform to the content or style of the test.

Response:

There is only so much instructional time available and choices must be made as to how it is used. (Of course, some new school designs extend the school day or year to ameliorate this problem.) If non-tested subjects are being dropped, either they, too, should be tested or, perhaps, educators and policy makers are signaling that, in a world of tough choices among competing priorities, some subjects must in fact take a backseat to others. A state or school system could easily add high-stakes tests in art, music, language, and civics, or any other subjects. Attaching high stakes to tests in some subjects and not others would be interpreted by most as a signal that the former subjects are considered to be more important. Perhaps that's actually true. Especially where students are sorely deficient in basic skills and need extra instruction in them, it is likely that few parents would object to such priorities. Survey results show clearly that the public wants students to master the basics skills first, before they go on to explore the rest of the possible curriculum.[78] If that means spending more time on "the basics," so be it. As for subject content being narrowed or made shallow in anticipation of a test, a better response than eliminating the test might be to replace it with one that probes deeper or more broadly.

3a. Emphasis on Lower-Order Thinking in Instruction

In her talk at the AERA press conference, Lorrie Shepard further asserted:

> High-stakes testing misdirects instruction even for the basic skills. Under pressure, classroom instruction is increasingly dominated by tasks that resemble tests. . . . Even in the early grades, students practice finding mistakes rather than do real writing, and they learn to guess by eliminating wrong answers. . . .
>
> In an extensive eighteen-month observational study, for example, Mary Lee Smith and her colleagues found that because of external tests, elementary teachers had given up on [students'] reading real books, writing, and undertaking long-term projects and were filling all available time with word recognition; recognition of errors in spelling, language usage, and punctuation; and arithmetic operations. . . .[79]

Response:

Critics like Smith and Shepard say that intensive instruction in basic skills denies the slow students instruction in the "the neat stuff" in favor of "lower-order thinking."[80] They argue that time for preparing students for high-stakes tests reduces "ordinary instruction." They cannot abide the notion that preparing students for a standardized test could be considered instruction because it is not the kind of instruction that they favor.[81]

Instruction to which teachers may resort to help students improve their scores on standardized tests tends not to be constructivist. It is the type of instruction, however, that teachers feel works best for knowledge and skill acquisition. Teachers in high-stakes testing situations do not deliberately use instructional practices that impede learning; they use those that they find to be most successful.

These testing critics idealize the concept of teachers as individual craftspersons, responding to the unique needs of their unique pupils in unique ways with "creative and innovative" curriculum and instruction.[82] But the most difficult jobs in the world are those that must be created anew every day without any consistent structure and performed in isolation without collaboration or advice. In Public Agenda's research, "teachers routinely complained that teaching is an isolated and isolating experience."[83]

By contrast, teachers in other countries are commonly held to more narrowly prescribed curricula and teaching methods. Furthermore, because their curricula and instructional methods are standardized, they can work together and learn from each other. They seem not to suffer from a loss of "creativity and innovation"; indeed, when adjusted for a country's wealth, teachers in other nations are commonly paid more and usually have greater prestige.[84]

Critics like Shepard and Smith cannot accept that some teachers may *want* to conform to systemwide standards for curriculum, instruction, and testing. Standardization brings the security, convenience, camaraderie, and common professional development that accompany a shared work experience.[85]

3b. Emphasis on Lower-Order Thinking in Test Content

One CSTEEP study, funded by the National Science Foundation, analyzed whether several widely used commercial (and mostly multiple-choice) tests required higher- or lower-order thinking. A press account boasted, "In the most comprehensive study of its kind yet conducted, researchers from Boston College have found evidence to confirm the widespread view that standardized and textbook tests emphasize low-level thinking and knowledge and that they exert a profound, mostly negative effect on classroom interaction."[86]

Researcher Maryellen Harmon told a reporter, "None of [the test content] calls for high-order thinking that requires that they go in-depth into the concept, that they use math skills in non-conventional contexts, or pull together concepts from geometry and algebra."[87] Project director George Madaus was quoted as saying that the findings present a "depressing picture. . . . If this doesn't change, an inordinate amount of time, attention, and preparation will be given to the wrong domains in math and science, domains that are not reflecting the outcomes we want."[88]

Response:

Many readers would be astonished, as I still am, by the vehemence of some critics' ire toward something as seemingly dull and innocuous as item-response format. And many of the accusations leveled at multiple-choice items have little substance. For example, you can often find in CSTEEP and FairTest publications assertions that multiple-choice items demand only factual recall and lower-order thinking, while performance-based tests do neither. Both claims are without merit. It is the structure of the *question,* not the response format, that determines the character of the cognitive processing necessary to reach a correct answer.

Test items can be banal and simplistic or intricately complex, and either way, their response format can be multiple-choice or open-ended. There is no necessary correlation between the difficulty of a problem and its response format. Even huge, integrative tasks that require fifty minutes to classify, assemble, organize, calculate, and analyze can, in the end, present the test-taker with a multiple-choice response format. Just because the answer to the question is among those provided, it is not necessarily easy or obvious how to get from the question to the answer.

Anyone who still thinks that multiple-choice items demand only factual recall should take a trip to the bookstore and look at some SAT or ACT help books. I purchased a copy of the Cliffs Notes SAT prep book and randomly picked a page. It was in the math section and four items are posed. Here's one: "What is the maximum number of milk cartons, each 2" wide by 3" long by 4" tall, that can fit into a cardboard box with inside dimensions of 16" wide by 9" long by 8" tall?" Five possible answers are provided, but the correct one, obviously, cannot just be "recalled." Calculations are required. My solution was to calculate the area, in square inches, of a carton and the box, by multiplying the three dimensions in each case, then to divide the former area into the latter. I used pen and paper for two of the calculations and figured the other in my head. Interestingly, the Cliffs Notes book solves the problem graphically, by sketching a three-dimensional box and subdividing it along each dimension.[89]

Indeed, much of the Cliffs Notes book is devoted to convincing the student that there is usually more than one way to "construct" a response to a problem. The book contains sections that illustrate different approaches to solving similar problems. It's a very "constructivist" book; any student following its advice would make ample use—in taking the SAT—of pen, paper, calculator, formulas, diagrams, sketches, lateral thinking, meta-analysis, and other devices that constructivists hold dear. Students armed with multiple methods for solving problems, of course, will hit more correct answers on the SAT than students with fewer methods, other factors held equal. So, higher SAT scores should be taken as evidence of more higher-order thinking.

All the optical scanner will read in the end, however, is a sheet of circles, some filled in with pencil and others not. Moreover, all the computer will score in the end is the number of correct filled-in circles. The calculations, sketches, and diagrams the student used to solve the problems are left behind in the test booklet, on scratch paper, or in the student's head. Just because the optical scanner and computer do not see the process evidence of higher-order thinking, however, does not mean it did not take place.[90] Yet that is what the critics assume.

The most essential point for the critics in applying the "lower-order" label to multiple-choice and the "higher-order" label to performance tests seems to be that with open-ended questions, a student *shows* her work in the test-response book itself and a scorer can see how the test-taker has approached the problem through the exposition of the answer. This is undoubtedly helpful to teachers but far less necessary for purposes of informing parents, policy makers, admissions counselors, and so on.

CSTEEP's study of several commercially available (and mostly multiple-choice) math and science tests claimed to analyze whether the tests required higher- or lower-order thinking. The researchers defined higher-order thinking skills as having three characteristics: problem solving (the abilities to formulate problems, use a variety of problem-solving strategies in nonroutine situations, and verify and interpret results); reasoning (the abilities to infer, analyze, and use logic); and communicating (the abilities to speak, write, depict, or demonstrate ideas in prose, graphs, models, equations and to describe, explain, or argue a position).[91]

The first two characteristics are typically found in definitions of higher-order thinking.[92] The third was added by CSTEEP for the purposes of their study. The CSTEEP researchers crafted a definition of higher-order thinking that multiple-choice tests would invariably fail. According to the CSTEEP researchers, one is *not* communicating when filling in a bubble for a multiple-choice item, no matter what mental or physical processes may have been used in getting a student to that point; but one *is* communicating when writing a textual response to an open-ended prompt.[93] If the scorer cannot see the work, the work does not exist. Obviously, if one can define higher-order thinking skills any way one wishes, as these CSTEEP researchers did, one can define any type of testing one dislikes as embodying only lower-order thinking.

Even when defined without the communicating component, is higher-order thinking always a superior form of thinking, as testing critics imply? Consider the type of thinking surgeons do. They are highly paid and well-respected professionals. Their course of study, however, consists of a considerable amount of rote memorization, and their work entails a considerable amount of routine and factual recall (all lower-order thinking). Moreover, the medical college admissions test is largely multiple-choice, and tests administered during medical training largely elicit the recall of discrete facts.

If you were about to go under the knife, which kind of surgeon would you want? One who used only higher-order thinking, only "creative and innovative" techniques, and "constructed her own meaning" from every operation she performed?

Or would you prefer a surgeon who had passed her lower-order thinking exams—on the difference, say, between a spleen and a kidney—and used tried-and-true methods with a history of success, methods that other surgeons had used successfully?

Certainly, there would be some situations where one could benefit from an innovative surgeon. If *no aspect whatsoever* of the study or practice of surgery were standardized, however, there would be nothing to teach in medical school and your regular barber or beautician would be as well qualified to "creatively" excise your appendix as anyone else. Ideally, most of us would want a surgeon who possesses both lower and higher abilities.[94]

The surgery analogy also addresses another of the testing critics' arguments. They say that multiple-choice tests limit students to the "one correct answer" when there may be more than one valid answer and more than one way to get to each. Moreover, they say, students should not get an entire exercise counted wrong if they analyze most of the problem correctly, but make one careless error.

Most of us would sympathize with this sentiment, but we should remember that there are countless examples in real life where there *is* just one right answer or where one careless error can have devastating consequences—in brain surgery, for example.

4. Declining Achievement

Testing experts claim that high-stakes tests actually interfere with learning and student achievement in states that use them. In "High-Stakes Tests Do Not Improve Student Learning," FairTest asserted that states with high-stakes graduation exams tend to score lower on the NAEP. According to FairTest, this "contradicts the . . . common assumption of standards and tests-based school reform . . . that high-stakes testing . . . will produce improved learning outcomes."[95]

The FairTest solution is to restrict testing to occasional no-stakes monitoring with samples of students using the types of response formats that FairTest favors (no multiple-choice). Scores on "portfolios" of each student's best work would track individual student progress.[96] Indeed, the only state-testing program to garner the highest rating from FairTest was Vermont, which had a statewide portfolio program and no high-stakes or multiple-choice standardized testing.[97]

Response:

The claim that high-stakes tests inhibit learning is a weak argument supported by dubious research. The FairTest report provides a good example of just how simplistic that research can be. FairTest argues that states with high-stakes, minimum-competency-test graduation requirements tend to have lower average test scores on the NAEP. They make no effort, however, to control for other factors that influence test performance, and the relationship between cause and effect is just assumed to run in the direction FairTest wants.[98] Most honest observers would assume the direction of cause and effect to be just the opposite—poorly performing states initiate high-stakes testing programs in an effort to improve academic performance while high-performing states do not feel the need to.

The work of Cornell labor economist John Bishop does not get the press attention bestowed on FairTest. Yet in a series of solid studies conducted over a decade, Bishop has shown that when other factors that influence academic achievement are controlled for, students from states, provinces, or countries with medium- or high-stakes testing programs score better on neutral, common tests and earn higher salaries after graduation than do their counterparts from states, provinces, or countries with no- or low-stakes tests.[99]

Bishop recently turned his attention to the very same relationship that FairTest studied, except he looked at it in depth. He and his colleagues used individual-level data from the National Education Longitudinal Study that began in 1988 (NELS:88) and High School and Beyond (HSB), another longitudinal study that ran from 1980 to 1992. They controlled for socioeconomic status, grades, and other important factors, while comparing the earnings of graduates from "minimum-competency" testing states to those from non-testing states.[100] "They found that test-taking students earned an average of 3 percent to 5 percent more per hour than their counterparts from schools with no minimum-competency tests. And the differences were greater for women, with as much as 6 percent higher earnings for those who had taken the tests. Other evidence of the success of high-stakes state testing programs continues to surface.[101]

5. Standardized Tests Hurt Women and Minorities

As mentioned in the case study of high-stakes testing in Texas, the NAACP and the Mexican-American Legal Defense Fund both argued that the Texas Assessment of Academic Skills was biased against minorities.

The brunt of FairTest's attack on the SAT involves alleged bias as well. The argument is straightforward: On average, girls score worse on the SAT than boys, despite getting better grades in school. Therefore the SAT is gender-biased. Blacks and Hispanics score lower than whites. Therefore the SAT is race-biased.[102] FairTest argues that these biases depress minority and female college admissions.

Response:

After investigating why girls score worse on the SAT than boys despite getting better grades in school, the Educational Testing Service (ETS), the SAT's developer, concluded that the gender difference in SAT scores was almost entirely explained by high school course selection (for example, girls took fewer math and science courses than boys and so got lower SAT math scores).[103]

FairTest called the ETS explanation a "smokescreen."[104] Yet similar evidence is available for blacks and Hispanics: Almost all the SAT math score differences between them and their white counterparts disappear when they take as much algebra and geometry in high school as white students do.[105]

The charge that the use of SATs in college admissions artificially depresses minority admissions is also misguided. As David W. Murray writes in "The War on Testing":

> Nor is it even clear that relying more exclusively on grades would bump up the enrollment numbers of blacks and Hispanics, as many seem to think. While it is true that more minority students would thereby become eligible for admission, so would other students whose grade point averages (GPAs) outstripped their test scores. A state commission in California, considering the adoption of such a scheme, discovered that in order to pick students from this larger pool for the limited number of places in the state university system, the schools would have to raise their GPA cut-off point. As a result, the percentage of eligible Hispanics would have remained the same, and black eligibility actually would have dropped.[106]

There is a double sadness to the focus of some minority spokesmen on the messenger instead of the message. Black and Hispanic students in the United States generally receive an education inferior to what white students receive. This is a shame and a disgrace. By blaming standardized tests instead of the schools that are responsible for their students' poor achievement, however, these advocacy groups waste efforts that would be better expended reforming bad schools.

A Public Agenda survey of parents on education issues pertaining to race implies that the NAACP actions in Texas and other states against high-stakes standardized testing may not even reflect what most African Americans want. "Most African-American parents do not think standardized tests are culturally biased," reports Public Agenda, "and very few want race to be a factor when choosing the best teachers for their children . . . ."[107] When asked why, on average, black students don't do as well as whites on standardized achievement tests, only 28 percent say it is mostly because "the tests are culturally biased against black students." Forty-four percent of black parents say "the tests measure real differences in educational achievement," and 18 percent say the reason for this difference is a result of low expectations.[108]

6. Tests Are Too Costly

Some experts have criticized standardized tests as too costly. Daniel Koretz appeared before a Congressional committee to testify against President George H. W. Bush's national testing proposal and stressed cost as a major negative. He claimed that while costs of standard multiple-choice commercial tests range from $2 to $5 per student, the costs of performance-based national tests would be considerably more than $100 per student, perhaps as high as $325 per student.

Another study of the extent and cost of testing, by Walter Haney and George Madaus of CSTEEP, calculated a high estimate of $22.7 billion spent on standardized testing in a year.[109] U.S. schools, the CSTEEP report claimed, suffered from "too much standardized testing" that amounted to "a complete and utter waste of resources."[110] Their estimate breaks down to about $575 per student per year.

A CRESST report by Larry Picus, which counted cost components in much the same way as the CSTEEP study, estimated costs of a certain state test at between $848 and $1,792 per student tested.[111]

Response:

In the early 1990s, the U.S. General Accounting Office (GAO) surveyed a national sample of state and local testing directors and administrators to appraise the costs of then-current statewide and districtwide tests. Based on their responses, the GAO assumed that the tests President George H. W. Bush proposed would probably evolve, as many state exams had, from plans for a 100 percent performance-based format to a mixed format that includes multiple-choice items. Eleven state tests ranging from 20 percent to 100 percent performance-based cost an average of $33 per student, including the salary time of teachers and other staff engaged in test-related activity, as well as the purchase of test materials and services. The GAO estimated that slightly more than $500 million was spent by U.S. school systems on systemwide testing in a year, or about 0.2 percent of all spending on elementary and secondary schools.[112]

The GAO estimate of $33 per student contrasts with CRESST and CSTEEP estimates of $575 to $1,792. The GAO estimate of about $500 million for the total national cost of systemwide testing contrasts with a CSTEEP estimate 45 times higher.

Testing critics estimate standardized tests' costs so much higher because they count the costs of any activities *related to* a test as costs *of* a test. In the CRESST study of Kentucky's performance-based testing program, for example, teachers were asked to count the number of hours they spent preparing materials for classroom use that related to the testing program. In an instructional program that has the intention of unifying all instruction and assessment into a seamless web, where the curriculum and the test mutually determine each other, all instruction throughout the entire school year will be related to the assessment.

Furthermore, the Kentucky Instructional Results Information System (KIRIS) was a comprehensive program that included changes in curriculum, instruction, and evaluation. Assessment was just one component. All the changes were implemented at the same time, and some survey respondents could consider any or all KIRIS costs as related to the assessment. Given the manner in which it posed its questions, CRESST could not discern which were costs of the test and which were costs of other parts of the KIRIS program.

The CSTEEP study counted even more cost items, such as student time. Walter Haney and the other CSTEEP researchers assumed that the time spent on preparing for or taking a test holds no instructional value whatsoever. (I would guess that students probably learn more while preparing for or taking a test.) Then they calculated the present discounted value of that "lost" instructional time against future earnings, assuming all future earnings to be the direct outcome of school instruction. The

CSTEEP researchers also counted building overhead (maintenance and capital costs) for the time spent testing, even though those costs are constant and not affected by the existence of a test. In sum, CSTEEP counts any and all costs incurred simultaneously with tests, not just those caused by testing.

7. Other Countries Don't Test As Much As the United States

At the AERA press conference, CSTEEP's Madaus argued against proposals for a national examination system by claiming that "American students [were] already the most heavily tested in the world."[113] In a separate report, he also asserted that the trend in other developed countries is toward less standardized testing. He reasoned that other countries are dropping large-scale external tests because they no longer need them as selection devices because places in upper secondary programs are being made available to everyone and access to higher education programs has widened. Thus, he argued, a worldwide trend toward less external testing could be found at all levels of education, "even at the postsecondary level," and it was unidirectional—large-scale, external tests were being "abolished."[114]

Response:

Are U.S. students the "most heavily tested in the world"? No. U.S. students actually spend less time taking high-stakes standardized tests than do students in other developed countries. A 1991 survey for the Organisation for Economic Co-operation and Development revealed that "U.S. students face fewer hours and fewer numbers of high-stakes standardized tests than their counterparts in every one of the thirteen other countries and states participating in the survey and fewer hours of state-mandated tests than their counterparts in twelve of the thirteen other countries and states."[115]

What of Madaus's assertion of a trend toward less standardized testing in other countries?[116] The primary trend appears to be toward more testing, with a variety of new test types used for a variety of purposes. In a study I conducted, I found twenty-seven countries and provinces had increased or planned to increase ∴est-ing over the period 1974–1999, while only three decreased it. Altogether, fifty-nine tests were added and only five dropped.[117]

8. All Those Who Really Care about Children Oppose Testing

The panelists at the AERA press conference implied that they were speaking on behalf of teachers and students, defending them against politicians, mean-spirited conservatives, and the greedy testing industry.[118] The critics claimed that those who care about teachers and students see testing for what it really is and oppose it.

Regarding teachers, for example, Robert Stake, said, "[teachers] have essentially no confidence in testing as the basis of the reform of schooling in America."[119]

The laundry list of costs attributed to *students* from the use of standardized tests ranged from a change in instruction away from the "neat stuff" in the curriculum toward "lower-order thinking" to an increase in grade retention and dropout rates from the use of standardized tests in high-stakes situations. A CRESST study on the "unintended consequences of external testing" that Mary Lee Smith referred to at the conference claimed to find "stress, frustration, burnout, fatigue, physical illness, misbehavior and fighting, and psychological distress" among the effects of testing on young students.[120]

Response:

To learn the true attitudes toward testing among teachers, students, parents, and the public, I attempted to gather all relevant U.S. poll and survey items on student testing by collecting many surveys myself and searching the Roper Center archives. I discovered 200 items from seventy-five surveys over three decades.[121]

The results are fairly decisive. Majorities of the general public favor more testing, more high-stakes testing, and higher stakes in testing. The majorities have been large, often very large, and fairly consistent over the years, across polls and surveys, and even across respondent groups. Parents, students, employers, state education administrators, and even teachers (who exhibit more guarded opinions and sometimes fear being blamed if their students score badly on tests) consistently favor more student testing and higher stakes.

Twenty-seven polls taken between 1970 and 1999 asked specific respondents whether they thought education would improve if there were higher (student) stakes in school testing. The results of twenty-six of the twenty-seven polls said yes, in most cases by huge margins.

Which was the twenty-seventh study, the one claiming that respondents want lower stakes in student testing? It was a survey conducted by CSTEEP and funded by the National Science Foundation.[122] Its contrary conclusions may have a lot to do with its convoluted design. First, respondents were chosen selectively from urban, high-minority public school districts. High school teachers in the sample were limited to those with classes of "average and below average" students.[123] Moreover, the specific interview question that elicited opinions on the effects of mandated tests was, in my judgment, biased in a way that would generate negative answers. The question was: "Do you have any particular concerns or opinions about any of these standardized tests?" "Concerns" doesn't equal "criticisms" in meaning, but, in this context, it's pretty close.[124] Then the CSTEEP researchers classified as "negative" responses those that others might classify as neutral or positive. For example, if a teacher said that her students "didn't test well," it was interpreted by the researchers as a "major source of invalidity" and a "negative" comment, even though students can test poorly for dozens of reasons, including not studying and not paying attention in class.[125]

Do these CSTEEP researchers and the speakers at the aforementioned AERA press conference at least represent other "education establishment" organizations in opposing high-stakes standardized testing?

Far from it. The National Association of State Boards of Education has come out strongly in favor of greater use of high-stakes standardized testing.[126] So have state superintendents and governors. The American Federation of Teachers (AFT) has been the nation's most forceful and vocal advocate for greater use of high-stakes standardized student testing.

Nationwide polls of teachers conducted over three decades by the Carnegie Foundation for the Advancement of Teaching, Metropolitan Life Insurance Co., the AFT, and Public Agenda show strong teacher support for high-stakes standardized tests.[127]

Despite this widespread support for testing, press coverage of testing issues often seems one-sided *against* testing. It typically features a FairTest spokesperson as the antitesting alternative to some sincere, beleaguered state or local testing director just trying to do her job.

I telephoned a few newspaper reporters to try to understand why their stories on testing were set up this way. They replied that they do not know of any advocacy group on the other side of the issue that could balance FairTest's perspective. They added that FairTest is also reliable: They keep up with the issues, and they return telephone calls promptly. In his review of SAT critiques, Gregory Cizek expresses disappointment that "the measurement profession has made no corresponding, popular, accessible, public defense of its mission or of testing."[128]

While one sees only a handful of education-researcher experts speaking out in favor of high-stakes standardized tests, there are in fact hundreds of qualified testing experts working for national, state, or local agencies (not to mention the experts working for organizations that develop tests under contract to these government agencies) who are legally and ethically restricted from expressing their views regarding testing policy. The debate seems unbalanced only because one side is often missing from it, that of the pro-testing advocates who cannot speak out.

For a reporter who arrives at the office in the morning with no story and who cannot leave in the evening without one, FairTest is a godsend. The millions who favor testing have no comparable voice.

Testing in Perspective

That tests and test results can be misused is beyond dispute. Human beings are responsible for administering them and interpreting their results, and humans are imperfect creatures. There also is no denying that tests are imperfect measurement devices. If the items in the antitesting canon were also beyond dispute, one might well be disposed to give up on high-stakes standardized testing. But that would be an enormous mistake.

The critics would have us believe that all problems with high-stakes and standardized testing must always be with us, that is, that nothing can be changed or improved. They're wrong. Some of the alleged problems—that they hurt learning and are expensive, for example—are really not problems at all, as shown above. Other problems apply equally to the alternatives to testing. Still others are solvable and are being or have been solved by state, local, or national testing directors.

Probably the single most important recent innovation in relation to the quality and fairness of testing in the United States has been the addition of managerial and technical expertise in state education agencies. At that level, it is possible to retain an adequate group of technically proficient testing experts, adept at screening, evaluating, administering, and interpreting tests, who are not controlled by commercial publishers or naive about test results. They, along with governors and legislatures, are currently calling the shots in standardized testing. Some of the most important decisions affecting the design and content of the tests, the character of the testing industry, and the nature of its work are today being made by state testing directors.

These testing directors can, for example, deploy a number of relatively simple solutions to the problems of score inflation, curricular compression and teaching to the test, including: not revealing the contents of tests beforehand; not using the same test twice; including items on the test that sample broadly from the whole domain of the curriculum tested; requiring that nontested subjects also get taught (or testing them, too); and maintaining strict precautions against cheating during test administrations.

In North Carolina and other states, they do something else about score inflation: They keep raising the bar. As instruction and learning improve and scores rise, they boost their grading standards.[129] Their students' dramatic improvements on the independent NAEP offer evidence that the achievement gains are real, not a result of score inflation caused by narrowing the curriculum and teaching to the test.

In some states and countries, officials use "blended" or "moderated" scores for high-stakes decisions. The "blends" combine test scores with other measures, such as classroom grades and attendance records, so that instructional efforts will not focus exclusively on the standardized test and so that high-stakes decisions will not be based solely on single or even multiple attempts at passing a test.

One final argument against testing, the argument that using test results to evaluate schools leads to unfair comparisons between rich districts with highly educated parents and poor districts with less-well educated parents, can also be dealt with. There are at least two solutions to this problem. One is to set targets for schools based on their own past performance. Another is to calculate value-added test scores, as Tennessee and North Carolina do. This method estimates how much value a school adds to the level of achievement that would have been predicted (given the background and prior attainment of students), then adjusts a school's or district's test scores accordingly. Like any other system, value-added scoring can be abused; there's a particular danger in its being used to excuse the performance of school systems that have a large number of poor and minority children. Value-added scores can also be tricky to calculate. But many able and earnest analysts throughout the country are striving to make value-added systems work.

Although some of the "problems" with standardized testing turn out not to be problems, and others turn out to be solvable, a third set of problems is inherent and inevitable—but similar problems are also present in the alternatives to standardized tests.

The critics unfairly compare high-stakes standardized testing with their own notion of perfection. Administration of high-stakes tests will never be perfect. There will always be some teachers and pupils who cheat. There will always be some students who are better prepared to take a test than others, and so on.

Perfection, however, is not a reasonable standard of comparison for standardized testing. Too often, the alternative is a system of social promotion with many levels of (nominally) the same subject matter being taught, ranging from classes for the self-motivated kids to those for youngsters who quit trying years before and whom the system has ignored ever since.[130] Too often, the result is a system that graduates functional illiterates.

If *none* of the curriculum is tested, we cannot know if any of it works. Without standardized tests, no one outside the classroom can reliably gauge student progress. No district or state superintendent. No governor. No taxpayer. No parent. No student. Each has to accept whatever the teacher says, and without standardized tests, no teacher has any point of comparison, either.

Certainly, it is unfair to test what has not been taught, but no such claim can be made about testing what has been taught. And if what is tested is the curriculum, then attacks on teaching to the test seem silly because teachers are teaching what they should be teaching.

Eliminating high-stakes standardized testing would necessarily increase our reliance on teacher grading and testing. But are teacher evaluations free from all the complaints of the antitesting canon? Not exactly. Individual teachers also can narrow the curriculum to that which they prefer. Grades are susceptible to inflation with any teachers. Students get to know a teacher better and learn his idiosyncrasies. A teacher's grades and test scores are far more likely to be idiosyncratic and far less likely to be generalizable than the scores of any standardized test.[131]

Moreover, teacher-made tests are not necessarily any better-supplied with higher-order thinking than are standardized tests. Yet many test critics would bar all high-stakes standardized tests and have us rely solely on teacher evaluations of student performance. How reliable are those evaluations? Not very. There are a number of problems with teacher evaluations, according to research on the topic. Teachers tend to consider "nearly everything" when assigning marks, including student class participation, perceived effort, progress over the period of the course, and comportment, according to Gregory Cizek. Actual achievement vis-à-vis the subject matter is just one factor. Indeed, many teachers express a clear preference for noncognitive outcomes such as "group interaction, effort, and participation" as more important than averaging tests and quiz scores.[132] It's not so much what you know, it's how you act in class. Being enthusiastic and group-oriented not only gets you into the audience for television game shows, but it also, apparently, gets you better grades in school.

One study of teacher grading practices discovered that 66 percent of teachers feel that their perception of a student's ability should be taken into consideration in awarding the final grade.[133] Parents of students who assume that their children's grades represent subject matter mastery might well be surprised.

Conclusion: Two Views of Testing and Learning

There is perhaps no more concise exposition of the general philosophy undergirding opposition to standardized testing among education experts than that revealed in the Public Agenda survey of education school professors, *Different Drummers*.[134] Among the reasons most dislike standardized tests are their preferences for: "process over content"; "facilitating learning" rather than teaching; and "partnership and collaboration" over imparting knowledge.[135]

A large majority of education school professors surveyed felt that it was more important that "kids struggle with the process of trying to find the right answers" (86 percent) than that "kids end up knowing the right answers to the questions or problems" (12 percent): "[I]t is the process, not the content, of learning that most engages the passion and energy of teacher educators. If students learn how to learn, the content will naturally follow."[136]

The role of teachers in this education worldview, then, should be that of "facilitator," not "sage on the stage." When asked which statement was "closer to their own philosophy of the role of teachers," 92 percent of the education professors agreed that "teachers should see themselves as facilitators of learning who enable their students to learn on their own." Only 7 percent felt that "teachers should see themselves as conveyors of knowledge who enlighten their students with what they know."[137]

The constructivist criticism of any teaching or testing that fixes the manner of solving a problem and penalizes students for careless or minor errors is not shared by the public or even by students. In *Getting By,* Public Agenda reported that 79 percent of teens say "most students would learn more if their schools routinely assured that kids were on time and completed their homework . . . . [Sixty-one percent said] having their classwork checked regularly and being forced to redo it until it was correct would get them to learn a lot more. When interviewed in focus groups, teens often remembered "tough" teachers with fondness: "I had a math teacher [who] was like a drill sergeant. She was nice, but she was really strict. Now I don't have her this year, and looking back, I learned so much."[138]

In the real world, testing will continue. Testing experts have much to contribute to efforts that ensure testing is done well. Unfortunately, many of them share an ideological orientation that makes any type of standardized test impossible to swallow. Until these experts reexamine their most fundamental beliefs about teaching and learning, all the hard work of improving standardized tests will have to be done without them.

Notes

1. See Richard P. Phelps, "The Demand for Standardized Student Testing," *Educational Measurement: Issues and Practice* 17, no. 3 (fall 1998).
2. Steve Farkas, Jean Johnson, and Ann Duffett, *Different Drummers: How Teachers of Teachers View Public Education* (New York: Public Agenda, 1997), 20, 36.
3. Ibid., 20.
4. Ibid., 13–14.
5. Ibid., 13.
6. Ibid., 14.
7. See transcripts of the conference papers printed, along with an introduction, in "Accountability As a Reform Strategy," *Phi Delta Kappan* (November 1991): 219–51.
8. CRESST is headquartered at UCLA's education school, but associates with "partners" at the education schools of the universities of Colorado and Southern California, Arizona State University, and the RAND Corporation. CRESST publishes dozens of reports every year that are objective, often concentrating on psychometric methods. Some of the best psychometric research in the country is

produced by CRESST. The research that several of CRESST's affiliated scholars publish that relates to *testing policy,* however, typically subscribes to the canon.

9. CSTTEEP has recently changed its name to the National Board on Educational Testing and Public Policy (NBETPP). Not everyone associated with CSTEEP opposes testing. Indeed, the Third International Mathematics and Science Study (TIMSS), perhaps the standardized test most reviled by testing critics, was head-quartered at CSTEEP. TIMSS showed U.S. students performing more and more poorly in comparison with their international counterparts as grade levels advanced to the last year of high school. But another group of researchers at CSTEEP, not associated with TIMSS, devote themselves almost exclusively to antitesting research.

10. FairTest receives much of its financial support from the Ford Foundation, a great deal of exposure in the media, and a seat at the table with study commissions on testing policy as an interested "stakeholder"; for example, it was on the former Office of Technology Assessment's Advisory Panel for the report *Testing in American Schools: Asking the Right Questions.*

11. The actual number of standardized tests administered annually in the public schools at the time was around 40 million, not 100 million. Forty million tests for about 40 million students calculates to one test per student per year, and only one in four of those was for high stakes. See Richard P. Phelps, "The Extent and Character of Systemwide Student Testing in the United States," *Educational Assessment* 4, no. 2: 89–121.

12. Noe Medina and Monty D. Neill, *Fallout from the Testing Explosion: How 100 Million Standardized Exams Undermine Equity and Excellence in America's Public Schools* (Cambridge, Mass.: FairTest, 1990).

13. Daniel M. Koretz, "State Comparisons Using NAEP: Large Costs, Disappointing Benefits," *Educational Researcher* 20, no. 3 (April 1991): 19.

14. Ibid., 19–21.

15. Ibid., 20.

16. See also Richard M. Wolf, "What Can We Learn from State NAEP?" *Educational Measurement: Issues and Practice;* Bruce J. Biddle, "Foolishness, Dangerous Nonsense, and Real Correlates of State Differences in Achievement," *Phi Delta Kappan* (Bloomington, Ind.: Phi Delta Kappa online article, August 8, 1998).

17. Koretz, "State Comparisons Using NAEP: Large Costs, Disappointing Benefits," 20.

18. Gary Phillips, "Benefits of State-by-State Comparisons," *Educational Researcher*

20, no. 3 (April 1991), 17–19.

19. Ibid., p. 17. See also George Bohrnstedt, Project Director, *The Trial State Assessment: Prospects and Realities* (Stanford, Calif.: National Academy of Education, 1993).

20. James W. Pellegrino, Lee R. Jones, and Karen J. Mitchell, *Grading the Nation's Report Card: Evaluating NAEP and Transforming the Assessment of Educational Progress* (Washington, D.C.: National Academy Press, 1998), 2.

21. Ibid.

22. FairTest, "How the States Scored" (Cambridge, Mass.: FairTest, summer 1997).

23. Robert C. Johnston, "In Texas, the Arrival of Spring Means the Focus Is on Testing," *Education Week* 17, no. 33 (April 29, 1998): 20.

24. Ibid., 21.

25. Lonnie Harp, "OCR Probes Bias Complaint Against Texas Exit Test," *Education Week on the Web* (February 7, 1996).

26. Linda Jacobson, "State Graduation Tests Raise Questions, Stakes," *Education Week on the Web* (June 24, 1998).

27. "ED Clears Texas Tests" in "News in Brief," *Education Week on the Web* (August 6, 1997).

28. Johnston, "In Texas, the Arrival of Spring Means the Focus Is on Testing," 21.

29. Ibid., 1, 20, 21; "Pass or Fail," *Teacher Magazine: Education Week on the Web* (September 1994); Lonnie Harp, "Final Exam," *Teacher Magazine: Education Week on the Web* (September 1994); Lonnie Harp, "Texas Politicians Wrangle Over School Rankings," *Education Week on the Web* (September 14, 1994); Robert C. Johnston, "Texas Governor Has Social Promotions in His Sights," *Education Week on the Web* (February 11, 1998).

30. See "Pass or Fail," *Teacher Magazine: Education Week on the Web* (September 1994); Harp, "Final Exam"; Harp, "Texas Politicians Wrangle Over School Rankings"; Johnston, "Texas Governor Has Social Promotions in His Sights."

31. They have eased one requirement, however. The "no pass, no play" rule, originally recommended by an education reform commission chaired by Ross Perot, barred students who were failing courses from participating in team sports for six weeks. That has been reduced to three weeks as other, broader requirements have been put in place. See Harp, "Texas Politicians Wrangle Over School Rankings"; Lonnie Harp, "Texas Lawmakers Reach Accord on Overhaul of Education Laws," *Education Week on the Web* (May 31, 1995).

32. See Kathleen Kennedy Manzo: "N.C. Consensus Pushes for New Set of Reforms," *Education Week on the Web* (April 9, 1997); "Quality Counts, '98: North

Carolina Summary," *Education Week on the Web;* "High Stakes: Test Truth or Consequences," *Education Week,* 17, no. 8 (October 22, 1997); "N.C. Gets First School-by-School Performance Results," *Education Week* (September 3, 1997): 26; "Struggling N.C. Schools Buoyed by State Teams," *Education Daily* (July 10, 1998): 4.

33. Marzo, "Struggling N.C. Schools Buoyed by State Teams," 4.

34. Ibid., 4.

35. Telephone conversations with Vanessa Jeter and Janet Byrd of the North Carolina Department of Public Instruction (October 19, 1998).

36. David Molpus, "Improving High School Education," *National Public Radio Morning Edition* (September 15, 1998).

37. Ibid.

38. Manzo, "High Stakes: Test Truths or Consequences," 1, 2.

39. Ibid., 3.

40. Ibid., 3.

41. Ibid., 2.

42. Ibid., 1.

43. Ibid., 2.

44. Ibid., 4.

45. Telephone conversations with James Causby, superintendent of the Johnson County Schools (September 24, 1998).

46. Richard M. Jaeger, "Legislative Perspectives on Statewide Testing" in "Accountability As a Reform Strategy," *Phi Delta Kappan* (November 1991): 242.

47. Ibid.

48. Ibid.

49. George F. Madaus, "The Effects of Important Tests on Students: Implications for a National Examination System," *Phi Delta Kappan* (November 1991): 228; Lorrie A. Shepard, "Will National Tests Improve Student Learning?" *Phi Delta Kappan* (November 1991): 234.

50. See Indicator C3 in Organisation for Economic and Co-operative Development, "Education at a Glance: OECD Indicators 1997" (Paris: OECD, 1997). The United States has a lower percentage of 16-year-old students enrolled than do Austria, Belgium, Canada, the Czech Republic, Denmark, Finland, Germany, the Netherlands, Norway, New Zealand, and Sweden, all countries with high-stakes secondary-level exit exams. Rates in Hungary and Ireland are similar to ours. Switzerland and the United Kingdom are the only countries, among those

included, with high-stakes exit exams and lower enrollment rates than the United States. Comparisons at age 17 are similar. The conclusion: Students drop out in the United States for reasons other than not passing an exit exam.

51. J. B. Erickson, *Indiana Youth Poll: Youths' Views of High School Life* (Indianapolis: Indiana Youth Institute, 1991), 33.

52. Bryan W. Griffin and Mark H. Heidorn, "An Examination of the Relationship Between Minimum Competency Test Performance and Dropping Out of High School," *Educational Evaluation and Policy Analysis* 18, no. 3 (fall 1996): 243–52.

53. C. Boyden Gray and Evan J. Kemp Jr., "Flunking Testing: Is Too Much Fairness Unfair to School Kids?" *Washington Post,* 19 September 1993, C3.

54. FairTest, "Testing Our Children: North Carolina" (Cambridge, Mass.: FairTest, summer 1997).

55. See Indicators 8 and 9 in U.S. Department of Education, National Center for Education Statistics, *State Indicators in Education 1997,* NCES 97–376, by Richard P. Phelps, Andrew Cullen, Jack C. Easton, and Clayton M. Best, Project Officer, Claire Geddes (Washington, D.C.: 1997).

56. While the SAT tends to be more visible, about half of state colleges and well over one-third of all U.S. colleges use the competing American College Test (ACT). Some colleges allow applicants to submit either test.

57. FairTest, "FairTest Fact Sheet: The SAT" (Cambridge, Mass.: FairTest, Summer 1997): 2.

58. They don't mention, however, the continual *growth* in the number of colleges *using* the SAT—more than a hundred added since 1990, bringing the total to 1,450 four-year institutions. See Charles A. Kiesler, "On SAT Cause and Effect," *Education Week* (May 13, 1998): 43.

59. See Debbie Goldberg, "Putting the SAT to the Test," *The Washington Post Education Review* (October 27, 1996): 20–21; Many colleges have complained to the National Association for College Admission Counseling (NACAC) about their presence on "The List" of colleges that FairTest claims waive the SAT requirement. Many colleges FairTest includes waive the requirement only for a few students under extraordinary circumstances (for example, disabilities, remote foreign locations, and so on) (telephone conversation with NACAC officials, August 14, 1998).

60. See, for example, Joyce Slayton Mitchell, "A Word to High School Seniors— SATs Don't Get You In," *Education Week* (May 29, 1998): 33; also National Association for College Admission Counseling, "Members Assess 1996

Recruitment Cycle in Eighth Annual NACAC Admission Trends Survey," *News from National Association for College Admission Counseling* (October 28, 1996): 2, 4.

61. National Association for College Admission Counseling, "Members Assess 1996 Recruitment Cycle in Eighth Annual NACAC Admission Trends Survey," 2, 4.

62. See Warren W. Willingham et al., *Predicting College Grades* (New York: The College Board, 1990), chapters 5 and 12; also Thomas F. Donlon, ed., *The College Board Technical Handbook for the Scholastic Aptitude Test and Achievement Tests* (New York: The College Board, 1984), chapter 8.

63. Actually, one could make the same (poor) argument about high school grade-point averages. After all other predictive factors are accounted for, including SAT or ACT scores, high school GPA explains only another several percentage points of the variation in first-year college grades. So, why bother with the GPA? See also Gerald W. Bracey, "The $150 Million Redundancy," *Phi Delta Kappan* 70, no. 9 (May 1989): 698–702; Lucy May, "Tests Don't Have All the Answers to How Kentucky Kids Rank," *The Lexington Herald-Leader,* July 6, 1995; Edward B. Fiske, "Questioning an American Rite of Passage: How Valuable Is the SAT?" *New York Times*, January 18, 1989, B10. Walt Haney of Boston College is often quoted on this issue. See, for example, May, "Test Don't Have All the Answers to How Kentucky Kids Rank"; Debbie Goldberg, "Putting the SAT to the Test"; Peter Sacks, "Standardized Testing: Meritocracy's Crooked Yardstick," *Change* (March/April 1997): 26.

64. Lucy May, "Tests Don't Have All the Answers to How Kentucky Kids Rank," 44, 45.

65. Even 15 percent underestimates the predictive power of the SAT or ACT. Because colleges publish the mean and range of the admissions test scores of their first-year class, a high school senior can pick potential colleges in whose range his test score fits, and he is more likely to be admitted. Likewise, colleges can focus their recruiting efforts where they are likely to find attractive applicants who can succeed on their campuses and who might be willing to come. This represents an added benefit of the SAT—applicants and colleges don't waste time chasing after poor matches. Technicians call this benefit "restriction of range" or, more generally, "allocative efficiency." Allocative efficiency is very difficult to estimate, but the Educational Testing Service has calculated that just for the colleges alone it must add at least another two percentage points of predictive power to the additional 15 percent already accounted for by SAT scores.

66. At best, a student's high school record explains only 44 percent of the variation

in first-year college grades. SAT scores alone explain 42 percent of the variation. To a large extent, however, high school record and SAT scores represent the same thing, mastery of academic subject matter. Thus when high school record and SAT scores are used together in equations to predict students' first-year college grades, the two predictive factors overlap. If SAT scores are put in the equation first, high school record adds only a comparatively smaller amount of predictive power. After subtracting the proportion of predictive power that the two predictive factors share in common, SAT scores predict an additional 15 percent of the variation in first-year college grades. This 15 percent predicted by the SAT represents 34 percent of the variation in first-year college grades explained by high school record alone (which was 44 percent). Thus, if we put high school record in the prediction equation first, SAT scores represent a 34 percent incremental increase in predictive power when added to the equation. See Willingham et al., *Predicting College Grades,* chapters 5 and 12.

67. The annual survey by the National Association for College Admission Counseling shows that their members consider the following criteria the most important in determining admission (by percentage, mentioning each criterion of considerable or moderate importance): grades in college prep courses, such as Advanced Placement courses (90); admission test scores, such as the SAT or ACT (82); grades in all subjects (79); class rank (71); essay or writing sample (53); counselor recommendation (66); teacher recommendation (55). (National Association for College Admission Counseling, "Members Assess 1996 Recruitment Cycle in Eighth Annual NACAC Admission Trends Survey," 2, 4.)

68. To some extent, the criticisms are tautological. A CSTEEP study of several commercially available math and science tests, managed by George Madaus and funded by the National Science Foundation, concluded that the tests promoted "test preparation" practices. Eighty-one percent of math teachers and 53 percent of science teachers engaged in some form of "test preparation," according to CSTEEP. However, the researchers "coded 'test preparation' as 'present' when the teacher or administrator made an explicit link between a particular activity and test scores, or gave such evidence in spite of denying test preparation." Thus, if a teacher taught an ordinary math or science lesson and hoped that it would improve students' performance on a test, that's "test preparation." Mary Maxwell West and Katherine A. Viator, *The Influence of Testing on Teaching Math and Science in Grades 4–12: Appendix D: Testing and Teaching in Six Urban Sites* (Boston: CSTEEP, October 1992), 27–28.

69. Mary Lee Smith et al. *Reforming Schools by Reforming Assessment: Consequences of*

the Arizona Student Assessment Program (ASAP): Equity and Teacher Capacity Building, CSE Technical Report 425 (Los Angeles: CRESST, March 1997), 2.

70. The history of the large-scale, standardized use of portfolios is spare and brief (FairTest, "Testing Our Children: Introduction" [Cambridge, Mass.: FairTest, 1998], 2). There appear to be many problems with a sole reliance on portfolios to measure student progress: They're far more susceptible to cheating, coaching, gaming, and outright plagiarism than are standardized tests. (See "Test Violations Uncovered" in "News in Brief," *Education Week on the Web* [August 6, 1997]: 5; Maryl Gearhart and Joan L. Herman, "Portfolio Assessment: Whose Work Is It?" *Evaluation Comment* [CSE, CRESST, winter 1996]; and Daniel M. Koretz, "Sometimes a Cigar Is Only a Cigar" in *Debating the Future of American Education,* ed. Diane Ravitch [Washington, D.C.: Brookings Institution, 1995]: 160–62.) Moreover, they reward occasional, exceptional brilliance and not steady competence, and they are difficult to score with consistency (Daniel Koretz et al., *The Reliability of Scores from the 1992 Vermont Portfolio Assessment Program,* Technical Report No. 355 [Los Angeles: CRESST, December 1992). These sound like the same tenor of criticisms that FairTest, the most prominent advocate for the exclusive use of portfolios, makes of standardized tests.

71. One can also find elements of other theories and philosophies in the critics' rhetoric—that of "multiple intelligences," popularized by Howard Gardner, and what E. D. Hirsch labels "romantic progressivism," for example. As this article is not meant to focus on philosophy, however, I have kept this digression spare.

72. Daniel M. Koretz, Robert L. Linn, Stephen B. Dunbar, and Lorrie S. Shepard, "The Effects of High-Stakes Testing on Achievement: Preliminary Findings About Generalization Across Tests" (paper presented at the 1991 annual meeting of the AERA, Chicago, April 3–7). See also Robert L. Linn, "Assessments and Accountability," *Education Researcher* (March 2000): 4–16.

73. See a discussion of the phenomenon that includes the physician John Jacob Cannell and many others in full-issue coverage in *Educational Measurement: Issues and Practice* (summer 1988).

74. Test publishers make economic and logistical trade-offs by using convenient samples, such as Chapter 1 students they are already testing to meet Chapter 1 requirements, as norming samples.

75. See Gary W. Phillips and Chester E. Finn Jr., "The Lake Wobegon Effect: A Skeleton in the Testing Closet?" *Educational Measurement: Issues and Practice* (summer 1988): 10–12.

76. Ibid.

77. Shepard, "Will National Tests Improve Student Learning?" 233, 234.

78. Farkas, Johnson, and Duffet, *Different Drummers,* 7; Jean Johnson and John Immerwahr, *First Things First: What Americans Expect from the Public Schools* (New York: Public Agenda, 1994).

79. Shepard, "Will National Tests Improve Student Learning?" 233–34.

80. See, for example, Mary Lee Smith, "Put to the Test: The Effects of External Testing on Teachers," *Educational Researcher* 20, no. 5 (June 1991); "Meanings of Test Preparation," *American Educational Research Journal* 28, no. 3 (fall 1991); "The Role of Testing in Elementary Schools," CSE Technical Report 321, Los Angeles, UCLA, May 1991; and Lorrie Shepard et al. "Effects of High-Stakes Testing on Instruction," paper presented at the Annual Meeting of the AERA, Chicago, April 1991.

81. See, for example, Shepard, "Will National Tests Improve Student Learning?" 233, 234.

82. See, for example, the example on the first two pages of Mary Lee Smith, "Put to the Test: The Effects of External Testing on Teachers," *Educational Researcher* 20, no. 5 (June 1991).

83. Farkas, Johnson, and Duffett, *Different Drummers: How Teachers of Teachers View Public Education,* 12.

84. See OECD, *Education at a Glance,* 1997, p. 200, for the salary figures. See also John H. Bishop: "Impacts of School Organization and Signaling on Incentives to Learn in France, the Netherlands, England, Scotland, and the United States," working paper no. 94-30, Center for Advanced Human Resource Studies, New York State School of Industrial and Labor Relations, Cornell University (Ithaca, N.Y.: December 1994) and "Incentives for Learning: Why American High School Students Compare So Poorly to Their Counterparts Overseas," working paper no. 89-09, Cornell University School of Industrial and Labor Relations (1989) for discussions of the relationship of external tests and teacher status.

85. See Richard P. Phelps, "Benchmarking to the World's Best in Mathematics," *Evaluation Review* 25, no. 4 (August 2001); Linda Ann Bond and Darla A. Cohen, "The Early Impact of Indiana Statewide Testing for Educational Progress on Local Education Agencies," *Advances in Program Evaluation,* in ed. Rita G. O'Sullivan and Robert E. Stake, Vol.1, Part B, 1991, 87–88; or see James Stigler's work comparing time use in U.S., German, and Japanese lower secondary mathematics and science classes, in James W. Stigler and James Hiebert, "Understanding and Improving Classroom Mathematics Instruction: An Overview of the TIMSS Video Study," *Phi Delta Kappan* (Bloomington: Phi

Delta Kappa, September 1997): 14–21.

86. Robert Rothman, "Study Confirms 'Fears' Regarding Commercial Tests," *Education Week* 12, no. 7 (October 21, 1992): 1, 13.

87. Malcolm Gladwell, "NSF Faults Science and Math Testing," *Washington Post,* 16 October 1992, A1, A4.

88. Ibid., 1.

89. Jerry Bobrow, *Cliffs SAT I Preparation Guide* (Lincoln, Neb.: Cliffs Notes, 1994) 63.

90. They are made explicit, however, in the cognitive laboratory testing that some multiple-choice tests undergo when they are developed.

91. Maryellen C. Harman and Claudette Fong-Kong Mungal, *The Influence of Testing on Teaching Math and Science in Grades 4–12: Appendix B: An Analysis of Standardized and Text-Embedded Tests in Mathematics* (Boston: CSTEEP, October 1992): 5.

92. Here's another definition of higher-order thinking that can be used as a point of comparison: "Students engage in purposeful, extended lines of thought during which they: identify the task or problem type; define and clarify essential elements and terms; judge and connect relevant information; and evaluate the adequacy of information and procedures for drawing conclusions and/or solving problems. In addition, students become self-conscious about their thinking and develop self-monitoring problem-solving strategies. Commonly specified higher-order reasoning processes are: cognitive: analyze, compare, infer/interpret, evaluate; metacognitive: plan, monitor, review/revise." (Edys S. Quellmalz, "Needed: Better Methods for Testing Higher-Order Thinking Skills," *Educational Leadership* 43, no. 2 [October 1985]: 30)

93. See George F. Madaus, Mary Maxwell West, Maryellen C. Harmon, Richard G. Lomax, and Katherine A. Viator, *The Influence of Testing on Teaching Math and Science in Grades 4-12: Executive Summary* (Chestnut Hill: CSTEEP, Boston College, October 1992); and West and Viator, *The Influence of Testing on Teaching Math and Science in Grades 4-12: Appendix D: Testing and Teaching in Six Urban Sites.*

94. E. D. Hirsch, of course, makes a more detailed and eloquent argument for the acceptance of both process and content as necessary components of intelligence. See E. D. Hirsch Jr., *The Schools We Need and Why We Don't Have Them* (New York: Doubleday, 1996).

95. Monte Neill, *High Stakes Tests Do Not Improve Student Learning* (Cambridge: FairTest, 1998).

96. FairTest, "Testing Our Children: Introduction" (Cambridge: FairTest, 1998): 2.

97. FairTest, "How the States Scored," and "Vermont," *FairTest Examiner* (summer 1997): 1–3.

98. Neill, *High Stakes Tests Do Not Improve Student Learning.*

99. See, for example, John H. Bishop, "A Steeper, Better Road to Graduation," *Education Next* (winter 2001).

100. John H. Bishop, "Diplomas for Learning, Not Seat Time: The Impacts of New York Regents Examinations," working paper no. 97-31, Cornell University, School of Industrial and Labor Relations, Center for Advanced Human Resource Studies (1997), 11–17.

101. See, for example, Ludger Woessman, "Why Students in Some Countries Do Better," *Education Next* (summer 2001); Richard P. Phelps, "Benchmarking to the Best in Mathematics: Quality Control in Curriculum and Instruction Among the Top Performers in the TIMSS," *Evaluation Review* 25, no. 4 (August 2001); Debra Viadero, "Assessment Payoff," *Education Week* (September 10, 1997): 32; as well as the work of Robert Costrell, Julian Betts, Thomas Dee, David Grissmer, Anne Danenberg, and others.

102. FairTest, "FairTest Fact Sheet: The SAT" and "SAT, ACT Bias Persist," *FairTest Examiner* (Cambridge: FairTest, fall, 1995).

103. Nancy Cole and Warren Willingham, *Gender and Fair Assessment* (Princeton: ETS, 1997).

104. "ETS Gender Bias Report a 'Smokescreen.'" *FairTest Examiner* (Cambridge: FairTest, fall 1997).

105. Sol Pelavin and Michael Kane, *Changing the Odds* (New York: The College Board, 1990).

106. David W. Murray, "The War on Testing," *Commentary* (September 1998): 34–37; see also Jessica L. Sandham, "Ending SAT May Hurt Minorities, Study Says," *Education Week* (January 14, 1998): 5.

107. "Diversity Takes Back Seat to Standards in New Poll," *Education Daily* (July 30, 1998): 3, 4.

108. Steve Farkus, Jean Johnson, Stephen Immerwahr, and Joanna McHugh, *Time to Move On: African-American and White Parents Set an Agenda for Public Schools* (New York: Public Agenda, 1998): 16, 17.

109. Walter M. Haney, George F. Madaus, and Robert Lyons, *The Fractured Marketplace for Standardized Testing* (Boston: Kluwer, 1993): 119.

110. Ibid., 122.

111. Lawrence O. Picus and Alisha Tralli, *Alternative Assessment Programs: What Are*

the True Costs? CSE Technical Report 441 (Los Angeles: CRESST, February 1998: 47.

112. See Richard P. Phelps, "Estimating the Cost of Standardized Student Testing in the United States," *Journal of Education Finance* 25, no. 3 (winter 2000). See also U.S. General Accounting Office, *Student Testing: Current Extent and Expenditures, with Cost Estimates for a National Examination,* Report GAO/PEMD-93-8 (Washington, D.C.: Author, 1993): 66; and U.S. Department of Education, National Center for Education Statistics, *Digest of Education Statistics 1997,* by Thomas D. Snyder and Charlene M. Hoffman, Washington, D.C.: U.S.GPO, 1997, Table 33.

113. Madaus, "The Effects of Important Tests on Students: Implications for a National Examination System," 227.

114. George F. Madaus and Thomas Kellaghan, "Student Examination Systems in the European Community: Lessons for the United States" (contractor report submitted to the Office of Technology Assessment, June 1991).

115. See Richard P. Phelps, "Are U.S. Students the Most Heavily Tested on Earth?" *Educational Measurement* 15, no. 3 (fall 1996); see also Richard P. Phelps, "Benchmarking to the Best in Mathematics: Quality Control in Curriculum and Instruction Among the Top Performers in the TIMSS," *Evaluation Review* 25, no. 4 (August 2001).

116. Madaus and Kellaghan, "Student Examination Systems in the European Community: Lessons for the United States."

117. See Richard P. Phelps, "Trends in Large-Scale Testing Outside the United States," *Educational Measurement* 19, no. 1 (spring 2000). The study included OECD countries, plus Russia and China.

118. On the latter point, one speaker, Linda Darling-Hammond, then of Columbia University Teachers College, now at Stanford University, said, "In contrast to testing in most other countries, testing in the U.S. is primarily controlled by commercial publishers and nonschool agencies that produce norm-referenced, multiple-choice instruments designed to rank students cheaply and efficiently." (Linda Darling-Hammond, "The Implications of Testing Policy for Quality and Equality," *Phi Delta Kappan* [November 1991]: 220).

119. Robert E. Stake, "The Teacher, Standardized Testing, and Prospects of Revolution," *Phi Delta Kappan* (November 1991): 246.

120. Mary Lee Smith and Claire Rottenberg, "Unintended Consequences of External Testing in Elementary Schools," *Educational Measurement: Issues and Practice* (winter 1991): 10, 11.

121. See Phelps, "The Demand for Standardized Student Testing."

122. Mary Maxwell West and Katherine A. Viator, *Teachers' and Administrators' Views of Mandated Testing Programs* (Boston: CSTEEP, October 1992), Table 3.

123. Ibid., 2.

124. Ibid., 6.

125. Ibid., 39, 40. Other sources of "test invalidity" included "kids are not on grade level," even though a student can be so because he doesn't study or pay attention in class; "kids don't try on tests," even though it can be the fault of the student that he doesn't try; or "tests have weird words, content unfamiliar to the students (language/culture bias)," even though words can be "weird" and "content unfamiliar" because a student doesn't do his reading, study, or pay attention in class.

126. National Association of State Boards of Education, The Full Measure: *Report of the NASBE Study Group on Statewide Assessment Systems* (Alexandria, Va.: Author, 1997); and Millicent Lawton, "State Boards' Leaders Call for Assessments Bearing Consequences," *Education Week on the Web* (October 22, 1997).

127. For an interesting study of the positive opinions of teachers and administrators toward one state test, see Linda Ann Bond and Darla A. Cohen, "The Early Impact of Indiana Statewide Testing for Educational Progress on Local Education Agencies," in *Advances in Program Evaluation* Vol.1, Part B, ed. Rita G. O'Sullivan and Robert E. Stake (1991), 78, 79, 87, 88.

128. Gregory J. Cizek, "The Case Against the SAT," book review, *Educational and Psychological Measurement* 50, no. 3 (autumn 1990): 705.

129. For example, see "State News Roundup," *Education Week on the Web* (June 8, 1994): 1.

130. According to Jeff Moss, the associate school superintendent for the Hoke County, North Carolina, schools, before the accountability reforms, "We had seven levels of instruction for a subject matter—such as seven levels of biology, seven levels of English I—which ranged from remedial to honors or college preparatory. So the teacher expectation was such that if I labeled you a basic student I needed to put you in basic English and not require much from you." See Molpus, "Improving High School Education."

131. For a comprehensive overview of the quality and reliability of teacher evaluations of student achievement, see Richard J. Stiggins and Nancy Faires Conklin, *In Teachers' Hands: Investigating the Practices of Classroom Assessment* (New York: SUNY Press, 1992).

132. Gregory J. Cizek, "Grades: The Final Frontier in Assessment Reform," *NASSP Bulletin* (December 1996).

133. Robert B. Frary et al., "Testing and Grading Practices and Opinions of Secondary

School Teachers of Academic Subjects: Implications for Instruction in Measurement," *Educational Measurement: Issues and Practice* (fall 1998): 23–30.

134. Farkas, Johnson, and Duffett, *Different Drummers: How Teachers of Teachers View Public Education.*

135. Ibid., 10–12.

136. Ibid., 10, 11.

137. Ibid., 11.

138. Ibid., 15, 16.

Part Two

Constructive Uses of Tests

Chapter 3

Early Reading Assessment

Barbara R. Foorman,
Jack M. Fletcher, and
David J. Francis

Early Assessment

When confronted with the large reported numbers of people who are reading-disabled (up to 17.5 percent nationally)[1] and poor readers (more than 64 percent of African-American and 60 percent of Hispanic children, according to the fourth-grade National Assessment of Educational Progress [NAEP]), policy makers want to know why these numbers are so large and whether reading problems can be prevented. These concerns prompted the U.S. Department of Education and the U.S. Department of Health and Human Services to establish a committee through the National Research Council to investigate the prevention of reading difficulties. The resulting report, *Preventing Reading Difficulties in Young Children,*[2] focuses on the conditions under

Supported by grants from the National Institute of Child Health and Human Development, R01 HD30995, "Early Interventions in Children with Reading Problems" and P01 21889, "Psycholinguistic and Biological Mechanisms in Dyslexia."

which reading success is likely to emerge. Success comes when teachers teach reading in a comprehensive way that emphasizes the importance of letter-sound relations and reading for meaning and that provides opportunities to practice. Those most at risk for reading difficulties are, as a group, children from low-income families. They live in poor neighborhoods, attend schools with low achievement, have limited English proficiency, and speak a dialect of English substantially different from the one spoken at school.[3] Researchers also have found that in addition to such family background, there are individual risk factors of reading difficulty: limited experience at home with reading and physical, language, or cognitive weaknesses involving "cognitive-linguistic processing, especially phonological awareness, confrontation naming, sentence/story recall, and general language ability."[4]

Given that the National Research Council report represents the consensus of empirical researchers on predicting success and failure in reading, how should the classroom teacher apply this knowledge? How does the kindergarten, first-grade, or second-grade teacher know which students are headed for reading success and which for reading failure? One answer is provided through early assessment of reading growth and outcomes.

In this chapter we divide the topic of early reading assessment into the following sections: (1) the importance of assessing early reading skills; (2) impediments to early reading assessment; (3) "formal" and "authentic" early reading assessments; and (4) the example of the Texas Primary Reading Inventory.

The Importance of Assessing Early Reading Skills

When children exhibit reading problems at an early age, these problems typically persist. There is little evidence that they catch up in reading skills, in spite of the widespread belief among educators in developmental delay—the late bloomer phenomenon. In one study from our group, 74 percent of children who were reading disabled in the third grade remained reading disabled in the ninth grade.[5] In fact, the presence of risk characteristics is apparent in kindergarten and grade one. Juel found that 88 percent of students who were poor readers in grade one were also poor readers in grade four; 87 percent of students who were good readers in grade one were also good readers in grade four.[6] (But see Phillips and colleagues for a different perspective.[7]) In short, first grade matters in determining a child's status as a reader. Torgesen[8] found similar stability in reading status from grade one through grade five, but this status was predictable based on kindergarten performance—confirming that kindergarten matters as well.

The good news is that recent research indicates that early intervention is effective. Torgesen and colleagues identified children in kindergarten who had poor phonological awareness, that is, they had difficulty blending and segmenting sounds in speech.[9] By second grade, one-on-one tutoring brought 75 percent of the children to grade-level reading. Vellutino and colleagues identified middle-class children with very low word recognition skills at the beginning of grade one.[10] After one semester of one-on-one tutoring, 70 percent were reading at grade level. After two semesters, more than 90 percent were at grade level.

Tunmer and colleagues show the benefits of adding explicit, systematic alphabetic instruction to Reading Recovery tutorials.[11] Foorman and colleagues found that classroom-level explicit instruction in phonological awareness and the alphabetic principle as part of a balanced approach to reading brought students in grades one and two in eight Title 1 schools to national averages.[12] Less explicit, inductive approaches were unable to show such gains.

In sum, it is important to assess reading skills early for three reasons. First, reading status is a stable characteristic from as early as first grade and becomes intractable after third grade. Second, the presence of risk characteristics is apparent in kindergarten and first grade. Third, early intervention in first and second grade is effective.

Impediments to Early Reading Assessment

The major impediment to assessing reading skill development early in school is the "wait and see" attitude apparent in many areas of early education. Consequently, children have to accumu-late sufficient failure on standardized achievement tests adminis-tered in second or third grade before they are eligible for special education testing. Identification of "learning disabilities"—the label under which children with reading disabilities are typically served—is largely based on a significant discrepancy between IQ and reading achievement. In the 1950s, Bond and Tinker argued in favor of an IQ-discrepancy definition, noting that a child with reading disability "is a child who is not reading as well as could be expected for one of his intellectual or verbal maturity."[13] They further indicated that children with IQ scores below 95 should not be considered disabled in reading because "they are reading about as well as can be expected in view of their limited intellec-tual ability."[14] Much of the broad acceptance of IQ discrepancy models was fueled by the Isle of Wight studies by Rutter and Yule.[15] These studies presumably showed that reading skills had a bimodal distribution, with a longer tail representing children who were generally behind in reading relative to age but not IQ (low achievers). These children were contrasted to children with "specific" forms of reading disability reflected by poor reading in relation to expectations based on IQ (discrepant). These two groups of children were further shown to differ in gender, prog-nosis, reading and spelling characteristics, and language skills.

None of these findings has held up in research in the 1980s and 1990s.[16] The viability of IQ-discrepancy models is widely questioned. This has major implications for existing policy because the implementation of special education standards for children with reading disabilities still makes use of an IQ-dis-crepancy model. Interestingly, these concerns about IQ-discrep-ancy have come about despite major improvements in how IQ-discrepancy is modeled. For example, the types of definitions used in the 1950s, which typically involved a grade-below defin-ition, have been widely questioned because of problems with their psychometric properties.[17] There is a significant literature on measuring IQ-discrepancy. The bulk of the evidence found in the literature clearly indicates that regression-based models that adjust for the correlation of IQ and achievement are the most appropriate.[18] However, much of the research simply does not show major variations in the phenotypic characteristics of reading disability according to any definition.

In the last decade there has been much more attention paid to the assessment of domain-specific skills that are related to reading disability and a general deemphasis on the role of IQ tests.[19] This has happened largely because of a shift from organismic neuropsychological models to cognitive models of reading disability. There are multiple cognitive models of reading (for example, dual route, connectionist, and interactive). These models have been applied to reading disability with varying degrees of success.[20] In addition, research in the 1990s reflects the emphasis on the need for larger, well-defined samples, stronger hypothesis formulation, and the importance of a multivariate rather than univariate approach to research design. The following characteristics of the disabled reader have emerged from this recent research:[21]

1. Reading problems in most children occur at the level of the single word and involve word recognition skills. The best predictor of poor reading comprehension skills is deficient word recognition ability. Text reading problems account for far fewer cases of reading disability than problems with the development of word recognition skills.[22]

2. Word recognition problems are primarily associated with difficulties in segmenting words and syllables into phonemes. Deficits in phonological awareness characterize most poor readers, whether they are children, adolescents, or adults (at all levels of intelligence) or from economically disadvantaged or non-English speaking backgrounds. Individuals with reading disability have difficulty mapping speech into print.[23]

3. Reading ability lies along a natural, unbroken continuum. There is no natural demarcation on this continuum that separates good and poor readers, and a major research topic is the severity of impairment of reading skills that constitutes a disability. Most of the more current research in the

area of reading disabilities operates, at least implicitly, from a dimensional rather than a categorical model.[24]

4. Reading difficulties occur with equal frequency in boys and girls. The puzzle is that schools identify four times more boys than girls.[25] Vernon said that this was because of boys' behavioral characteristics.[26] He noted that reports of differences between the sexes were most likely related to the use of clinic samples, and, like Shaywitz and colleagues,[27] he further noted that boys were "most resistant to school teaching and discipline"—resulting in referral to a clinic.

5. As stated early in this chapter, children's early reading problems typically persist throughout their schooling. There is little evidence that they catch up in reading skills.

6. Reading disability is best identified through domain-specific assessments of reading and reading-related skills.[28] IQ tests are not necessary for the identification of reading disability. Models for identification based on IQ discrepancy lack validity. Stated another way, there is little evidence for differences between IQ-discrepant and low-achieving children on multiple dimensions, including the cognitive characteristics of reading disability, response to intervention, and long-term outcomes.[29]

7. There are multiple distal causes of reading disability, including (a) neurological; (b) familial; (c) economic (low income) and linguistic (low English proficiency and dialect differences); and (d) instructional:

   (a) Because of improvements in definition and measurement, major advances have been made in understanding the neurobiological correlates of reading disability. In particular, researchers have studied brain metabolism using positron emission tomography and functional magnetic resonance imaging. Such research shows that when adults with reading disability complete word-recognition tasks that separate the phonological, orthographic, and semantic components of word recognition, several of the neural networks that they use are different from those used by good readers.[30] Previous studies had reported problems with brain structure, but these problems are subtle, and differences are less robust than differences apparent in studies of brain function. Although researchers in the 1950s were interested in brain damage as a cause of phonological reading disability, it is clearly not a major cause. In fact, brain injury often results in preservation of word recognition skills and is more likely to lead to impairment at the level of text processes.[31]

(b) It has long been known that reading problems run in families. Recent studies have shown specific genetic loadings at chromosome 6 and 15.[32] However, several combinations of genes appear to be involved and the penetrance is low. Environmental factors clearly have significant influences on reading outcomes, and heritability accounts for about 50 percent of the variability.

(c) In addition to research on neurobiological factors, recent research also clearly establishes the importance of environmental factors for the development of reading disability. This is apparent in the large number of minority children with poor reading achievement on the National Assessment of Educational Progress (NAEP). The child's early literacy environment has a significant influence on reading outcomes.[33]

(d) The influence of instructional factors is underestimated. Recent studies have shown that intervention, particularly if it is early, can succeed in improving the word recognition skills of children with reading disability.[34]

8. Studies show that interventions that focus specifically on word recognition skills appear to help children overcome the most common forms of reading disability. The best available data suggests that this instruction needs to be explicit, must emphasize the alphabetic principle, and requires some intensity. Success has been reported both in

classroom level studies and in tutorial and pullout models.[35] The interventions that are successful provide an explicit focus on alphabetic decoding and word recognition skills, but are also characterized by an emphasis on reading connected text, writing, and reading then discussing intellectually challenging literature. This reflects a broad view of the reading process and the importance of applications of skills, particularly for children with reading disability. It is clear that many children with reading disability read and write less than other children, particularly if they are in traditional school-based remedial programs. Outcomes in any reading program are tied to the amount of practice, so it is important to get children to read and write and apply the skills they learned in the intervention program.

This summary makes clear that oral language skills and reading skills are related. The relationship does not apply solely to children who have speech and language disorders, although this is a population that is at substantial risk for the development of reading problems. Recent epidemiological studies suggest that approximately 50 percent of children with a history of an oral language disorder will develop a reading disability.[36]

Language factors do appear to account both for success and failure in the acquisition of reading skills. This point, argued most persistently by Vellutino in the 1970s,[37] is clearly the predominant view today among reading researchers. Researchers understand that reading is an unnatural outgrowth of language. Reading and writing are scaffolded onto oral language. Children do not acquire reading skills through exposure to literature, and reading does not develop naturally as does oral language. Reading must be taught, and the component of reading that requires the most explicit instruction is the relationship between print and speech at the level of the single word. The pivotal role of phonological awareness skills in the acquisition of reading ability is now well established and represents the most robust proximal cause of reading failure.[38]

Much of this summary of research on reading disability is based on children and adults identified as "reading disabled." Yet there is little evidence that the causes of reading problems in children who come from environments with limited literacy exposure are different from the causes of reading problems in children who come from non-English speaking backgrounds. In recent research on intervention with samples in which children from linguistically and culturally diverse backgrounds predominated, the evidence for word-level deficiencies in the early grades and the mediating effects of improvements in phonological processing skills is impressive.[39] This is not to say that word-level skills are all that teachers need to address or that addressing these skills will eliminate reading failure. Rather, the point is that the development of word-level skills is necessary—but not sufficient—for preventing reading failure. Instructional programs at all levels must integrate alphabetic instruction with opportunities to read connected text and an emphasis on meaning. Nonetheless, this summary makes it clear that we know a great deal about the characteristics of the disabled reader. We know the importance of prevention and early intervention. The question becomes how to identify children at risk for reading disabilities so that instructional support may be provided early on.

Formal and Authentic Reading Assessments

In the past, testing of early literacy was remarkably unconnected to teaching practices, although some claimed that testing harmed teaching and learning.[40] The source of this prevalent disconnection was the schism in the discipline of psychology between behaviorists and rationalists. As a result, on the one hand, a professional class of testers administered formal tests of skills as part of the accountability system, whereas on the other hand, constructivist teachers spent time filling out informal inventories. Those using either of these approaches typically missed the central purpose of assessment: setting individual learning objectives on the basis of systematically gathered information. In the following section, we discuss examples of "formal" and "authentic" assessment of early reading and then examples of attempts to merge the two.

Formal reading tests

We use the term "formal" to designate tests that are part of the accountability system (and, therefore, are high stakes). Formal tests can be norm-referenced or criterion-referenced. Norm-referenced tests are standardized on a clearly defined group, termed the norm group, and scaled so that each individual score reflects a rank within the norm group.[41] Criterion-referenced tests rate students against the content being assessed.[42]

Formal reading assessments are generally well-known, so are not be described in detail here. The Stanford Achievement Test-10 is an example of a well-known group-administered, norm-referenced achievement test. The Woodcock-Johnson[43] is a well-known individually administered achievement test. In both cases, students' word identification and passage comprehension scores are reported in relation to students of the same age or grade. In contrast, Texas uses the Texas Assessment of Knowledge and Skills (TAKS), a group-administered criterion-referenced test, as its accountability device. Scores on the TAKS reflect the percentage of items passed.

All of these formal tests use a multiple-choice format. In an attempt to go beyond the declarative knowledge tapped by multiple-choice formats, performance-based assessments, in which the student constructs an original response (that is, displays procedural knowledge) and the examiner observes the process of construction, have become popular alternatives. Assessment of writing fits well into this format. Reading comprehension also fits well if longer passages are used and students are asked to write responses to questions rather than to select the best alternative. The NAEP and the New Standards Project[44] are examples of national performance-based assessments.

Performance assessments that measure children's mastery of specific curriculum objectives through formal and informal approaches are not discussed in this chapter. The many curriculum-based assessments found in basal reading programs used to monitor student progress and make placement decisions are examples of this kind of performance assessment. These assessments rarely present evidence of reliability or validity and generally do not measure transfer of knowledge independently of the specific curriculum. Interestingly, hybrid approaches do exist that measure students' mastery of a curriculum and transfer of knowledge. One notable example, that of Fuchs and Fuchs, also has excellent reliability and validity, with a strong empirical basis of support.[45]

For the present discussion, we see no inherent reason why the value of the procedural knowledge tested by performance assessment would negate the value of declarative knowledge. For example, it is important to assess vocabulary knowledge prior to instruction in reading. Yet, in order to construct an original response, the student needs to write definitions or give them orally. Written and oral responses are complex tasks all by themselves because they require more than just vocabulary knowledge. Moreover, scoring of written and oral responses is time-consuming and often unreliable. In fact, the judicious use of multiple-choice formats to assess declarative knowledge may be the most valid, reliable, and useful way to proceed. Thus, performance assessment should be used as an addition to rather than a replacement for more traditional formats.[46] Similarly, performance-based assessments and authentic assessments can be complementary. The research literature provides several examples of combined assessments of reading and literacy skills.[47] Linn and colleagues remind us, in their writings on complex, performance-based assessment, that:

> Serious validation of alternative assessments needs to include evidence regarding the intended and unintended consequences, the degree to which performance on specific assessment tasks transfers, and the fairness of the assessments. Evidence is also needed regarding the cognitive complexity of the processes students employ in solving assessment problems and the meaningfulness of the problems for students and teachers. In addition, a basis for judging both the content quality and the comprehensiveness of the content coverage needs to be provided. Finally, the cost of the assessment must be justified.[48]

Authentic assessment. Performance assessments are "authentic" to the degree that they "reflect the actual learning and instructional activities of the classroom and out-of-school worlds."[49] The term "authentic assessment" covers a wide territory with great variability in how formal the test procedures are. Some authentic assessment is rather formal, and some is quite informal. At the least formal end of the continuum are portfolios of student work. The use of portfolios that has proved most enduring is as a component of local assessment systems agreed upon by parents, teachers, administrators, and school board members. Six examples of authentic assessment systems, some of which are implemented on a large-scale basis, are described here.

1. *Observation Survey*[50] This diagnostic battery of tests, developed in New Zealand and used in the Reading Recovery program in that country and in the United States, is the blueprint for many current authentic literacy assessments. Part I of the battery uses a technique called "running records." A teacher listens to a child read and takes notes ("running records") of oral reading errors and self-corrections. Part II of the battery includes letter identification and concepts about print, word reading, writing, and dictation. No inter-rater reliability is reported for the running records in Part I; however, excellent reliability is reported for the tests in Part II in multiple studies with different sample sizes and compositions: test-retest, .73–.98; internal consistency, .84–.97. Concurrent validity is reported as correlations of letter identification with word reading ($r = .96$), concepts about print with word reading ($r = .79$), and word reading with the Schnoell Reading-1 Test ($r = .90$). Evidence for predictive validity can be found in a study reporting that Reading Recovery brought 35 percent of children served through the one-on-one tutorial to the classroom average.

   Marie Clay's work is commendable for its attention to issues of validity and reliability, authenticity, and professional development.[51] Becoming a Reading Recovery tutor requires one year of intensive clinical work. Tutors have to learn to observe children, code running records, administer the diagnostic tests, and apply results to instructional planning. The expense of year-long teacher training and one-on-one tutoring has resulted in many adaptations of the model under other names. These adaptations typically include the same 30-minute lesson cycle for tutorials: rereading of a previously read book; independent reading of a newly introduced book with a running record taken; letter identification exercises, if necessary; writing and reading of sentence strips; cutting up and reassembling words on sentence strips; and introduction of a new book with scaffolded reading.

Program developers of Reading Recovery report positive long-term gains on concepts of print and dictation.[52] However, external evaluations do not report strong transfer to other reading measures.[53] Moreover, Iversen and Tunmer found that children were "recovered" at a faster rate if the lesson cycle included systematic instruction in letter-sound patterns.[54] Finally, Center and colleagues[55] and Tunmer and colleagues[56] found that children with poor metalinguistic knowledge were less likely to be successful in Reading Recovery. That may explain why approximately 27 percent of children served are dismissed from the program without being recovered.[57]

2. South Brunswick, New Jersey, Schools' *Early Literacy Portfolio*[58] This suburban district of seven elementary schools developed a portfolio system for children in kindergarten and first and second grades that consisted of these components:

- Writing samples
- Story retelling records
- Oral reading records
- An invented spelling activity
- Sight word inventories
- Interviews with parents and students
- Self-portraits

Teachers collected documentation for each of these components at the middle and end of each year. They rated the quality of the documentation according to a 6-point scale referenced to expected literacy performance at each phase of development. These ratings were used to monitor student progress and to meet local and state evaluation requirements. Each year teachers met across schools to blindly rate each other's portfolios in order to check inter-rater reliability of scoring. Reliability has been high (.90s).

Salinger and Chittenden[59] interviewed teachers about their use of the portfolio system. The profile of a student's strengths and weaknesses across the seven components mattered more to teachers than the developmental scale. This profile helped teachers plan for instruction and for meetings with parents. Teachers' biggest complaints concerned management and time.

Compiling multiple documents for each child at the middle and end of the school year requires organization and time. Moreover, some experienced teachers admitted that the portfolio was redundant with what they already knew about their students through instruction. But for new and developing teachers, portfolios provide a mechanism whereby they spend individual time with each student and reflect on the impact of their instruction on literacy development.

3. *The Primary Language Record,* developed in London and used at P.S. 261 in New York City,[60] consists of writing samples, running records, interviews with parents and students, and classroom observations. In California the PLR has been adapted by classroom teachers and renamed the California Learning Record(CLR).[61] Five developmental levels of reading proficiency have been defined for kindergarten through third grade, fourth through eighth grade, and high school.

The K-3 scale is described in the 1996 moderation report:[62]

a. Beginning reader: Uses just a few successful strategies for tackling print independently. Relies on having another person to read the text aloud. May still be unaware that text carries meaning.

b. Not-yet-fluent reader: Tackles known and predictable text with growing confidence but still needs support with new and unfamiliar ones. Has a growing ability to predict meanings and developing strategies to check predictions against other cues, such as the illustrations and the print itself.

c. Moderately fluent reader (partially proficient): Well launched on reading but still needs to return to a familiar range of reader text. At the same time, is beginning to explore new kinds of texts independently and is beginning to read silently.

d. Fluent reader (proficient): A capable reader who now approaches familiar texts with confidence but still needs support with unfamiliar materials. Is beginning to draw inferences from books and stories. Reads independently. Chooses to read silently.

e. Exceptionally fluent reader (advanced): An avid and independent reader who is making choices from a wider range of material. Able to appreciate nuances and subtlety in text.

Inter-rater reliability for placement of students into these levels of proficiency was 85 percent within a school site and 70 percent to 80 percent across sites within a region. Teacher reports are used as evidence of the impact of the CLR upon classroom instruction and are collected annually as part of the moderation process.

4. *The Primary Assessment of Language Arts and Mathematics (PALM)* was designed in Austin, Texas, by researchers and teachers to include three components: (a) curriculum-embedded assessments, (b) taking-a-closer-look assessments, and (c) on-demand assessments.[63] The curriculum-embedded assessments consist of the ongoing gathering of evidence to document progress in the curriculum. This evidence consists of work samples, classroom observations, and anecdotal records. The taking-a-closer-look assessments include

informal reading inventories, running records or miscue analyses of oral reading, and think-aloud and reflective problem-solving strategies—all tools that teachers might use to gain further information about individual students. On-demand assessments for the PALM include: a personal journal; a response journal for both a book read aloud by the teacher and a free-choice book read independently; an adaptation of the K-W-L (know, want to learn, learned) model for expository text;[64] an oral reading of a familiar and an unfamiliar passage scored for accuracy, rate, and self-correction; and an inventory of reading attitudes and habits and of self-concept.

Hoffman and colleagues found that teachers could implement the PALM and use the results to plan instruction.[65] However, no evidence of reliability is provided. Evidence of concurrent validity was established with the Iowa Test of Basic Skills (ITBS). Hoffman and colleagues also found that the PALM accounted for 86 percent of the variance in the ITBS reading score.[66] However, as Pearson points out, such overlap with the ITBS may not be a blessing.[67] Given the time-consuming nature of the PALM, one might argue that the ITBS is a cost-effective substitute. The issue is an empirical one: Which assessment approach has more utility— the PALM or the ITBS—in assuring that students become successful readers one year and two years later? This is an issue both of predictive validity and diagnostic utility. In other words, which approach reliably identifies students in need of additional assistance if they are to become successful readers and which approach provides teachers with information about the nature of the assistance needed? The PALM clearly provides information directly relevant to the content of instructional assistance. However, a longitudinal study of student growth and outcomes is needed to address whether the PALM has predictive validity.

5. *The Work Sampling System*[68] Meisels's Work Sampling System involves elementary school teachers' documenta-

tion and evaluation of ongoing student work with the goal of improving instructional practices and student learning. Three forms of documentation are used: checklists, portfolios, and summary reports. The checklists consist of performance indicators for seven major curriculum areas drawn from national and state curriculum standards. For example, "Understands and interprets a story or other text" is one indicator from the first-grade checklist. Teachers check the three-level mastery scale—Not Yet, In Process, and Proficient—in fall, winter, and spring assessments to trace student performance. Detailed developmental guidelines accompany each checklist area in order to promote consistency of interpretation and evaluation across teachers, students, and schools.

In Meisels's system, portfolios consist of two types of student work: core items and individualized items. Core items represent performance in five domains—language and literacy, mathematical thinking, scientific thinking, social studies, and the arts. Individualized items reflect a child's goals, interests, and abilities in various curricular areas, such as first attempts at acrylic painting or writing a story. The inclusion of core items provides for structured sampling of performance across students. Individualized items provide the opportunity to represent student strengths and to enable students to take an active role in evaluating their own work.

Summary Reports transform information from teacher observations, checklists, and portfolios into evaluation of student performance across the curriculum. Teachers complete these reports three times a year, writing an evaluation in narrative form and completing a rating scale for each of the five domains. The ratings are: (1) not yet accomplished, (2) accomplished, or (3) highly accomplished. A total summary score is created by summing ratings across domains and across the three subscales—observations, checklists, and portfolios.

Meisels and colleagues examined the Work Sampling System's reliability and validity with 100 kindergartners.[69] Results showed that the checklist and summary report (including portfolio ratings) had high internal and moderately high inter-rater reliability. Also, the Work Sampling System accurately predicted performance on the norm-referenced battery of individually administered achievement tests, controlling for sex, age, and initial ability.

6. *Phonological Awareness and Literacy Screening (PALS)* PALS was developed at the University of Virginia with funds from the state in order to develop a tool that teachers could use to identify kindergarten and first-grade students who might benefit from additional instruction. There are two parts to PALS—phonological awareness (PALS I) and literacy screening (PALS II). PALS I assesses ability to identify rhyme units and to isolate beginning sounds, in an individual or small group format. PALS II assesses (1) alphabet knowledge, (2) knowledge of letter sounds, (3) concept of word, (4) sense of story, and, in first grade, (5) word recognition. Letter knowledge is assessed through recognition of upper- and lowercase letters and production of a subset of letters. Knowledge of letter sounds is assessed through (a) production of letter sounds in isolation, (b) ability to categorize beginning sounds, and (c) ability to use knowledge of letter sounds to attempt to spell. Concept of word is measured by ability to track words in familiar text as well as ability to use context to identify individual words within a line of text. Sense of story is measured through story retelling. Word recognition in first grade is assessed with graded word lists.

University of Virginia researchers received PALS scores from 52,094 kindergarten and first-grade children in the 1997–1998 and 1998–1999 school years, with more than 90 percent of school divisions in Virginia returning data. Item reliabilities were determined for grade, gender, socioeconomic status, and geographical region, yielding Cronbach's Alphas ranging from .83 to .89. Ethnicity was available in the 1998–1999 administration. Inter-rater reliability of .99 for each subtest was obtained when teams of two adults (not the actual teachers) administered the PALS screening to the same children in six schools across three regions in Virginia in the fall of 1999. Construct validity was addressed through factor analysis of the 1997 PALS data. Both kindergarten and first-grade data were best represented by a single-factor solution that accounted for 64 percent to 74 percent of the total variance in the children's scores on all tasks in both the phonological awareness and literacy screening components. The subtasks contributing the most to the one-factor solution were rhyme, beginning sounds, lowercase alphabet recognition, letter sounds, and spelling. These were retained in the current version of PALS. Of these five subtasks, lowercase alphabet recognition, letter sounds, and spelling contributed the most to the unitary factor. Concurrent validity was established with medium to high correlations (.67 to .81) with Stanford-9 subtests of sounds and letters, word reading, and sentence reading administered to 127 first-graders in the fall of 1997.

These examples show that a number of authentic assessment systems are available. Mostly, they are local efforts to engage teachers in collecting evidence upon which to base individual curricular decisions. Three of the six systems presented are large-scale applications—the CLR, the Work Sampling System, and PALS. The latter two systems have been the most responsive to psychometric concerns regarding validity and reliability. Pearson regards validity as the ultimate criterion for judging the worth of a test and, therefore, for judging the worth of an assessment system.[70] He lists the following as the important questions to ask in determining the validity of a test:

1. Does it measure the intended trait? (construct validity)
2. Is it consistent with the curriculum? (content validity)

3. Does it behave like other measures of this domain? (concurrent validity)

4. Does it result in appropriate decisions for users? Do they get what they need? (consequential validity)

5. How much effort is required to obtain the information? (feasibility)

6. How do users judge the quality and appropriateness of the information they receive? (utility)[71]

In judging the validity of an assessment system, Pearson raises these three questions:

1. Are all of the important dimensions of the domain assessed? This question speaks to the issue of domain or content validity. The items being from the appropriate domain is not enough to establish their system validity. For the system to be valid, the entire domain must be adequately represented.

2. Are the clients of the system getting the information they need in order to answer the questions they want answered? This question speaks to the criterion of utility and emphasizes the "tailoring" of the information to the audience who will use it.

3. Are clients making the right decisions? This question addresses issues of consequential validity. It must be answered by examining the impact of such assessments on the lives of individuals and groups who are affected by the results of the assessments. The ultimate test is whether appropriate placements and instructional decisions are made. Particularly important to examine are egregious misapplications of the system; other things being equal, we want assessments that do no harm.

These are important and clearly articulated aspects of validity, but Pearson fails to list one kind of validity important to early reading assessment—predictive validity. Does the test or the system predict future reading performance? To address predictive validity, longitudinal studies of individual growth and outcomes in reading are required. Currently, the only early reading assessment with evidence of predictive validity is the Texas Primary Reading Inventory (TPRI).[73] However, let us address the notion of reliability, for it is conspicuously missing from Pearson's discussion.

"Reliability" measures the consistency or reproducibility of test scores. In practical terms, reliability is the extent to which a student's score remains constant when the same test is given under a variety of conditions. The reliability of an instrument is important in school settings because educators and parents want to make sure that a student's score is representative of the student's ability and not a reflection of random error. "Internal consistency" provides an estimate of the error in using the subset of items on the test instead of using all possible items from the domain of items. "Alternate forms reliability" estimates the error in using two forms for measuring the same trait. "Test-retest reliability" is an estimate of the error associated with testing over time. "Inter-rater reliability" reflects the consistency with which different raters score a student.

Recently, some researchers have reduced the importance of reliability relative to validity. For example, Tierney offers thirteen principles of assessment,[74] one of which is: "Some things that can be assessed reliably across raters are not worth assessing; some things that are worth assessing may be difficult to assess reliably except by the same rater" (384). Difficult as it may be to achieve high inter-rater reliability, the concept of consistency and reproducibility is essential if a test is to be considered valid. If classroom teachers are inconsistent in setting learning objectives based on assessment results, then the validity of the assessment instrument can be questioned. In short, validity can be no stronger than reliability. A test can be reliable, but not valid, as the first part of Tierney's statement says. However, tests can never be valid and unreliable. Hence, we urge educators not to abandon the notion of reliability just because it may be hard to achieve. Rather, we urge educators to gather evidence of reliability so that we can fully address issues of validity.

Texas Primary Reading Inventory

All school districts in Texas are required to administer an early reading diagnostic instrument for students in kindergarten, grade one, and grade two according to Texas Education Code 28.006. This requirement developed out of the 75th Texas Legislature with the passage of House Bill 107 in May 1997. Texas Education Code 28.006 is explicitly *not* part of the accountability or teacher appraisal or incentive system in Texas. Assessment results are to be reported to parents, superintendents, school boards, and the Commissioner. The state does not mandate what assessment is used, but does provide support for assessments on a list from the Texas Education Agency that includes instruments that can be individually administered by a teacher and that have evidence of reliability and validity.

In order to facilitate this mandated diagnosis of early reading skills and comprehension development, the Texas Education Agency (TEA) contracted with the Center for Academic and Reading Skills to revise an early diagnostic reading instrument developed by the TEA known as the Texas Primary Reading Inventory. There are more than 1,000 school districts in Texas, with almost one million children in kindergarten, first grade, and second grade, taught by more than 45,000 teachers. During 1998–1999—the first year of implementation of Education Code 28.006—approximately 80 percent of school districts adopted the TPRI. During 1999-2000, 85 percent of school districts adopted the TPRI and many piloted a Spanish reconstruction called the Tejas LEE. During 2000-2001, over 90 percent of school districts adopted the TPRI and the Tejas LEE, and in 2001–2002 the percentage rose to 95 percent. In the 2004–2005 edition, a third-grade screen and inventory and a progress-monitoring booklet were added to meet the requirements of the Reading First component of the ESEA's No Child Left Behind legislation. The TPRI was developed as a large-scale example of an early reading instrument that attempts to bring psychometric rigor to informal assessment, as PALS in Virginia attempts to do. In this section we will describe in detail the development and implementation of the TPRI.

Development of the TPRI

In revising the TPRI, we (a) added a screening component to identify those students who had high probabilities of success at the end of grades one and two, and (b) modified the inventory portion to be aligned with the new state curriculum standards and to be more easily scored by teachers. The screen consists of those measures most predictive of reading success in our longitudinal sample of more than 900 children in kindergarten through grade two and parallels closely the work of Torgesen and Vellutino and colleagues.[75] These measures are: phonological awareness and its theoretically related construct of letter-sound knowledge in kindergarten and the beginning of grade one; and word reading at the beginning and end of grade one and beginning of grade two. For children still developing these screening concepts, the inventory is administered to set learning objectives. These administration procedures are described in Figure 3.1.

The components of the TPRI are defined in the teacher guides for kindergarten, first, and second grades as follows:

- Book and print awareness – knowledge of the function of print and of the characteristics of books and other print materials

- Phonemic awareness – the ability to detect and identify individual sounds within spoken words

- Graphophonemic knowledge – the recognition of the letters of the alphabet and the understanding of sound-symbol relationships

- Reading accuracy and fluency – the ability to read grade-appropriate text accurately and fluently

- Reading comprehension – the understanding of what has been read

All tasks in the TPRI consist of five questions, with concept development indicated by four out of five correct. The book and print awareness task, inspired by Clay's Concepts of Print,[76] asks the teacher to select a short storybook and to ask the child to

FIGURE 3.1   Flowchart of components of the TPRI

Texas Primary Reading Inventory

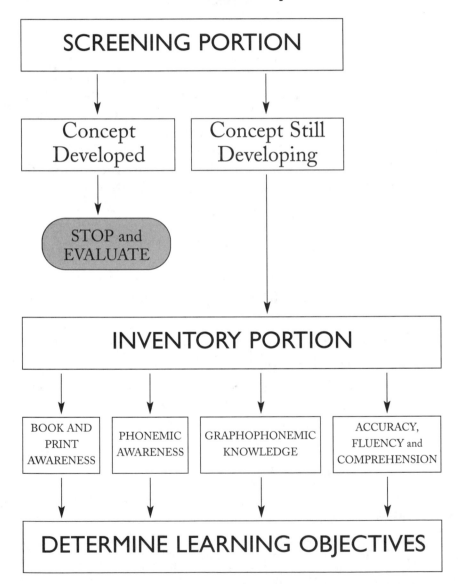

point to the place where the teacher starts reading, to point to the start and end of a sentence, and to point to a word, a letter, and a capital letter. This task is included in the kindergarten inventory as a warm-up activity. It is not scored because of lack of inter-rater reliability in the validation study.[77]

The phonemic awareness tasks on the kindergarten inventory are (a) rhyming, and (b) blending word parts. In the rhyming task, the teacher gives the child three rhyming words (for example, hill, fill, dill) and the child is to produce a word, real or made up, that rhymes with these three. In the second task, the teacher pronounces a single-syllable word broken into the initial sound (onset) and the final pattern (the rhyme), such as /h/-/ouse/ or /ch/-/in/. The child's job is to put the word-parts back together. These two tasks also appear on the first-grade inventory. Additional phonemic awareness tasks on the first-grade inventory are blending phonemes in spoken words (/s/-/u/-/n/→"sun") and detecting initial sounds (say "sit" without the /s/→"it") and final sounds (say "beef" without the /f/→"bee").

The graphophonemic knowledge tasks vary in format from kindergarten through grade two. In kindergarten there are two tasks—letter-name identification and letter-to-sound linking. In the letter-name identification task, the teacher presents in random order the letters of the alphabet in uppercase and lowercase, asking for each letter's name. In the letter-to-sound linking task, the teacher first asks the child to isolate the first sound in a word ("lamp"→/l/). Then the teacher shows the child three letters (c, o, l) and asks the child to point to the letter that makes that sound. Stuart found this kind of letter-to-sound linking task to be more predictive of successful reading than Clay's screening battery.[78] There may be kindergartners who know letter names and can rhyme and blend onset-rhymes, but are not yet success-ful at linking letters to sounds. For them, instruction should focus on alliterative games and building words with a small set of taught letter-sounds.

In first grade the graphophonemic tasks require the student to write spelling patterns. The tasks progress from initial con-sonant substitution to final consonant substitution to medial vowel substitution. For example, in the initial consonant substitution the teacher places a spelling pattern in front of the child (__ad) and spreads out seven consonant letters (d, f, h, m, p, s, t). Then the teacher asks the child to make the word "mad," followed by four additional words (dad, fad, tad, had). More difficult tasks require the substitution of initial and final blends (making "drip" from the pattern __ip and making "list" from the pattern li__). The second-grade inventory also includes four spelling tasks that cover long and complex vowel spellings, compound words, consonant digraphs, past tense, homophones, plurals, consonant doubling, and inflectional endings.

Comprehension tasks in kindergarten and first and second grades consist of narrative and expository passages drawn from children's books. During the 1998–1999 and 1999–2000 school years, passages from real books rather than artificially constructed passages were used in an attempt to provide an authentic performance measure of reading/listening comprehension. However, in our implementation study of 6,000 children in randomly selected schools in urban, suburban, and rural Texas, we found that the vast majority of first-graders could not read the authentic text said to be at first-grade level. Therefore, for the 2000–2001 edition of the TPRI we constructed first-grade passages that progress in difficulty across the year with respect to word properties of sound-spelling patterns and word frequency. Students are placed in passages at their instructional level based on their performance on a list of words linked empirically to oral reading accuracy in the passages. Instructional level is defined as the level at which oral reading accuracy ranges from 90 percent to 94 percent.

In administering the TPRI, the question is whether the graphophonemic knowledge assessed in the inventory and the attention and memory skills not assessed in the inventory—but required of any complex performance—will transfer to the comprehension tasks. In kindergarten, children listen to the teacher read a passage, then they answer questions. In first and second grades the children are asked to read the passage and to answer orally the questions the teacher asks. If a student miscalls more than three words in the first sentence, then the teacher turns the task into a listening comprehension exercise. However, the new procedure of placing students in instructional-level text through performance on a word list minimizes the need for listening comprehension in grades one and two. As the student reads the passage aloud, the teacher notes miscalled words by slashing them in the student booklet. After five seconds have elapsed, the teacher provides the student with the word. When the student has finished reading the passage, the teacher can count the number of miscalled words and circle the reading accuracy level—frustrational (more than 10 percent), instructional (6 percent to 10 percent errors), or independent (less than 6 percent errors).

In the 2000–2001 edition of the TPRI, we added reading fluency rate. Teachers are provided with a stopwatch to time the students while they read a passage aloud. In order to calculate reading fluency rate, teachers are told to (a) determine the number of words read correctly and multiply by 60 and (b) divide this number by the number of seconds it took the student to read the passage. The reading rate goal is 60 WPM by the end of first grade and 90 WPM by the end of second grade.

Several passages are provided for the beginning, middle, and end of the year for first and second grades (with kindergarten having only middle and end-of-year passages) so that the teacher can note progress on increasingly complex texts. In the 2004–2005 edition, fluency probes are provided so that fluency may be monitored as often as twice a month for at-risk students. Passage complexity is determined empirically through an item development study, rather than by readability. Readability formulas are typically based on the number of words, syllables, and sentences in the text being evaluated. We found that the formulas produced highly variable results for beginning reading passages such as those used in the TPRI. The five questions that follow the TPRI passage to assess comprehension vary in the extent to which the answer is explicitly stated in the passage. Roughly, three of the five questions are explicit and two are implicit. Implicit questions require the student to make an inference about events, themes, or characters. Here, as an example of this procedure, we provide one of the passages used for the beginning of the first grade in the first edition of the TPRI. The passage is from *Danny and the Dinosaur,* by Syd Hoff (and used by permission of HarperCollins Publishers):

> One day Danny went to the museum. He wanted to see what was inside. He saw Indians. He saw bears. He saw Eskimos. He saw guns. He saw swords. And he saw . . . DINOSAURS! Danny loved dinosaurs. He wished he had one. "I'm sorry they are not real," said Danny. "It would be nice to play with a dinosaur." "And I think it would be nice to play with you," said a voice.

After reading or listening to this passage, the child is asked to answer these questions:

1. Where did Danny go?

   Correct: To the museum

2. Tell me two things that Danny saw at the museum.

   Correct: Two of the following: Indians, bears, Eskimos, guns, swords, dinosaurs

3. What did Danny love most?

   Correct: Dinosaurs

4. What did Danny want to do with the dinosaurs?

   Correct: To play

5. What do you think talked to Danny? (Note: If the student answers "a voice," ask them whose voice.)

   Correct: A dinosaur

These five questions serve as a probed retelling. Full story retelling places demands on discourse skills that may interfere with assessment of reading comprehension. However, as Morrow points out, "Retelling allows the child to reconstruct meaning and personalize information."[79]

To investigate whether story retelling contributes to sense of story above and beyond the five questions in the TPRI and to examine the effect of reading the passage in the TPRI booklet, in the actual storybook, or in a guided reading context, we con-

ducted a small study with 124 first-graders as part of the validation study.[80] Each child read two short passages taken from children's literature books, answered five comprehension questions,
and retold the story they had just read. Reading rate and accuracy
were recorded for each child for each passage. There were no dif-
ferential effects of context on reading comprehension as measured by comprehension questions or retell scores. That is,
reading a storybook passage printed in the TPRI booklet versus
reading the passage in the storybook with or without adult scaf-
folding made no difference in the number of story grammar elements in first-graders' retells or number of comprehension
questions answered correctly. For one passage—the one that was
above a first-grade level—there were significant effects of fluency
(that is, reading rate) on answering comprehension questions and
on retell scores. Specifically, speed and accuracy of decoding
explained 13 percent of the variance in correctly answering comprehension questions and 10 percent of the variance in retelling
scores. Moderate correlations were found among formal and
informal measures of reading comprehension.

Validation of the TPRI

The TPRI screen provides extensive psychometric data. The
screen is based on empirically based predictors of reading success
at the end of grades one and two. These predictors were derived
from a study that had a modified, longitudinal, time-sequential
design in which 945 children in kindergarten and first and second grades were evaluated on reading and reading-related skills
four times yearly for one to three years. In addition, achievement
tests were administered at the end of first and second grades. The
participating children were in regular education in three elementary schools. The percentage of participation in the federal lunch
program at the three schools was 13 percent, 15 percent, and 30
percent. The student populations varied in socioeconomic status
from lower-middle to upper-middle class. The sample was
approximately half boys and half girls. The ethnic composition of
the sample was diverse, with the following breakdown in kindergarten: 54 percent Caucasian, 18 percent African-American,

15 percent Hispanic, 12 percent Asian, and 1 percent other. Children were excluded from the sample if they had severe emotional problems, uncorrected vision problems, hearing loss, or acquired neurological disorders or were classified at the lowest level of English as a second language (ESL). Children who were at ESL levels 2, 3, and 4 were included in the sample.

The items on the screen were those items selected on the basis of Item Response Theory (IRT) from a larger battery of items that discriminate success and failure on reading outcomes at the end of grades one and two.[81] The larger battery included measures of visual-motor integration, visual-spatial skill, expressive and receptive syntax, phonological memory, vocabulary, attention, IQ, rapid naming, letter names and letter sounds knowledge, phonological awareness, word reading, and spelling. For kindergarten, we attempted to predict outcomes using the Woodcock-Johnson PsychoEducational Test Battery Basic Reading cluster. For predictions involving first- and second-graders, the Woodcock-Johnson Broad Reading cluster, which consists of letter-word identification and word attack measures and a cloze-based passage comprehension measure, was used. The criteria for risk were arbitrarily set at grade equivalents of 1.4 or lower at the end of grade one and 2.4 or lower at the end of grade two on the Woodcock-Johnson. In first grade this grade equivalent represents the 22nd percentile for Basic Reading and the 18th percentile for Broad Reading. In second grade it represents the 35th percentile. The cut-point was deliberately set higher in grade two because of the greater stability in the prediction equations and the reduction in time available for a student to reach the Texas Reading Initiative goal of being on or above grade level by the end of third grade.

Separate analyses were conducted on the five assessment time-points. We attempted to establish a series of prediction equations that helped select variables contributing uniquely to the prediction. Decisions about effective predictors were based on both the accuracy of individual child predictions and the relation of false positive and false negative errors. The goal in selecting the best prediction set was to maximize identification, minimize the number of predictors, and produce the lowest possible false positive errors rate, keeping false negative error rates below 10 percent. False positives and false negatives are inherent to any assessment device and are inevitably linked. To use screening as an example, false negatives occur when a child meets criteria on the screening but fails to learn to read; a false positive occurs when a child does not meet criteria on the screening but nevertheless becomes a successful reader. A false negative error is more serious because these children do not receive the additional assistance they require at the earliest possible time, which makes their problems more difficult to remediate at a later time. False positive errors are a concern because they place an increased demand on scarce resources. False positives in kindergarten and the beginning of first grade may reflect the assessment of children from poor neighborhoods or who have limited English proficiency whose opportunity to become literate comes from instruction at school. False positive rates in kindergarten ranged from 44 percent in December to 38 percent in April, to 36 percent in first grade, and to less than 15 percent at the beginning of second grade.[82]

In order to collect reliability and validity data for the TPRI inventory, a field study was conducted in four Houston Independent School District elementary schools that were also participating in a much larger study of early reading funded by the National Institute of Child Health and Human Development (NICHD). The field study involved thirty-two kindergarten and first-grade teachers, 128 kindergarten students, and 144 first-grade students. In each classroom, eight students were randomly selected from the sample of all NICHD students to participate in the field study. We trained the teachers to administer the TPRI, then provided substitutes so that these teachers could administer the TPRI screen and inventory to their own students on one day and to the students in the neighboring classroom on the next day. We included this step to obtain inter-rater of scoring between a teacher who knows the student well and another teacher of the same grade who does not know the student well.

Included in the analyses of the field study data were (a) concurrent validation of the TPRI with well-known individually administered word recognition and comprehension measures (that is, the letter-word identification and passage comprehension from the Woodcock-Johnson),[83] (b) internal consistency of items, and (c) inter-rater reliability judgments. These judgments were obtained in three ways. First, to examine scoring accuracy, a teacher's ability to apply scoring criteria was compared with an expert's scoring of the same protocol. Second, to examine objectivity of scoring, teachers administered the TPRI to students who were either from their own classroom or from the neighboring teacher's classroom. Third, to see if they agreed on interpretation of results, teachers were asked to rate the importance of various instructional strategies for an individual student, based on that student's TPRI results, then to prioritize those strategies on one week's lesson plans.

The evidence for reliability for the items in the screen and inventory was very good. Median internal consistencies were .89 for the end of kindergarten, .80 for the beginning of first grade, .74 for the end of first grade, and .68 for the beginning of second grade. The median lower-bound estimate of test-retest reliability was .60. Only the subtest for book and print awareness had unacceptably low internal consistency, test-retest reliability, and inter-rater reliability. Evidence for the TPRI's construct validity was provided through correlations with the Woodcock-Johnson (WJ) reading scores and scores from the Gray Oral Reading Test-III (GORT-III). In second grade, the correlations with the WJ ranged between .26 and .61, and correlations with the GORT-III ranged between .23 and .56, depending on the TPRI passage. In first grade, the correlation with WJ was .48 and the correlations with GORT-III comprehension, reading rate, and reading accuracy ranged from .41 to .52 on the passage with adequate reliability. The passage from *Danny and the Dinosaur* had inadequate reliability because the children were very familiar with the story. In kindergarten, there were no additional measures of reading comprehension. The strongest correlation with the two passages in the TPRI listening comprehension subtest was provided by the Peabody Picture Vocabulary Test-Revised (PPVT-R). Correlations ranged from .41 to .65 in kindergarten. In first grade, the correlations of TPRI reading comprehension with the PPVT-R ranged from .32 to .38; in second grade, the range was .53 to .63 (see the TPRI technical manual for details).

Teachers participating in this field study also provided their opinions about training issues and test administration issues. Overall, teachers responded positively to the presentation format and informational content of the TPRI training. At least 70 percent found the directions and the format of the teacher's guide and student booklet clear. The majority of teachers felt that all parts of the TPRI were easy to administer and were useful. They rated the TPRI very helpful for identifying strengths and weaknesses of students not previously taught and were very likely to recommend the TPRI to another teacher or administrator. Most teachers responded that gathering materials for administration of the TPRI and planning individual instruction based on TPRI results would be relatively easy. Forty percent were familiar with other reading assessments and reported that when comparing the TPRI with the other assessments, the TPRI was better in terms of ease of administration, usefulness for planning instruction, identification of students' reading strengths and weaknesses, and worthwhile use of instructional time. The majority of teachers did not think that changes should be made to either the screening or the inventory portions of the instrument.

Professional Development

If teachers rather than testing professionals are to administer the assessment, then professional development is necessary. Typically, teacher certification does not require coursework in assessment, diagnosis, and intervention. These courses are more commonly found at the master's degree level. The areas of the TPRI in which teachers require the most training the TPRI are: (a) pronunciation of speech sounds in the phonemic awareness and letter-sound tasks; (b) learning to assess rather than to coach; and (3) developing intervention strategies based on the results of assessment. Teacher certification typically does not include information about phonology. Therefore, something as seemingly simple as pronouncing letter-sounds requires professional development. For example, it should be pointed out that the letter *p* represents /p/, not "puh;" the letter *m* represents /m/ or /mmmmm/, but not "muh."

Coaching occurs because teachers are used to teaching rather than assessing and also because many teachers feel that assessment and instruction should occur concurrently. However, there is a time for teachers to step back from classroom instruction and put on the assessor's hat to see if knowledge and skills transfer to new contexts. If teachers are not willing to do this, assessment might be taken out of their hands. This would be unfortunate because it is teachers who are in the best position to use results of assessment to affect instruction.

To help with intervention strategies, we have developed an Intervention Activities Guide as part of the TPRI kit that links results from the TPRI with specific classroom activities. But the first line of defense is prevention. As teachers in Texas align their curriculum with the adopted state curriculum standards (the Texas Essential Knowledge and Skills [TEKS]), they will find the components of the TPRI inventory closely aligned with TEKS objectives. Examples of the link between curricular standards and the TPRI are provided in Figure 3.2.

Linking TPRI to instruction

The TEKS and the TPRI go hand in hand. As Simmons and Resnick point out,[84] "without performance standards the meaning of content standards is subject to interpretations" (12). Thus, performance on the TPRI inventory provides a concrete demonstration of the knowledge and skills supposedly covered in the classroom curriculum. By readministering the inventory at midyear and end-of-year, teachers can determine progress toward the standards. Because the items on the kindergarten and first- and second-grade screens predict that students will be on or above grade level at the end of first and second grades, teachers have a gauge with which to calibrate benchmark expectations from year to year. Thus, no child should fall through the cracks because he or she appears to be making sufficient progress on the inventory. The end-of-year screen in kindergarten and first

FIGURE 3.2   TPRI inventory and related instruction areas

TPRI Components   **Examples of related areas**
                                            for instruction

Book and print awareness   Print conventions and format
The ability to attend to the   Book conventions
conventions and formats of   Word awareness, word length
print   Recognition and production of letters

Phonemic Awareness   Listening skills
The ability to attend to the   Oral language development
sound structure of spoken   Letter names and sounds
language   Rhymes, alliteration
                                            Sentences, words, and syllables
                                            Initial/final phoneme identification
                                            Phoneme blending and segmentation

Graphophonemic knowledge   Familiarity with letters and
Recognition of letters and   letter clusters
understanding of sound-   Sound-letter relationships
spelling relations   Word decoding
                                            Recognition/production of spelling
                                                patterns
                                            Recognition of morphological units
                                            Writing conventions

Comprehension   Listening comprehension
Literal and inferential   (memory and attention)
understanding of text   Reading fluency and accuracy
                                            Prior knowledge and vocabulary
                                                development
                                            Comprehension monitoring and
                                                self-questioning
                                            Story structure
                                            Predicting, inferencing, identifying
                                                main idea and details
                                            Reading practice

grade and the beginning-of-year screen in first and second grades provide safeguards. In fact, the identification of risk is so accurate at the beginning of second grade (above 85 percent) that further evaluation is warranted. That student will be well below grade level unless intervention is undertaken.

Conclusions

We have argued for the importance of assessing early reading skills by pointing out (a) the intractable nature of reading problems identified in third grade and beyond, (b) the presence of risk characteristics in kindergarten and grade one, and (c) the effectiveness of early intervention. The major impediments to assessing early reading skills are (a) the "wait and see" adage or "late bloomer" attribution espoused by some early childhood educators and (b) the need to accumulate sufficient failure on standardized achievement tests before an IQ test is administered to determine eligibility for special education. We have described six early assessment systems. Three of these were local efforts that engage teachers in collecting evidence upon which to base individual curricular decisions. Three were large-scale efforts—the California Learning Record, the Work Sampling System, and the Phonological Awareness and Literacy Screening currently under development in Virginia. Both the Work Sampling System and PALS have demonstrated evidence of validity and reliability. Finally, we have presented the Texas Primary Reading Inventory in detail as an example of a large-scale statewide assessment aligned to state curriculum standards and based on psychometric evidence that includes predictive validity. The items on the short screening component of the TPRI allow a teacher to know quickly which students are on track to becoming successful readers one year and two years later. That prediction allows the teacher to administer the more time-consuming inventory to the students potentially at risk so that instructional objectives can be established and monitored for progress.

Because the false positive rate is relatively large in kindergarten and first grade, early reading assessment should *not* be part of the accountability system. In other words, many kindergartners and first-graders will appear to be at risk for reading failure when, in fact, they turn out to become successful readers. However, by the beginning of second grade, the false positive rate is below 15 percent. Therefore, a second-grader who does not meet the criterion on the TPRI screen is a candidate for further evaluation and intervention to avoid being well below grade level at the end of the year. Thus, the performance on the Texas Primary Reading Inventory not only signals the need for early intervention, it holds the promise of preventing reading difficulties from occurring by maximizing the individual student's opportunities to learn in the classroom.

Assessment of early reading skills is useful only to the extent that (a) assessment results can be put in the hands of the teacher and used to plan instructional objectives and (b) the results enhance instructional outcomes by providing information to parents, teachers, administrators, and policy makers on the efficacy of different programs and decisions. Here Linn and colleagues and Pearson's notion of consequential validity is important.[85] Assessment for the sake of assessment is not meaningful. In the area of reading, assessment decisions must be linked to decision-making processes that will enhance reading outcomes for children. Decisions to assess early reading skills should be linked to the teacher's ability to plan instructional objectives. The use of assessments for accountability must not be punitive, but linked to the statewide curriculum and goals for all participants in the educational community. In the area of early reading assessments, the goal should be prevention so that accountability goals can be met later in schooling. This is consistent with the Reading First component of the Elementary and Secondary Education Act's No Child Left Behind legislation that requires assessment in K–3 classrooms for screening, diagnosis, progress monitoring, and outcome.

Notes

1. Sally E. Shaywitz, "Dyslexia," *Scientific American* 275 (1996): 98–104.
2. Catherine E. Snow, M. Susan Burns, and Patricia Griffin, *Preventing Reading Difficulties in Young Children* (Washington, D.C.: National Academy of Science, 1998).

3. Ibid.
4. Ibid.
5. David J. Francis, Sally E. Shaywitz, Karla K. Stuebing, Bennett A. Shaywitz, and Jack M. Fletcher, "Developmental Lag Versus Deficit Models of Reading Disability: A Longitudinal Individual Growth Curves Analysis," *Journal of Educational Psychology* 88 (1996): 3–17.
6. Connie Juel, "Learning to Read and Write: A Longitudinal Study of 54 Children from First Through Fourth Grades," *Journal of Educational Psychology* 80 (1988): 437–47.
7. Linda M. Phillips, Stephen P. Norris, Wendy C. Osmond, and Agnes M. Maynard, "Relative Reading Achievement: A Longitudinal Study of 187 Children from First Through Sixth Grades," *Journal of Educational Psychology* 94 (2002): 3–13.
8. Joseph K. Torgesen, "The Prevention and Remediation of Reading Disabilities: Evaluating What We Know from Research," *Journal of Academic Language Therapy* 1 (1997): 11–47.
9. Joseph K. Torgesen, Richard K. Wagner, Carol A. Rashotte, Elaine Rose, Patricia Lindamood, Tim Conway, and Cyndi Garvan, "Preventing Reading Failure in Young Children with Phonological Processing Disabilities: Group and Individual Responses to Instruction," *Journal of Educational Psychology* 91 (1999): 579–93; Joseph K. Torgesen, A. W. Alexander, Richard K. Wagner, Carol A. Rashotte, K. S. Voeller, and Tim Conway, "Intensive Remedial Instruction for Children with Severe Reading Disabilities: Immediate and Long-Term Outcomes from Two Instructional Approaches," *Journal of Learning Disabilities* 34 (2001): 33–58.
10. Frank R. Vellutino, Donna M. Scanlon, Edward Sipay, Sheila Small, Alice Pratt, Rusan Chen, and Martha Denckla, "Cognitive Profiles of Difficult-to-Remediate and Readily Remediated Poor Readers: Early Intervention As a Vehicle for Distinguishing Between Cognitive and Experimental Deficits As Basic Causes of Specific Reading Disability," *Journal of Educational Psychology* 88 (1996): 601–38.
11. Sandra Iversen and William Tunmer, "Phonological Processing Skills and the Reading Recovery Program," *Journal of Educational Psychology* 85 (1993): 112–26; William E. Tunmer, James W. Chapman, Henry Ryan, and Jane E. Prochnow, "The Importance of Providing Beginning Readers with Explicit Training in Phonological Processing Skills," *Australian Journal of Learning Disabilities* 3 (1998): 4–14 (hereafter cited as "The Importance of Providing Training in Phonological Processing Skills").
12. Barbara R. Foorman, David J. Francis, Jack M. Fletcher, Chris Schatschneider,

and Paris Mehta, "The Role of Instruction in Learning to Read: Preventing Reading Failure in At-Risk Children," *Journal of Educational Psychology* 90 (1998): 38–55.

13. Gerald Bond and Miles A. Tinker, *Reading Difficulties: Their Diagnosis and Correction* (New York: Appleton-Century-Crofts, 1957), 82.

14. Ibid., 70.

15. Michael Rutter and William Yule, "The Concept of Specific Reading Retardation," *Journal of Child Psychology and Psychiatry* 16 (1975): 181–97.

16. Jack M. Fletcher, Sally E. Shaywitz, Donald P. Shankweiler, Leonard Katz, Isabelle Y. Liberman, Ann Fowler, David J. Francis, Karla K. Stuebing, and Bennett A. Shaywitz, "Cognitive Profiles of Reading Disability: Comparisons of Discrepancy and Low Achievement Definitions," *Journal of Educational Psychology* 85 (1994): 1–18; Jack M. Fletcher, David J. Francis, Sally E. Shaywitz, Barbara R. Foorman, Karla K. Stuebing, and Bennett A. Shaywitz, "Intelligent Testing and the Discrepancy Model for Children with Learning Disabilities," *Learning Disabilities Research and Practice* 13 (1998): 186–203; Keith E. Stanovich and Linda S. Siegel, "Phenotypic Performance Profiles of Children with Reading Disabilities: A Regression-Based Test of the Phonological-Core Variable Difference Model," *Journal of Educational Psychology* 86 (1994): 24–53; Karla K. Stuebing, Jack M. Fletcher, J. M. LeDoux, G. Reid Lyon, Sally Shaywitz, and Bennett Shaywitz, "Validity of IQ-Discrepancy Classifications of Reading Disabilities: A Meta-Analysis," *American Educational Research Journal* 39 (2001): 469–518.

17. Cecil R. Reynolds, "Critical Measurement Issues in Learning Disabilities," *Journal of Special Education* 18 (1984): 451–76.

18. Rutter and Yule, "The Concept of Specific Reading Retardation."

19. Jack M. Fletcher, G. Reid Lyon, Marcia Barnes, Karla K. Stuebing, David Francis, Richard K. Olson, Sally E. Shaywitz, and Bennett A. Shaywitz, "Classification of Learning Disabilities: An Evidenced-Based Evaluation" in *Identification of Learning Disabilities: Research to Practice,* ed. R. Bradley, L. Danielson, and D. Hallahan (Mahwah, N.Y.: Erlbaum, 2002): 185–250; G. Reid Lyon, Dwayne Alexander, and Stephen Yaffe, "Progress and Promise in Research on Learning Disabilities," *Learning Disabilities* 8 (1997): 1–6; G. Reid Lyon, Jack M. Fletcher, Sally E. Shaywitz, Bennett A. Shaywitz, Joseph K. Torgesen, Frank B. Wood, Ann Schulte, and Richard Olson, "Rethinking Learning Disabilities" in *Rethinking Special Education for a New Century,* ed. C. E. Finn Jr., R. A. J. Rotherham, and C. R. Hokanson Jr. (Washington, D.C.: Thomas B. Fordham Foundation and

Progressive Policy Institute, 2001): 259–87; David L. Share, Robert McGee, and Philip D. Silva, "I.Q. and Reading Progress: A Test of the Capacity Notion of I.Q.," *Journal of the American Academy of Child and Adolescent Psychiatry* 28 (1989): 97–100; Stuebing, Fletcher, et al., "Validity of IQ-Discrepancy Classifications"; Joseph K. Torgesen, and Richard K. Wagner, "Alternative Diagnostic Approaches for Specific Developmental Reading Disabilities," *Learning Disabilities Research & Practice* 13 (1998): 220–32.

20. Barbara R. Foorman, "The Relevance of a Connectionistic Model of Reading for 'The Great Debate,'" *Educational Psychology Review* 6 (1994): 25–47; Michael W. Harm and Mark S. Seidenberg, "Phonology, Reading Acquisition, and Dyslexia: Insights from Connectionist Models," *Psychological Review* 106 (1999): 491–528; David C. Plaut, James L. McClelland, Mark S. Seidenberg, and Kathleen Patterson, "Understanding Normal and Impaired Word Reading: Computational Principles in Quasi-Regular Domains," *Psychological Review* 103 (1996): 56–115; Keith Rayner, Barbara Foorman, Charles A. Perfetti, David Pesetsky, and Mark S. Seidenberg, "How Should Reading Be Taught?" *Scientific American* (2002): 84–91; Stanovich and Siegel, "Phenotypic Performance Profiles."

21. Jack M. Fletcher and G. Reid Lyon, "Reading: A Research-Based Approach" in *What's Gone Wrong in America's Classrooms*, ed. W. M. Evers (Stanford, Calif.: Hoover Institution Press, 1998), 49–90.

22. Shaywitz, "Dyslexia"; Keith E. Stanovich, "Cognitive Science Meets Beginning Reading," *Psychological Science* 2 (1991): 70–81; Frank R. Vellutino, "Introduction to Three Studies on Reading Acquisition: Convergent Findings on Theoretical Foundations of Code-Oriented Versus Whole-Language Approaches to Reading Instruction," *Journal of Educational Psychology* 83 (1991): 437–43.

23. David L. Share and Keith E. Stanovich, "Cognitive Processes in Early Reading Development: A Model of Acquisition and Individual Differences," *Issues in Education: Contributions from Educational Psychology* 1 (1995): 1–57.

24. Sally E. Shaywitz, Michael D. Escobar, Bennett A. Shaywitz, Jack M. Fletcher, and Robert Makuch, "Distribution and Temporal Stability of Dyslexia in an Epidemiological Sample of 414 Children Followed Longitudinally," *New England Journal of Medicine* 326 (1992): 145–50.

25. Sally E. Shaywitz, Bennett A. Shaywitz, Jack M. Fletcher, and Michael D. Escobar, "Prevalence of Reading Disability in Boys and Girls: Results of the Connecticut Longitudinal Study," *Journal of the American Medical Association* 264 (1990): 998–1002.

26. Magdalen D. Vernon, *Backwardness in Reading: A Study of Its Nature and Origin* (London: Cambridge University Press, 1958).

27. Shaywitz, Shaywitz, et al., "Prevalence of Reading Disability in Boys and Girls."

28. Lyon, Fletcher, et al., eds., "Rethinking Learning Disabilities"; Torgesen and Wagner, "Alternative Diagnostic Approaches"; Share, McGee, and Silva, "I.Q. and Reading Progress."

29. Fletcher, Lyon, et al., *Classification of Learning Disabilities;* Fletcher, Shaywitz, et al., "Cognitive Profiles;" Stuebing, Fletcher, et al., "Validity of IQ-Discrepancy Classifications;" Stanovich and Siegel, "Phenotypic Performance Profiles."

30. G. Reid Lyon and Judith Rumsey, eds., *Neuroimaging: A Window to the Neurological Foundations of Learning and Behavior in Children* (Baltimore: Paul C. Brookes, 1997). Sally E. Shaywitz, Bennett A. Shaywitz, Ken R. Pugh, Robert K. Fulbright, Robert T. Constable, William E. Mencl, Donald P. Shankweiler, Alvin M. Liberman, Pawel Skudlarski, Jack M. Fletcher, Leonard Katz, Karen E. Marchione, Cheryl Lacadie, Carol Gatenby, and John C. Gore, "Functional Disruption in the Organization of the Brain for Reading in Dyslexia," *Proceedings of the National Academy of Sciences* 95 (1998): 2636–41. Panagiotis G. Simos, Jack M. Fletcher, Barbara R. Foorman, David J. Francis, E. M. Castillo, M. F. Davis, Patricia G. Mathes, Carolyn A. Denton, and Andrew C. Papanicolaou, "Brain Activation Profiles During the Early Stages of Reading Acquisition," *Journal of Child Neurology* 17 (2002): 159–63.

31. Jack M. Fletcher, Bonnie Brookshire, Timothy P. Bohan, Michael Brandt, and Kevin Davidson, "Early Hydrocephalus" in *Syndrome of Nonverbal Learning Disabilities: Neurodevelopmental Manifestations,* ed. B. P. Rourke (New York: Guilford Press, 1995), 206–38.

32. Lon Cardon, S. D. Smith, David Fulker, B. S. Kimberling, Bruce Pennington, and J. C. DeFries, "Quantitative Trait Locus for Reading Disability on Chromosome 6," *Science* 226 (1994): 276–79. Elena L. Grigorenko, Frank B. Wood, Marianne S. Meyer, Lesley A. Hart, William C. Speed, Arlene Shuster, and Donna Pauls, "Susceptibility Loci for Distinct Components of Developmental Dyslexia on Chromosomes 6 and 15," *American Journal of Human Genetics* (1997).

33. Catherine E. Snow, M. Susan Burns, and Patricia Griffin, *Preventing Reading Difficulties in Young Children* (Washington, D.C.: National Academy of Sciences, 1998).

34. Foorman, Francis, et al., "The Role of Instruction." Maureen W. Lovett, Lea Lacerenza, Susan L. Borden, Jan C. Frijters, Karen A. Steinbach, and Maria De Palma, "Components of Effective Remediation for Developmental Reading Disabilities: Combining Phonological and Strategy-Based Instruction," *Journal of Educational Psychology* 92 (2000): 263–83. Torgesen, "Prevention and Remediation." Torgesen, Wagner, et al., "Preventing Reading Failure." Torgesen,

Alexander, et al., "Intensive Remedial Instruction." Vellutino, Scanlon, et al., "Cognitive Profiles."

35. Foorman, Francis, et al., "The Role of Instruction in Learning to Read." Lovett, Lacerenza, et al., "Components of Effective Remediation." Torgesen, "Prevention and Remediation." Torgesen, Wagner, et al., "Preventing Reading Failure." Torgesen, Alexander, et al., "Intensive Remedial Instruction." Vellutino, Scanlon, et al., "Cognitive Profiles."

36. J. Bruce Tomblin and Xuyang Zhang, "Language Patterns and Etiology in Children with Specific Language Impairment" in *Neurodevelopmental Disorders: Contributions to a New Framework,* ed. H. Tager-Flusberg (Cambridge, Mass.: MIT Press, 1999), 361–82.

37. Frank R. Vellutino, Dyslexia: *Theory and Research* (Cambridge, Mass.: MIT Press, 1979).

38. Keith E. Stanovich, "Romance and Reality," *The Reading Teacher* 47 (1994): 280–9.

39. Foorman, Francis, et al., "The Role of Instruction in Learning to Read." Torgesen, "Prevention and Remediation." Torgesen, Wagner, et al., "Preventing Reading Failure." Torgesen, Alexander, et al., "Intensive Remedial Instruction."

40. Lorie Shepard, "What Policy Makers Who Mandate Tests Should Know About the New Psychology of Intellectual Ability and Learning" in *Changing Assessments: Alternative Views of Aptitude, Achievement and Instruction,* ed. B. R. Gifford and M. C. O'Connor (Boston, Mass.: Kluwer Academic Publishers, 1992), 301–28.

41. Jerome Sattler, *Assessment of Children,* 3rd ed. (San Diego, Calif.: Author, 1992).

42. Anne Anastasi, *Psychological Testing,* 5th ed. (New York: Macmillan, 1982).

43. Richard W. Woodcock, Kevin S. McGrew, and Nancy Mather, *Woodcock-Johnson* 3 (Itasca, Ill.: Riverside Publishing, 2001).

44. Lauren B. Resnick and Daniel P. Resnick, "Assessing the Thinking Curriculum: New Tools for Educational Reform" in *Changing Assessments,* ed. Gifford and O'Connor, 37–76.

45. Lynn S. Fuchs and Doug Fuchs, "Treatment Validity: A Unifying Concept for Reconceptualizing Identification of Learning Disabilities," *Learning Disabilities Research and Practice* 13 (1998): 45–58.

46. William A. Mehrens, "Using Performance Assessment for Accountability Purposes," *Educational Measurement: Issues and Practice* (spring 1992): 3–9. Reprinted in this volume.

47. Lauren Leslie and Joanne Caldwell, *Qualitative Reading Inventory* 2 (New York:

HarperCollins, 1995). Leslie M. Morrow, Michael Pressley, Jeffery K. Smith, and Michael Smith, "The Effect of a Literature-Based Program Integrated into Literacy and Science Instruction with Children from Diverse Backgrounds," *Reading Research Quarterly* 32 (1997): 54–77.

48. Robert L. Linn, Eve L. Baker, and Samuel B. Dunbar, "Complex Performance-Based Assessment: Expectations and Validation Criteria," *Educational Leadership* (1991): 15–21.

49. Elfrieda H. Hiebert, Sheila W. Valencia, and Peter P. Afflerbach, "Definitions and Perspectives." in *Authentic Reading Assessment: Practices and Possibilities,* ed. S. W. Valencia, E. H. Hiebert, and P. P. Afflerbach (Newark, Del.: International Reading Association, 1994), 6–21. Grant Wiggins, "Teaching to the Authentic Test," *Educational Leadership* 45 (1989).

50. Marie M. Clay, *Reading Recovery: A Guidebook for Teachers in Training* (Portsmouth, N.H.: Heinemann, 1993). Marie M. Clay, *The Early Detection of Reading Difficulties,* 3rd ed. (Portsmouth, N.H.: Heinemann, 1985).

51. Clay, *Reading Recovery: A Guidebook.*

52. Gay Sue Pinnell, Carol A. Lyons, Diane E. DeFord, Anthony S. Bryk, and Melvin Selzer, "Comparing Instructional Models for the Literacy Education of High-Risk First-Graders," *Reading Research Quarterly* 29 (1994): 8–38.

53. Tom Nicholson, "A Comment on Reading Recovery," *New Zealand Journal of Educational Studies* 24 (1989): 95–97. Valerie Robinson, "Some Limitations of Systemic Adaptation: The Implementation of Reading Recovery," *New Zealand Journal of Educational Studies* 24 (1989): 35–45.

54. Iversen and Tunmer, "Phonological Processing Skills."

55. Yola K. Center, Kevin Wheldall, Louella Freeman, Lynne Outhred, et al., "An Evaluation of Reading Recovery," *Reading Research Quarterly* 30 (1995): 240–63.

56. Tunmer, Chapman, et al., "The Importance of Providing Training in Phonological Processing Skills."

57. Snow, M. Burns, and Griffin, *Preventing Reading Difficulties.*

58. Terry Salinger and Edward Chittenden, "Analysis of an Early Literacy Portfolio: Consequences for Instruction," *Language Arts* 71 (1994): 446–52.

59. Ibid.

60. Mary A. Barr, S. Ellis, H. Tester, and A. Thomas, *The Primary Language Record: Handbook for Teachers* (Portsmouth, N.H.: Heinemann, 1988). Beverly Falk, "Using Direct Evidence to Assess Student Progress: How the Primary Language Record Supports Teaching and Learning." in *Assessing Reading 1: Theory and Practice,* ed. C. Harrison and T. Salinger (New York: Routledge, 1998), 152–65.

61. Mary A. Barr, ed., *California Learning Record: Handbook for Teachers* (San Diego: Center for Language in Learning, 1995).

62. Mary A. Barr and P. J. Hallam, *California Learning Record*, 1996 Moderation Report (San Diego: Center for Language in Learning, 1996).

63. James Hoffman, Nancy Roser, and Jo Worthy, "Challenging the Assessment Context for Literacy Instruction in First Grade: A Collaborative Study" in Assessing *Reading* 1, ed. Harrison and Salinger: 166–81.

64. Donna M. Ogle, "K-W-L: A Teaching Model That Develops Active Reading of Expository Text," *The Reading Teacher* 39 (1986): 564–70.

65. Hoffman, Roser, and Worthy, "Challenging the Assessment Context."

66. Ibid.

67. P. David Pearson, "Standards and Assessment: Tools for Crafting Effective Instruction?" in *Literacy for All: Issues in Teaching and Learning,* ed. F. Lehr and J. Osborn (New York: Guilford Publications, Inc., 1998): 264–88.

68. Samuel J. Meisels, "Using Work Sampling in Authentic Assessments," *Educational Leadership* (winter 1996–97): 60–65.

69. Samuel J. Meisels, F. Liaw, Anthony Dorfman, and Robert Nelson, "The Work Sampling System: Reliability and Validity of a Performance Assessment for Young Children," *Early Childhood Research Quarterly* 10 (1995): 277–96.

70. Pearson, "Standards and Assessment."

71. Ibid.

72. Ibid.

73. *Texas Primary Reading Inventory Technical Manual* (Austin, Tex.: Texas Education Agency, 1998). (Available at www.trpi.org under Researchers/Psychometrics.)

74. Robert J. Tierney, "Literacy Assessment Reform: Shifting Beliefs, Principled Possibilities, and Emerging Practices," *The Reading Teacher* 51 (1998): 374–91.

75. *Texas Primary Reading Inventory Technical Manual.* Chris Schatschneider, Jack Fletcher, David Francis, Coleen Carlson, and Barbara Foorman, "Kindergarten Prediction of Reading Skills: A Longitudinal Comparative Study," *Journal of Educational Psychology* (in press). Torgesen, "Prevention and Remediation." Vellutino, Scanlon, Edward Sipay, et al., "Cognitive Profiles."

76. Clay, *Reading Recovery: A Guidebook.*

77. *Texas Primary Reading Inventory Technical Manual.*

78. Morag Stuart, "Prediction and Qualitative Assessment of Five- and Six-Year-Old Children's Reading: A Longitudinal Study," *British Journal of Educational Psychology* 65 (1995): 287–96. Marie M. Clay, *Reading Recovery: A Guidebook.*

79. Leslie M. Morrow, "Assessing Children's Understanding of Story Through Their

Construction and Reconstruction of Narrative" in *Assessment for Instruction in Early Literacy*, ed. L. M. Morrow and J. K. Smith (Englewood Cliffs, N.J.: Prentice-Hall, Inc., 1990), 110–34.

80. Patricia McEnery, *The Role of Context in Comprehension of Narrative Text in First-Graders*. Unpublished doctoral dissertation (University of Houston, Houston, Tex., 1998).

81. Schatschneider, Fletcher, et al., *Kindergarten Prediction of Reading Skills*.

82. Jack Fletcher, Barbara Foorman, Amy Boudousquie, Marcia Barnes, Chris Schatschneider, and David Francis, "Assessment of Reading and Learning Disabilities: A Research-Based Intervention-Oriented Approach," *Journal of School Psychology* 40 (2002):27–63. Schatschneider, Fletcher, et al., *Kindergarten Prediction of Reading Skills*.

83. Richard W. Woodcock and M. Bonner Johnson, *Woodcock-Johnson Psychoeducational Battery* 3 (Allen, Tex.: DLM Teaching Resources, 2001).

84. Warren Simmons and Lauren Resnick, "Assessment As the Catalyst of School Reform," *Educational Leadership* (February 1993): 11–15.

85. Linn, Baker, and Dunbar, "Complex Performance-Based Assessment." Pearson, "Standards and Assessment."

Chapter 4

Science and Math Testing: What's Right and Wrong with the NAEP and the TIMSS?

Stan Metzenberg

Consider the question:

In the human body the digestion of proteins takes place primarily in which two organs?

A) Mouth and stomach

B) Stomach and small intestine

C) Liver and gall bladder

D) Pancreas and large intestine

The correct answer is B, and 66 percent of U.S. students in eighth grade answered it correctly on the National Assessment of Educational Progress (NAEP) Science Test administered in 2000.[1] It also is a very good question. It is stated in plain language and has a single correct answer. The distracters (incorrect answers) would be plausible to a person who has not learned the material well.

Perhaps more important, the content being tested is a foundation for future study. In high school, these sixty-six out of 100 students can go on to learn how proteins in the food we eat are broken into amino acids by the action of enzymes, such as pepsin (in the stomach) and trypsin (in the intestine). They can learn how the release of these enzymes is regulated, how each enzyme works in different conditions of acidity, and how the amino acids released during digestion are absorbed into the blood vessels in the intestinal walls. It's a truly beautiful system.

The reader may think it vain for a biologist to wax poetic over the details of digestive physiology, as these matters do not weigh heavily on the minds of most adults. Can there really be a credible link between testing eighth-grade students on their knowledge of the small intestine and international competitiveness? Questions of this type are usually delivered with a smirk and by the outcomes-based educator. A century ago, it would have been, "Does the future laborer really need to memorize Latin clauses for later regurgitation? *Tu quidem non es qui hoc crederes!*" Educational policy is regularly mauled by this *reductio ad absurdum* argument, and building a stronger line of defense ought to be a key goal of reformers. The rational response is as follows: Science disciplines the mind and is an important element of a sound, basic education. If the student has reached eighth grade without receiving a foundation for the core content of high school, then there is an immediate educational problem that will indeed lead to later problems with international competitiveness. Without an objective test of knowledge, there can be no diagnosis, and without diagnosis there can be no rescue of the student. *Quod erat demonstratum.*

Not all tests are good tests (see George K. Cunningham's chapter on the Kentucky system). The opening example of a good question, taken from the NAEP Science Test, is, unfortunately, a rare exception. Consider the following four items from the same eighth-grade NAEP Science Test. These are numbers eight through eleven out of a group of thirteen questions that refer to a diagram of a pond ecosystem:[2]

8. If all of the small fish in the pond system died one year from a disease that killed only the small fish, what would happen to the algae in the pond? Explain why you think so.

_____

_____

What would happen to the large fish? Explain why you think so.

_____

_____

9. Suppose that one spring a new type of large fish was put into the pond. So many were put in that there were twice as many fish as before. By the end of the summer, what would happen to the large fish that were already in the pond? Explain why you think these new large fish would have this effect.

_____

_____

10. If a rainstorm washed some fertilizer from a nearby field into the pond, what would happen to the algae in the pond system after one month? Why do you think the fertilizer would affect the algae this way?

_____

_____

11. What effect would the fertilizer have on the bacteria in the mud at the bottom of the pond after one month? Why do you think the fertilizer would affect the bacteria this way?

_____

_____

These questions do not have simple answers, nor do they even have single correct answers. The scoring guide is poorly constructed, giving the greatest reward to answers that are superficial. In question 8, the student is expected to write that the large fish will starve when the small fish die (and not be tempted to think that the fish might switch their diet to other animals pictured in the diagram, such as frogs and insects). In question 9, the student is expected to write that the "new type of large fish" that is added to the pond will compete with the old type of large fish. This is not only an unwarranted assumption about resource usage, but doubly confusing because the large fish still ought to be dead from the previous question. When a rainstorm washes "some fertilizer" into the pond in question 10, the student is expected to assume that the concentration of nutrients for the algae increases and not that the accompanying rainwater causes an overall dilution of nutrients. And finally, in question 11 the student is to believe that the bacteria in the mud at the bottom of the pond will be greater in number one month after the rainstorm and not hesitate to make such a prediction with so little data at hand. A correct answer on question 10 is critical for answering question 11, and this lack of independence between questions is a serious problem with the way the NAEP Science Test was constructed.

Question 11 verges on being unanswerable, for scientist and student alike. Approximately 69 percent of U.S. students gave answers that were deemed "incorrect" or "unsatisfactory" by the scoring panel, 21 percent gave answers that were considered "partial," and 10 percent were scored as "omitted item" or "off task." Last but not least, the percentage of eighth-grade students in the nation with "complete" answers on question 11 was reported to be 0 percent (after rounding). This is a strong indication that the question is defective in some way and that it should have been excluded from the test form after scientific or psychometric review.

These kinds of testing defects may arise, in part, from the over-powering interest of educators in what they call higher-order thinking and conceptual understanding. A straightforward question on a test, especially one that has a single correct answer, is likely to be discounted as "mere recall." This attitude leads to the administration of test items that are fundamentally superficial, though they may hold the pretense of showing conceptual understanding.

For example, on the eighth-grade NAEP Mathematics Test, the following problem appears:

   6. A poll is being taken at Baker Junior High School to determine whether to change the school mascot. Which of the following would be the best place to find a sample of students to interview that would be most representative of the entire student body?

A) An algebra class
B) The cafeteria
C) The guidance office
D) A French class
E) The faculty room

This particular question is classified by the NAEP writers as one that measures "students' conceptual understanding," though many readers might rightly wonder why it belongs on a mathematics test. Regarding this question, the NAEP writers go on to explain that:

> Students demonstrate conceptual understanding in mathematics when they provide evidence that they can recognize, label, and generate examples of concepts; use and interrelate models, diagrams, manipulatives, and varied representations of concepts; identify and apply principles; know and apply facts and definitions; compare, contrast, and integrate related concepts and principles; recognize, interpret, and apply the signs, symbols, and terms used to represent concepts.[3]

As to the aspects of data analysis, statistics, and probability being tested, they write, "This question also focuses on the subtopic of using measures of central tendency (that is, mean, median, range) to describe statistical relationships."[4] The test authors seem to have overestimated the mathematical value of the question and overlooked its apparent technical defects. The wording of the test item is likely to be misinterpreted by many students, because not all schools have each of the five named locations, nor would all use these exact titles for the sites (a cafeteria might be called a lunch room). Of those schools that even have a mascot, not all would be so progressive as to ask students for their opinions, which may explain why "The faculty room" was the most common incorrect answer nationally. Not all students are in settings in which the principal or teacher would even permit "An algebra class" or "A French class" to be interrupted by such a frivolous poll, and that may also have affected the students' thinking.

Just as there is grade inflation in the classroom, there seems to be cognitive inflation in test frameworks and in state and national standards of learning. There is one peculiar characteristic of these types of writings, for example, the just-quoted passage from the NAEP writers, and that is the feverish use of action verbs. Students are to "recognize, label, and generate," or "compare, contrast, and integrate," or "recognize, interpret, and apply." The swarms of verbs usually arrive in groups of three or more, like horsemen of the apocalypse, and they drive away the teaching and testing of foundational knowledge. The recommendations are sometimes explicit on this matter, as in the National Science Education Standards, which call for "less emphasis on knowing scientific facts and information" and "more emphasis on understanding scientific concepts and developing abilities of inquiry."[5]

Ideally, test items would be grounded in a wide range of cognitive levels, but would also be consistent with the goals of scientists and mathematicians to explain real or abstract structures in the simplest terms. On the NAEP test items, half of the student's job may be untangling the awkward English. For example, in the aforementioned NAEP Science Test question regarding stocking a pond with a new type of large fish, the second sentence reads: "So many were put in that there were twice as many fish as before." In the NAEP Mathematics Test for eighth-grade students, the following question appears:[6]

> There are 50 hamburgers to serve 38 children. If each child is to have
> at least one hamburger, at most how many of the children can have
> more than one?
>   A) 6
>   B) 12
>   C) 26
>   D) 38

This is cognitively a bit more difficult to solve than the question "50 - 38 = ?," but much of the burden for the student is in understanding the language rather than understanding the mathematics.

It may be fashionable to test students using word problems that are believed to measure higher-order thinking and to demand a constructed response rather than a selected response, but these practices may affect the validity of the test for students who have limited reading and writing skills. Validity, to a psychometrician, means that the test "actually measures the traits, knowledge, or skills it is intended to measure."[7] A test of science or mathematics that requires extensive reading or writing is partly a test of the intended content area and partly a test of the language skills needed to comprehend and complete the test form. The correlation shown in Figure 4.1 between state-level scores on the eighth-grade NAEP Science Test (1996) and the eighth-grade NAEP Reading Test (1998) is significant (r = 0.93, n = 36) and reproducible between test administrations.[8] A similar significant correlation exists between state-level performance on the eighth-grade NAEP Mathematics Test (2000) and NAEP Reading Test (1998) scores (r = 0.94, n = 34).

FIGURE 4.1   NAEP Reading and Science Scores Are Correlated

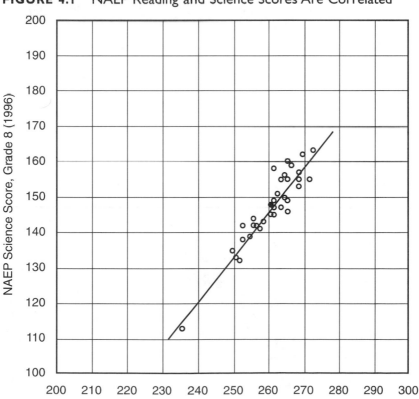

Other standardized tests yield similar findings. For example, in the Chicago Public High Schools the correlation between reading and math scores on the Illinois Goals Assessment Program (IGAP) test was significant in 1997 and 1998, with correlation coefficients of r = 0.95 and r = 0.97, respectively. In Figure 4.2, the change in reading and math scores for each school is shown in the form of individual arrows, with the tail of the arrow representing the reading and math scores in 1997 and the arrowhead representing the same paired data in 1998.[9] Of the sixty schools reporting data in both years, only one showed an increase in math score without an accompanying increase in reading score. It seems unlikely that pure mathematical ability is so closely tied to reading ability, and more probable that learning math (which may require

FIGURE 4.2   Correlated Improvement in Reading and Math IGAP Scores, Chicago Public High Schools, 1997–1998

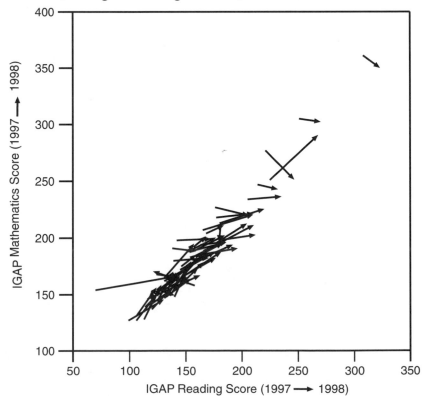

reading the textbook) and taking an exam in math (which may require comprehension of the test) is sensitive to language skills.

A similar effect may be at play in the correlation between reading and science scores or all three may be under the control of an unknown general variable, some sort of common currency of academic ability.[10] It is unlikely to be that simple, and policy makers should carefully consider the more probable sources of the correlation. If the reading and writing demands of the test are more significant than the mathematics and science challenges, then these tests are partially invalid because they do not measure what they purport to measure. Alternatively, the correlation may show that reading ability is a strong determinant of the ability to learn other subjects. If students learn most of their science and math by reading, then constructivist curricula that rely heavily on hands-on activities and other manipulative projects may not be fully effective.

The awareness of constructivist methods of teaching is fairly widespread, as 84 percent of the eighth-grade math teachers reported being at least "somewhat knowledgeable" about the National Council of Teachers of Mathematics (NCTM) Curriculum and Evaluation standards in 1996, and 65 percent reported having attended some sort of professional development workshop or activity designed to help implement those standards.[11] Fourth-grade teachers were less familiar with the NCTM standards, with only 55 percent reporting that they are "somewhat knowledgeable" and only 40 percent reporting attending an NCTM-aligned workshop or activity[12] (though fourth-graders performed relatively better according to the international comparison done in the Third International Mathematics and Science Study [TIMSS]).

Among eighth-grade math teachers, 67 percent report having their students solve problems in groups at least once or twice a week, and 94 percent reported a frequency of at least once or twice a month.[13] One must be wary of drawing any firm conclusions from these types of survey data, as they may depend on perception as much as reality. For example, as shown in Table 4.1, when fourth-grade students and teachers are both asked how often the students discuss solutions to mathematics problems with other students, the teachers report a relatively high frequency and the students report a relatively low frequency.

Perhaps these differ because the teachers report on the class average, whereas the student responses reflect the behaviors of individuals. Alternatively, as this question regards a teaching practice that is in high fashion, perhaps some teachers respond in the way they think they ought to and not in a way that reflects their own practice. One might find these data to be no more credible than the body weights people claim for their driver's licenses! If departments of motor vehicles want the truth, they must start weighing license applicants when their pictures are taken, and if educational policy makers want the truth, they must videotape the teaching (see the chapter by Alan Siegel on the TIMSS videotape studies).

Within an educational setting, it should be considered that some populations of students may be more sensitive to unsuitable teaching methods than others. The aforementioned correlation in reading and math ability in the Chicago Public Schools appears

TABLE 4.1

Question: **In this mathematics class, how often do you [the students] discuss solutions to mathematics problems with other students?**

	STUDENT RESPONSES[59]		TEACHER RESPONSES[60]	
Responses	*Prevalence*	*NAEP Score of Students by Response Type*	*Prevalence*	*NAEP Score of Teachers' Classes by Response Type*
Never or hardly ever	33%	222	6%	219
Once or twice a month	18%	227	22%	221
Once or twice a week	29%	224	37%	221
Almost every day	19%	217	35%	227

less strong in the schools performing in the top 10 percent. Four out of the top six schools showed a decrease in math score accompanied by an increase in reading score (these arrowheads point to the "southeast" on the graph, rather than to the usual "northeast"). Perhaps these students have reached a threshold reading ability at which comprehension of the textbook and examination is no longer problematic, so reading and math scores become independent variables. Alternatively, the top-performing students may have been negatively affected by the National Science Foundation's (NSF) Systemic Initiative Grant that was implemented at that time in the Chicago schools and that embraced the constructivist teaching methods recommended by the NCTM.[14]

According to the science teachers answering survey questions on the 1996 NAEP Science Test, hands-on methods of teaching science are widespread, with 86 percent of eighth-grade science teachers claiming to place "moderate" or "heavy" emphasis on developing students' laboratory skills and techniques.[15] Again, these responses are sensitive to perceptions and the psychology of surveys, but the reports from students raise some question about the value of hands-on science investigations in the classroom.

As Table 4.2 shows, student scores appear to decrease as the frequency of designing and carrying out science investigations increases, and it may be because these activities and projects do not involve much reading. Perhaps the best hands-on science program would be one in which students can get their "hands on" a good textbook.

TABLE 4.2

Question: When you study science in school, how often do you design and carry out your own science investigations?[61]

Responses	Prevalence	Student NAEP Science Score
Never or hardly ever	63%	151
Once or twice a month	23%	151
Once or twice a week	10%	142
Almost every day	5%	137

In California, poor reading skills have been the legacy of the whole-language movement, and while the picture is now becoming brighter for students in lower elementary grades, many of the students entering middle/junior high and high schools are deficient in reading–language arts skills. The numbers of students enrolled in Reading Improvement/Developmental Reading courses has increased dramatically in California, from 183,422 in the school year 1997–98 to 481,950 in 2002–3.[16] In seventh grade nearly one out of every four students is enrolled in this class. The effect of this problem on science instruction is difficult to measure because many districts continue to use hands-on kits for science instruction that have minimal reading materials for students. In 2002, California adopted the Science Curriculum Framework, which sets guidelines for K–8 instructional materials. With this document come new policies for teaching science.[17] The state-adopted science materials in grades K–8 are required to have expository text and cannot be based on more than 20 percent to 25 percent hands-on activities. Also, the new state-adopted language arts materials are required to address those K–3 science content standards that lend themselves to instruction during the language arts time period.[18] This is intended to protect that instructional time needed to develop language skills and is likely to be a wise investment over time.

This movement in California educational policy was partly in response to the 1994 NAEP Reading scores, which placed the state near the bottom of the national standings. One of the benefits of state, national, and international testing is that it can provide jurisdictions that are falling behind with a sense of reality and can have a positive effect on the curriculum. Enrollment in integrated math and integrated science courses[19] dropped significantly in California between 1998 and 2002,[20] and this may have been a rational response to the NAEP Science and Mathematics tests and the TIMSS report in 1998. Despite their good performance in the fourth-grade TIMSS Science Test,[21] U.S. students scored closer to the international average in the eighth-grade exam[22] and well below average in the terminal year of secondary school.[23] The poor performance of high school seniors in the United States was accompanied by an unrealistic view of their own prowess, and perhaps educational policy makers similarly had inflated opinions. For example, students in each nation were asked to respond on a Likert Scale to the statement "I have usually done well in mathematics,"—as Table 4.3 shows, their actual national test scores did not reflect their level of self-confidence.

In a broader look at the responses, 75.9 percent of the U.S. students either agreed or strongly agreed with the statement that they had usually done well in mathematics, and only 24 percent either disagreed or strongly disagreed. The United States may have taken the prize for "most deluded nation" on this particular matter, since their scores were so low; however the source of this delusion is not entirely clear. It may be that U.S. teachers are heaping students with undeserved accolades and top marks or that the national standards against which U.S. students are judged are woefully low. If U.S. students think that mathematics is primarily about passing out hamburgers and finding the best place to poll students about a new school mascot, then they may be truly surprised by the expectations placed on students in other countries.

The TIMSS test and survey results were reported by the Washington, D.C.–based National Center for Education Statistics (NCES), a federal entity that is part of the U.S. Department of Education. Examples of their publications include the *Pursuing Excellence* series of reports.[24] NCES work

TABLE 4.3

Statement: I [the student] have usually done well in mathematics.

TIMSS Nations	Students strongly agreeing with the statement[62]	Students' average mathematics general achievement score
Netherlands	13.4%	560
Sweden	16.2%	552
United States	23.6%	461
Cyprus	20.8%	446

should be distinguished from the TIMSS reports published by
education researchers at Michigan State University (MSU), a
group that calls itself the "U.S. TIMSS National Research
Center."[25] The MSU group is funded by the NSF and publishes
highly interpretive reports on U.S. student achievement, some of
which predate the TIMSS study.[26] Examples of their work
include *A Splintered Vision*,[27] which argued that U.S. science and
mathematics curricula show an intention to cover many more
topics than other nations' and that these topics are presented in a
fragmented and unfocused way in textbooks. In addition to the
content differences between the NCES and MSU reports, there
is a significant difference in how the two groups reached conclusions and how they brought results to the attention of the public.
Whereas the NCES reported with some restraint, "Our analysis
of TIMSS data does not suggest any single cause of this level of
U.S. performance,"[28] the MSU group opined, "What is surprising is not the profoundly disappointing results but rather failing
to realize how predictable those results were given what we
already knew."[29] Adding to the confusion, the MSU group had
hired the New York–based public relations firm of Hill and
Nolton, and the group's press release from East Lansing was
timed for the exact hour that the U.S. Commissioner of
Education Statistics made his statement, at 11:00 a.m. EST on
February 24, 1998.

The MSU group had considerable success in getting their
message to stick in the public's minds, with their claim that the
U.S. curriculum is "a mile wide and an inch deep."[30] Such a
statement has broad appeal because scientists and mathematicians may agree with the "inch deep" part, finding contemporary teaching to be superficial in content, and outcomes-based
educators agree with the "mile wide" part, finding the academic
curriculum in need of severe pruning. There are many factors
that indubitably influence the performance of students in science and mathematics, and it should be remembered that curriculum is but one. Without compelling evidence of a
cause-and-effect relationship, TIMSS scores cannot be used to
measure the relative values of national curricula, and this is a

critical error in the development of the MSU group's methodology. It was simply taken *a priori* that an analysis of curriculum would provide invaluable information for interpreting achievement results.[31]

The problem with the MSU group's TIMMS report is far more than mere data-dredging, however. Of particular concern is the apparent lack of detachment of the researchers from the selection of data used. In *A Splintered Vision*, the MSU group stated that "the TIMSS curriculum analysis was based primarily on state curriculum frameworks or guides and on supporting opinion by experts in mathematics and science education."[32] As a general rule, researchers cannot avoid having predilections or hopes about their results, and that is why it is critical that they blind themselves to the process of selecting the data. In the MSU study, one of the principal investigators was also the U.S. National Research coordinator. As such, he was responsible for designating the panel of curriculum experts that would develop the General Topic Trace Mapping data for the United States[33] and was involved in selecting the U.S. curricular documents to be analyzed.[34] To explain this another way, a researcher should never poll himself and become a data point in his own study.

The selection and sampling of documents (curricular guides and textbooks) in the MSU study was a key element in defining its data set. The MSU report indicates that their group of researchers "drew an appropriate random sample of state curriculum guides in 1992–93," but this comment has this footnote attached to it: "Selecting documents for the U.S. Curriculum Analysis presented considerable challenges given the nature of curriculum policy making and textbook markets in this country."[35] Random sampling and selection cannot both have happened. A further statement, "Documents were sampled rather than surveyed exhaustively,"[36] suggests that once a curriculum guide was chosen for analysis, there may have been additional, potentially uneven methods for selecting the portions of the text to be reviewed and coded. In the final analysis, twenty-two mathematics curriculum guides derived from thirteen different states were used to represent the United States in the study.[37]

A second type of data entering into the MSU group's study, the "supporting opinion by experts," may similarly have been selectively chosen. Most nations were represented by a single individual[38] and that individual had primary control of the data and opinion representing his or her country. The representatives were often the National Research coordinators; however, there was considerable variation as to whether the representatives were national education ministers or academics. With variation in mathematics and science expertise, these appointed individuals might have varied widely in their perceptions of their native countries and the content fields of mathematics and science.

The coding of the curriculum guides and textbooks was a process by which the intended curriculum was evaluated by reviewers, and code numbers expressing the mathematics content were assigned.[39] The taxonomic framework containing the code numbers is the organizing structure for all of the data collected on the curriculum guides and textbooks and is divided into ten major groups, as shown in Table 4.4 (the deeper branches of the taxonomic tree are not shown).

TABLE 4.4

CONTENT

  1.1   Numbers

      1.1.1   Whole numbers

      1.1.2   Fractions and decimals

      1.1.3   Integer, rational, and real numbers

      1.1.4   Other numbers and number concepts

      1.1.5   Estimation and number sense

  1.2   Measurement

      1.2.1   Units

      1.2.2   Perimeter, area and volume

      1.2.3   Estimation and errors

1.3 Geometry: Position, visualization, and shape

1.3.1	Two-dimensional geometry: Coordinate geometry

1.3.2	Two-dimensional geometry: Basics

1.3.3	Two-dimensional geometry: Polygons and circles

1.3.4	Three-dimensional geometry

1.3.5	Vectors

1.4 Geometry: Symmetry, congruence, and similarity

1.4.1	Transformations

1.4.2	Congruence and similarity

1.4.3	Constructions using straight-edge and compass

1.5 Proportionality

1.5.1	Proportionality concepts

1.5.2	Proportionality problems

1.5.3	Slope and trigonometry

1.5.4	Linear interpolation and extrapolation

1.6 Functions, relations, and equations

1.6.1	Patterns, relations, and functions

1.6.2	Equations and formulas

1.7 Data representation, probability, and statistics

1.7.1	Data representation and analysis

1.7.2	Uncertainty and probability

1.8 Elementary analysis

1.8.1	Infinite processes

1.8.2	Change

1.9 Validation and structure

1.9.1	Validation and justification

1.9.2	Structuring and abstracting

1.10 Other content

1.10.1	Informatics

These ten major groupings of content are unevenly distributed across the mathematics field, and considerable weight is given to measurement, estimation, data representation, and validation.

Beyond the primary groupings of content, the secondary and tertiary taxonomic levels are also unevenly allotted. Under category *1.1 Number*, the five subcategories are divided into a total of twenty additional codes (not shown). Fine distinctions are drawn at this tertiary level between the content areas of common fractions (*1.1.2.1*), decimal fractions (*1.1.2.2*), relationships between common and decimal fractions (*1.1.2.3*), percentages (*1.1.2.4*), properties of common and decimal fractions (*1.1.2.5*), and rational numbers (*1.1.3.2*). The major category *1.1 Number* is the only one that was divided to this third taxonomic level, and consequently it represents nearly half of the framework branches at their highest degree of specificity. Algebraic issues (*1.6 Functions, relations and equations*) merits only two subcategories overall, whereas proportionality (*1.5 Proportionality*) is specified by four subcategories, geometry (*1.3 Geometry: Position, visualization, and shape* and *1.4 Geometry: Symmetry, congruence, and similarity*) by eight, and number (*1.1 Number*) by twenty-five.

The MSU group did not force a one-to-one mapping between the curriculum material and the taxonomic scheme so as to take into account the "interrelatedness of content."[40] Individual "blocks" of content, small analytical segments of the books, were coded using the taxonomy, as shown here by one of their examples:[41]

> Problem: The product of 0.23 and 6.57 is closest to:
>   a. 0.0015   d. 15.0
>   b. 0.15   e. 150
>   c. 1.5

> Framework categories assigned:
>   1.1.2.2   Decimal fractions
>   1.1.5.3   Estimating computations

It is not clear why a reviewer would reject other potential classifications, such as *1.1.1.2 Operations* or *1.1.5.2 Rounding and significant figures*, or why a second- or first-generation taxonomic level might not be selected to code the task, such as *1.1.5 Estimation* and number sense or simply *1.1 Number*. This was a source of irregularity in their coded data because it led to differences in how countries evaluated the content of their own books. Reviewers in Korea, New Zealand, Switzerland, and the United States, to name a few, regularly used the a general level of specification (*1.1 Number*) to code data from seventh- and eighth-grade textbooks, whereas reviewers in other nations, such as Hong Kong, Cyprus, Spain, and Germany, applied the taxonomic framework differently.

The MSU group considered each taxonomic framework category to be a different "topic," meaning that a teacher who assigned the estimation problem shown above would have been instructing students in two different topics simultaneously (decimal fractions and estimating computations). Of course, the student would perceive it as a single-topic question—it is only the scheme developed by the MSU group that makes it two topics. By the taxonomy, a textbook in algebra might be coded as containing only three topics from *1.6 Functions, relations, and equations,* whereas another book that included an introduction to topics from *1.1 Number* might be coded as containing twenty-five. The MSU group reported that "the U.S. mathematics and science textbooks analyzed included far more topics than was typical internationally at all grade levels analyzed,"[42] but this statement depends on both the uneven taxonomic framework and the irregular methods by which the framework was applied during coding.

U.S. curriculum policy was characterized by the MSU group as being unfocused and incoherent; however, their method of aggregating the curriculum guides from thirteen states to represent the nation may have been the factor that created a lack of focus. The researchers in the MSU group did not seem to be unaware of the problem, as they wrote:

> Countries without national curriculum guides, but with multiple subsystems and their corresponding guides, could, when aggregated to the country level, produce longer durations for some topics. As a result, the country-level durations should not be interpreted as specific to individual students but rather to the country as a whole.[43]

No U.S. students experience the superimposed curricula of thirteen different states, and using that model as a representation of their schooling leads to a research artifact.

In remarks made at the Republican Governors' Conference in 1997[44] and to news organizations,[45] the MSU group voiced the opinion that a significant problem with U.S. textbooks is their sheer length. It was said that because of the large books "teachers in the United States are forced to deal superficially with subjects and then review them again yearly, wasting valuable instructional time." It is a question worth reviewing, because textbook page counts, unlike topic counts, are an objective measure. The MSU group has made their data set public,[46] so the number of pages in math textbooks from different nations can be analyzed for potential correlation with student performance. When this is attempted with the eighth-grade math textbooks from nineteen nations, as shown in Figure 4.3, the data are widely scattered, and there does not appear to be any credible correlation (r = -0.27).[47] For example, the number of pages in the math book from Singapore (278 pages, TIMSS score 630) is not significantly different from the number of pages in the math books of South Africa (360 pages, TIMSS score 354), even though their scores are dramatically different. The United States (TIMSS score 500) gave students large books, ranging in size from 545 pages to more than 700 pages, but scored similarly to Germany (TIMSS score 509), which had books one-fifth that size.

It may be a false assumption that U.S. teachers begin with a class in September on the first page of a book and continue teaching until they get to the 700th page sometime in June. Many sections of the book may be skipped during teaching, and there may, in fact, be benefits to the unused pages. Commercial textbooks may contain extra units so that they can be better applied to the focused curriculum in each school and so that they might provide better support for teaching students of varied achievement levels. The sizes and weights of books may be something that every educational policy maker can love to hate, but until the U.S. Surgeon General finds that eighth-grade student spines have become deformed from the extra burdens in backpacks, it is reasonable to doubt that the extra pages are harmful.

Although little credibility ought be given to the MSU group's counting of textbook "topics" because their taxonomic framework was subjectively and irregularly applied during coding, it is remarkable that the data in their files do not even support their own conclusions. As shown in Figure 4.4, the relationship between TIMSS scores and topic counts is again a scattered one without credible correlation (r = -0.21), as it was for the textbook page counts from each

FIGURE 4.3   TIMSS Math Scores Do Not Correlate with Number of Pages in National Textbooks

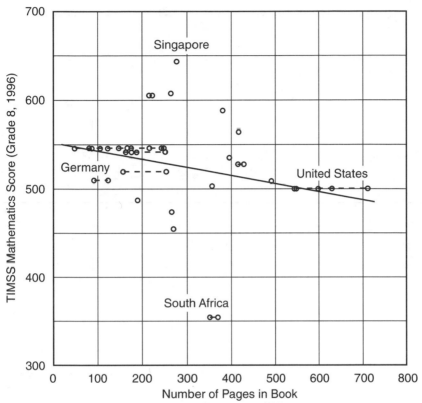

nation.[48] Singapore and South Africa, with widely different scores, have nearly identical numbers of topics in their textbooks, whereas the United States and Germany have nearly identical scores and widely different numbers of topics.

An attempt to correlate performance with coverage of specific topics would also fail. For example, Portugal (with a TIMSS score of 454) has considerably more textbook coverage of topics in the field of algebra than Singapore (with a TIMSS score of 630).[49]

The MSU group observed that according to its data, Japanese eighth-grade math books had long sequences of unbroken coverage of topics, whereas U.S. books tended to have shorter sequences on a single main topic and tended to break that sequence by attending to a different topic. A typical segment of twenty-five sequential blocks

FIGURE 4.4   TIMSS Math Scores Do Not Correlate with Number
of Topics in National Textbooks

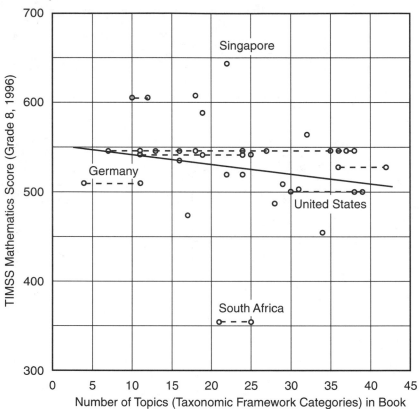

of data from a single U.S. and Japanese eighth-grade mathematics book are in Table 4.5 to illustrate this point. The U.S. reviewer encoded the twenty-five blocks from the U.S. book with one to two topics per block, and the sequence covers six different topics in total. The Japanese reviewer, on the other hand, gave each sequential block only one topic code per block, and within the twenty-five-block segment only one topic is covered.[50]

Both books are presenting the topic of algebra (equations and formulas). However, the reviewer of the U.S. book did not consistently encode the blocks as algebra (that is, the topic code *1.6.2 Equations and formulas* was omitted for blocks 5, 6, 11–18, 21,

TABLE 4.5 Twenty-five Sequential Topic Data Blocks from a U.S. Textbook and a Japanese Textbook

Block	United States book	Japanese book
1	1.3.1 (Coordinate geometry); 1.6.2 (Equations and formulas)	1.6.2 (Equations and formulas)
2	1.3.1 (Coordinate geometry); 1.6.2 (Equations and formulas)	1.6.2 (Equations and formulas)
3	1.1.3.3 (Real numbers); 1.6.2 (Equations and formulas)	1.6.2 (Equations and formulas)
4	1.1.3.3 (Real numbers); 1.6.2 (Equations and formulas)	1.6.2 (Equations and formulas)
5	1.1.3.3 (Real numbers)	1.6.2 (Equations and formulas)
6	1.1.3.3 (Real numbers); 1.3.1 (Coordinate geometry)	1.6.2 (Equations and formulas)
7	1.1.3.3 (Real numbers); 1.6.2 (Equations and formulas)	1.6.2 (Equations and formulas)
8	1.1.3.3 (Real numbers); 1.6.2 (Equations and formulas)	1.6.2 (Equations and formulas)
9	1.1.3.3 (Real numbers); 1.6.2 (Equations and formulas)	1.6.2 (Equations and formulas)
10	1.1.3.3 (Real numbers); 1.6.2 (Equations and formulas)	1.6.2 (Equations and formulas)
11	1.1.2.2 (Decimal fractions)	1.6.2 (Equations and formulas)
12	1.1.2.2 (Decimal fractions)	1.6.2 (Equations and formulas)
13	1.1.2.1 (Common fractions)	1.6.2 (Equations and formulas)
14	1.1.2.1 (Common fractions)	1.6.2 (Equations and formulas)
15	1.1.2.1 (Common fractions)	1.6.2 (Equations and formulas)
16	1.1.2.1 (Common fractions)	1.6.2 (Equations and formulas)
17	1.1.2.1 (Common fractions)	1.6.2 (Equations and formulas)
18	1.1 (Numbers)	1.6.2 (Equations and formulas)
19	1.6.2 (Equations and formulas)	1.6.2 (Equations and formulas)
20	1.6.2 (Equations and formulas)	1.6.2 (Equations and formulas)
21	1.1.3.3 (Real numbers)	1.6.2 (Equations and formulas)
22	1.1.3.3 (Real numbers); 1.3.1 (Coordinate geometry)	1.6.2 (Equations and formulas)
23	1.1.3.3 (Real numbers); 1.6.2 (Equations and formulas)	1.6.2 (Equations and formulas)
24	1.1.3.3 (Real numbers); 1.6.2 (Equations and formulas)	1.6.2 (Equations and formulas)
25	1.1.3.3 (Real numbers); 1.6.2 (Equations and formulas)	1.6.2 (Equations and formulas)

and 22). These differences in evaluation could be a result of different reviewing styles.

For example, if two individuals read Gertrude Stein's quotation "A rose is a rose is a rose" and evaluated it for its coverage of "roses," their conclusions might depend on their perspective. One reviewer might read the quotation one word at a time and think it fragmented, since "roses" were only intermittently addressed, and only three out of the eight words were on the topic. Another reviewer might read the phrase from a broader perspective and decide that all eight words were part of an ongoing discussion of roses. By the same token, an exposition on equations of functions might present a graph of a function on the real number plane, and one reviewer might think it part of the same topic (*1.6.2 Equations and formulas*), and another might code it as an interruption (*1.1.3.3 Real numbers* and *1.3.1 Coordinate geometry*). This appears to have been handled differently in each country and perhaps was related to the mathematics expertise of the reviewers. A reviewer without adequate expertise might read algebra books in much the same way as a "word-by-word automaton" would read Gertrude Stein.

In the evaluation of U.S. and Japanese eighth-grade textbooks, approximately 10 percent and 29 percent of the data blocks are coded as *1.6.2 Equations and formulas,* respectively.[51] The U.S. books' data blocks are a bit scattered (as in "a rose is a rose is a rose") compared with the Japanese books (as in "a a a rose rose rose is is"), but just as the complexion of the fairest Hollywood starlet might look coarse in an extreme close-up, the fragmentation of topics in these books needs to be studied from the right distance. Is the scattering of topics between data blocks real, or is it an artifact of noise created by the review? Data blocks typically represent only one-quarter to one-sixth of one textbook page in the MSU study, and this may be too fine-grained an analysis. A more appropriate view of the text might be to look at segments that amount to 1 percent of its length, which would amount to a few instructional days. If a topic such as *1.6.2 Equations and formulas* appears intermittently in the U.S. book, but frequently enough that a class is still effectively "on topic" for days, then the book may have a fairer complexion than was alleged.

In a reanalysis of the MSU group's data, 40 percent of the segments in the U.S. eighth-grade text contain the code *1.6.2 Equations and formulas*, with each "segment" taken to be 1 percent of the book.[52] That is to say, the "rose is a rose is a rose" looks considerably rosier at a reasonable distance than it does in the MSU group's close-up view of data blocks. Although it is possible that this indicates some sort of "complex signature"[53] of fragmentation in U.S. books, the chances of inconsistent treatment by different reviewers seems far greater. It hardly matters what the cause may be, however, because it is relatively easy to demonstrate that this type of fragmentation does not correlate with the TIMSS scores. The aforementioned U.S. book showed 10 percent coverage of *1.6.2 Equations and formulas* at the data block level and 40 percent coverage at the segmental level, so a "fragmentation index" of 4.00 is calculated for that book (that is, the index is simply the ratio, 40 percent divided by 10 percent). The Japanese book showed 29 percent coverage of the topic at the data block level and 31 percent coverage at the segmental level, so its fragmentation index is 1.07.

Figure 4.5 shows the fragmentation indices from the eighth-grade math books of nineteen countries, and it is apparent that they do not correlate to student performance on the TIMSS assessment (r = −0.16).[54] The South African books are less fragmented than the Singaporean books, though South Africa and Singapore place at the bottom and top of the TIMSS scoring respectively. The U.S. students score approximately as well on the TIMSS as German students, though the MSU TIMSS data indicate that their books are the most and least fragmented, respectively.

In their report *A Splintered Vision*, the MSU group created the impression, by anecdotal data taken only from the U.S. and Japanese books, that there might be a relationship between topic fragmentation and TIMSS performance.[55] Had they presented more than this small selection of their data on this particular question, the lack of correlation would have been immediately obvious.

FIGURE 4.5   TIMSS Math Scores Do Not Correlate with Topic Fragmentation in National Textbooks

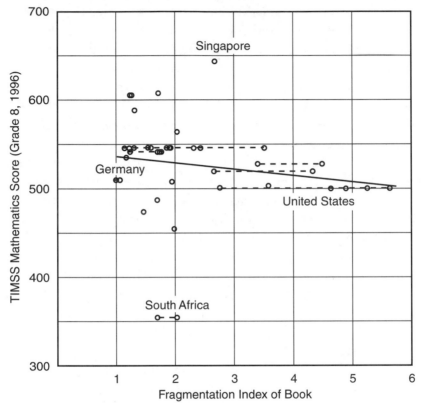

Summary and Recommendations

Testing in mathematics and science is a critical element of standards-based reform, but it is not without its shortcomings in practice. Individual standardized tests such as the NAEP need to be redesigned with greater care so that they are correct in content and are valid measures of knowledge and skills in their respective content areas. This may mean turning away from some fashionable types of questions that make it difficult to measure content knowledge and skills in isolation of more general language skills. The panels that construct these tests need to be stocked with the best content experts that the nation can provide. A working formula might be that for every ten panel members writing a test, five should have Ph.D. degrees in the subject (not in "education of the subject") and be active contributors to their fields. Four of the panel members should be full-time K–12 teachers in the subject area, with at least ten years' experience at the grade level being tested, and one of the panel members should be an iron-fisted psychometrician who knows that the test must be valid as well as reliable.

The survey data that accompany the NAEP and TIMSS tests should be analyzed for trends, but problems with the perception and psychology of the respondents may make it difficult to arrive at meaningful conclusions. There is no single cause of poor U.S. performance, and policy makers need to be cautious about any claim to the contrary. In particular, the findings of the Michigan State University TIMSS U.S. National Research Center are not credible. Their research design and methodology were flawed, and their own collected data do not support their published conclusions.

The MSU report *A Splintered Vision* expressed a view that national standards and reform were leading to progress and a wish that there could be greater local and state adherence to national reform guidelines.[56] The president of the National Academy of Sciences was similarly hopeful about the "pretty impressive" performance of fourth-grade students on the TIMSS and called for the nation not to step backward because of the poor twelfth-grade results. He said:

> Let me remind you that reform begins with the national education standards, and those standards must be implemented in the form of instructional materials, teaching methods, and assessments. Where such change has been made, for example, in elementary schools, we have preliminary indicators that education reform is working in those early grades.[57]

Was he right that the fourth-grade TIMSS results were a positive indication that national standards had benefited these fortunate students, and that eighth- and twelfth-grade students might soon be equally impressive?

The question was tested in 1999, when the United States participated in a follow-up TIMSS Repeat (TIMSS-R) study of eighth-grade students. This was a second look at the cohort of students who had been "pretty impressive" in 1995 and had now had four additional years of U.S. schooling. Unfortunately, by their TIMSS scores in eighth grade, they had sunk to the same level as the previous eighth-grade students of 1995.[58] U.S. students may simply travel along a well-worn path, from "pretty impressive" to "pretty mediocre." Making a better path for future students will depend on the collection of valid testing data and educational research that is open-minded and credible.

Notes

1. The NAEP test is developed by the National Assessment Governing Board. This question from the eighth-grade NAEP Science Test, Block: 2000-8S11 No.:12.
2. Questions from eighth-grade NAEP Science Test, Block: 2000-8S9, Nos.: 8–11.
3. Content classification for item on eighth-grade NAEP Mathematics Test, Block: 1996-8M3 No.:6.
4. Ibid.
5. National Research Council, National Science Education Standards (Washington, D.C.: National Academy Press, 1996), 113.
6. Questions from eighth-grade NAEP Mathematics Test, Block: 1992-8M5 No.:5.
7. Educational Testing Service: http://www.ets.org/aboutets/statist.html.
8. A correlation between the NAEP Science Test (2000) and NAEP Reading Test (1998) scores is similarly significant ($r = 0.91$, $n = 30$). The correlation can only be made using states that participated in both types of assessments and between years in which the tests were administered. The filled circle in Figure 4.1 represents the national average scores and was not part of the correlation coefficient r.
9. Data extracted from school-by-school reports provided by the *Chicago Times* web site, http://chicagotribune.com/ws/front/0,1413,66,00.html. Sixty high schools in the Chicago public schools system reported math and reading data in both years and were included. An additional twenty were excluded because they failed to report complete data for one or both years; these were typically charter schools and transition schools.
10. If it is really that simple, then one reading test would suffice for students each year, and a set of exchange rates could be used to predict accurately the scores on the other tests.
11. C. A. Shaughnessy, J. E. Nelson, and N. A. Norris, *NAEP 1996 Mathematics Cross-State Data Compendium for the Grade 4 and Grade 8 Assessment* (Washington, D.C.:

National Center for Education Statistics, 1997), Table 6.24.

12. Ibid., Tables 6.1 and 6.2.

13. Ibid., Table 6.37.

14. The NSF director has claimed that the math score increases in Chicago during this time period were a result of NSF Systemic Initiative funding, a questionable attribution given the correlation with reading that is shown. Rita R. Colwell and Eamon M. Kelly, *Science* 286 (1999):237.

15. National Center for Education Statistics, *NAEP 1996 Cross-State Data Compendium for the Eighth Grade Assessment (NCES98-482).* (Washington, D.C.: U.S. Department of Education, Office of Educational Research and Improvement), Table 5.1.

16. A course designed to provide instruction in basic language skills, integrating reading, writing, speaking, and listening while placing greater emphasis on individual student progress. In the California Basic Educational Data System (CBEDS), this course is CBEDS code number 2100. Data on specific course enrollment provided by the California Department of Education: http://data1.cde.ca.gov/dataquest.

17. California Department of Education *Science Framework for California Public Schools* (adopted by the State Board of Education, February 2002), http://www.cde.ca.gov/
cfir/science/.

18. California Department of Education *2002 K–8 Reading Language Arts English Language Development Adoption Criteria* (adopted by the State Board of Education, December 1999), http://www.cde.ca.gov/cfir/rla/2002criteria.pdf.

19. Integrated Mathematics 1 (CBEDS code 2425) course description: The course content includes functions, algebra, geometry, statistics, probability, discrete mathematics, measurement, number, logic, and language. The course emphasizes mathematical reasoning, problem solving, and communication through integration of the various strands, connections with other subject areas and real-life applications, use of technology, and exploratory and group activities. The course emphasizes algebra. Integrated Science 1 (CBEDS code 2626) course description: First-Year Coordinated/Integrated Science draws from the principles of several scientific disciplines—earth science, biology, chemistry, and physics—and organizes the material around thematic units. Common themes include systems, models, energy, patterns, change, and constancy. Students investigate applications of the theme using appropriate aspects from each discipline. http://www.cde.ca.gov/demographics/
coord/curriculum/subject-table.htm.

20. 1998 course enrollment figures for ninth grade: Integrated Mathematics – 69,208 students; Integrated Science I – 96,858 students. 2001 course enrollment figures

for ninth grade: Integrated Mathematics I – 22,695; Integrated Science I – 73,353. Data extracted from California Department of Education, demographic data files. http://www.cde.ca.gov/demographics/files/cbedshome.htm.

21. U.S. Department of Education, National Center for Education Statistics, *Pursuing Excellence: A Study of U.S. Fourth-Grade Mathematics and Science Achievement in International Context*, NCES 97-255 (Washington, D.C.: U.S. Government Printing Office, 1997).

22. U.S. Department of Education, National Center for Education Statistics, *Pursuing Excellence: A Study of U.S. Eighth-Grade Mathematics and Science Teaching, Learning, Curriculum, and Achievement in International Context*, NCES 97-198 (Washington, D.C.: U.S. Government Printing Office, 1996).

23. U.S. Department of Education, National Center for Education Statistics, *Pursuing Excellence: A Study of U.S. Twelfth-Grade Mathematics and Science Achievement in International Context*, NCES 98-049 (Washington, D.C.: U.S. Government Printing Office, 1998).

24. Ibid.

25. Also variously called the National Research Center for the Third International Mathematics and Science Study, and the U.S. National Research Center (http://ustimss.msu.edu/).

26. For example, the Survey of Mathematics and Science Opportunities (SMSO) project. William H. Schmidt et al., *Characterizing Pedagogical Flow* (Boston: Kluwer Academic Publishers, 1996).

27. William H. Schmidt, Curtis C. McKnight, and Senta A. Raizen, *A Splintered Vision—An Investigation of U.S. Science and Mathematics Education* (Boston: Kluwer Academic Publishers, 1997).

28. Pascal D. Forgione Jr., Ph.D., U.S. Commissioner of Education Statistics, National Center for Education Statistics (NCES), press release, "On the Release of U.S. Report on Grade 12 Results from the Third International Mathematics and Science Study (TIMSS)" (February 24, 1998), http://nces.ed.gov/Pressrelease/timssrelease.html.

29. William H. Schmidt, U.S. TIMSS National Research Coordinator, press release, "Are There Surprises in the TIMSS Twelfth-Grade Results?" (Michigan State University: February 24, 1998), http://ustimss.msu.edu/12gradepr.htm.

30. Ibid.

31. Leonard J. Bianchi, Richard T. Houang, Jacqueline Babcock, and William H. Schmidt, *User Guide for the TIMSS International Curriculum Analysis Database* (East Lansing: TIMSS International Curriculum Analysis Center, Michigan State University, December 1998), 1–2; and Schmidt, McKnight, Raizen, *A*

Splintered Vision—An Investigation of U.S. Science and Mathematics Education, 11.

32. Schmidt, McKnight, Raizen, *A Splintered Vision—An Investigation of U.S. Science and Mathematics Education,* 13.

33. Bianchi, Houang, Babcock, and Schmidt, *User Guide for the TIMSS International Curriculum Analysis Database,* 4–5.

34. Ibid., pp. 1–8.

35. Schmidt, McKnight, Raizen, *A Splintered Vision—An Investigation of U.S. Science and Mathematics Education,* 13.

36. Ibid.

37. Ibid., Appendix B; and William H. Schmidt et al., *Many Visions, Many Aims* Volume I (Boston: Kluwer Academic Publishers, 1997), Appendix G.

38. Bianchi, Houang, Babcock, and Schmidt, *User Guide for the TIMSS International Curriculum Analysis Database,* 1–11.

39. Schmidt, McKnight, and Raizen, *A Splintered Vision—An Investigation of U.S. Science and Mathematics Education,* 1 (footnotes).

40. David F. Robitaille, *Curriculum Frameworks for Mathematics and Science,* (Vancouver: Pacific Educational Press, 1993), 44.

41. Ibid., 56.

42. Schmidt, McKnight, and Raizen, *A Splintered Vision—An Investigation of U.S. Science and Mathematics Education,* 5.

43. Schmidt et al., *Many Visions, Many Aims* Volume I, 71.

44. Remarks to the Republican Governors' Conference (Miami: November 21, 1997), http://timss.msu.edu/republican.html.

45. Debra Viadero, "Surprise! Analyses Link Curriculum, TIMSS Test Scores," *Education Week* (April 2, 1997): http://www.edweek.org/ew/ew_printstory.cfm?slug=27timss.h16.

46. Available in .zip compression format from http://timss.msu.edu/cdata.html.

47. Eighth-grade textbooks from nineteen nations representative of the full range of TIMSS scores were included in this analysis, with some nations submitting multiple textbooks that are connected in the diagram by dashed lines. The nineteen nations were Canada, Cyprus, Czech Republic, Germany, Hong Kong, Japan, Korea, the Netherlands, Norway, New Zealand, Portugal, the Russian Federation, South Africa, Singapore, Slovenia, Spain, Sweden, Switzerland, and the United States of America. The solid line represents linear regression analysis, without significance in correlation (r = −0.27).

48. Nineteen representative nations, as described in the previous note. Data points from nations submitting multiple textbooks are connected in the diagram by dashed lines. The solid line represents linear regression analysis, without significance in correlation (r = −0.21).

49. In Portugal 50 percent, and in Singapore 30 percent of eighth-grade book topics are subcategories of *1.6 Functions and Equations.*

50. The twenty-five sequential blocks from each country represent: United States, a twenty-five-block portion of lessons 24–26 from book 840-10088; Japan, a twenty-five-block portion of lessons 10–14 from book 392-0M182C.

51. The percentages refer to U.S. book 840-10081 and Japanese book 392-0M182C, although the comparison is general to other examples.

52. The statistical analysis was programmed and performed as follows: A "moving window" of width 1 percent of the sequential blocks per textbook was passed over the MSU TIMSS block data, with starting position incremented by one block for each window movement. The topic codes contained in each window and numbers of window positions containing each topic code were recorded for analysis. The ratio between the fraction of windows (book segments) containing each topic code and the fraction of blocks containing each topic code represents a fragmentation index, normalized so that an unfragmented topic in a book would yield a score of 1.00.

53. An expression used to describe national differences in fragmentation: Schmidt, McKnight, and Raizen, *A Splintered Vision—An Investigation of U.S. Science and Mathematics Education,* 130.

54. Nineteen representative nations, as previously described. Method of statistical analysis as previously described. Data points from nations submitting multiple textbooks are connected in the diagram by dashed lines. The solid line represents linear regression analysis, without significance in correlation (r = –0.16).

55. Schmidt, McKnight, and Raizen, *A Splintered Vision—An Investigation of U.S. Science and Mathematics Education,* 98–102. The data on fragmentation that dealt solely with Japanese and U.S. books is in Exhibits 37–38, pp. 99–101.

56. Ibid., 10.

57. Bruce Alberts, president, National Academy of Sciences, press release, "Twelfth-Grade Results from the Third International Math and Science Study (TIMSS)" (Washington, D.C.: National Press Building, February 24, 1998). The full context of the quoted portion: "This ['12th-Grade Results from the Third International Math and Science Study'] may appear to give credence to the position that education reform is not working. Quite the contrary is true. Let me remind you that reform begins with the national education standards, and those standards must be implemented in the form of instructional materials, teaching methods, and assessments. Where such change has been made, for example, in elementary schools, we have preliminary indicators that education reform is working in those early grades;

recall that the fourth-grade results from these international tests for U.S. students were pretty impressive. In fact, today's test results underscore the importance of education reform. We cannot use these results as justification for standing still or taking a step backward—that would be a great disservice to our children, who are looking to us to provide them with the skills needed for success."

58. National Center for Educational Statistics, *Third International Mathematics and Science Study—Repeat* (Washington, D.C.: U.S. Department of Education, 2001), http://nces.ed.gov/timss/timss-r/.

59. National Center for Education Statistics, *NAEP 1996 Cross-State Data Compendium for the Grade 4 and Grade 8 Assessment* (NCES98-481) (Washington, D.C.: U.S. Department of Education, Office of Educational Research and Improvement, 1998), Table 6.11.

60. Ibid., Table 6.10.

61. National Center for Education Statistics, *NAEP 1996 Cross-State Data Compendium for the Grade 8 Assessment* (NCES98-482) (Washington, D.C.: U.S. Department of Education, Office of Educational Research and Improvement, 1998), Table 5.9.

62. Third International Mathematics and Science Study, *Student Background Variables—Students in the Final Year of Secondary School* (INTMSL4=1) (Boston: International Study Center, Lynch School of Education, Boston College), Question CSBMGOOD, Location SQ3-22A. http://isc.bc.edu/timss1/database/pop3/POP3ALMN.ZIP.

Chapter 5

Telling Lessons from the TIMSS Videotape

Remarkable Teaching Practices As Recorded from Eighth-Grade Mathematics Classes in Japan, Germany, and the United States

Alan R. Siegel

Why Another Study?

The outstanding performance of Japanese students on the Third International Mathematics and Science Study (TIMSS) examinations, along with the accompanying TIMSS videotape classroom studies, have generated widespread interest in Japanese teaching practices. Unfortunately, despite this excitement, the

It is a pleasure to thank Clilly Castiglia and Kevin Feeley of the NYU Center for Advanced Technology and the Media Research Lab, who graciously provided the VHS frame processing. The author would also like to thank Professor Michiko Kosaka for resolving several questions about the actual Japanese as recorded in the excerpts.

majority of ensuing education analyses and policy reports seem to be based on incomplete portrayals of the teaching as documented on videotape. Part of the problem is that the teaching is remarkably rich. As a consequence, short summaries and even quotes from original sources sometimes fail to provide a balanced characterization of the actual lessons and can even be just plain wrong.

These are strong words, and especially so if they happen to allege serious errors and misunderstandings in widely cited and highly respected studies. However, these studies, despite being based on common sources of information, do sometimes contradict each other, so some of the assertions cannot be right. On the other hand, it is only fair to point out that there are just a few such contradictions; most of the conclusions are consistent across all of the studies. But we also concur with the overall theme: The lessons as recorded in Japan are masterful. The main—and crucial—difference is in understanding the kind of teaching that made these lessons so remarkable.

For example, it is widely acknowledged that Japanese lessons often use very challenging problems as motivational focal points for the content being taught.[1] According to the recent Glenn Commission Report:

> In Japan, . . . closely supervised, collaborative work among students is the norm. Teachers begin by presenting students with a mathematics problem employing principles they have not yet learned. They then work alone or in small groups to devise a solution. After a few minutes, students are called on to present their answers; the whole class works through the problems and solutions, uncovering the related mathematical concepts and reasoning.[2]

This chapter resolves the crucial classroom question that the other reports left unanswered: How in the world can Japanese eighth-graders, with just a few minutes of thought, solve difficult problems employing principles they have not yet learned?

Background

The Third International Mathematics and Science Study comprises an enormously complex and comprehensive effort to assess primary and secondary school mathematics and science education worldwide. The examination phase began in 1995 with the testing of more than 500,000 students in forty-one countries[3] and continued with repeat testing (TIMSS-R) in 1999,[4] additional projects, and data analyses that are still a matter of ongoing research. As part of the TIMSS project, 231 eighth-grade mathematics lessons in Germany, Japan, and the United States were recorded on videotape during 1994–95. An analysis of these tapes, which includes a variety of statistics, findings, and assessments, was reported in the highly influential TIMSS Videotape Classroom Study by James Stigler and colleagues.[5] This study also provides a detailed description of its data acquisition and analysis methodologies. Subsequently, James Stigler and James Hiebert published additional findings in *The Teaching Gap*, which emphasizes the cultural aspects of teaching and offers suggestions about how to improve teaching in the United States.[6]

In addition, the project produced a publicly available videotape containing excerpts from representative lessons in geometry and in algebra for each of the three countries, along with a discussion of preliminary findings narrated by Dr. Stigler.[7] The excerpts of German and American lessons were produced in addition to the original 231 lessons, which are not in the public domain because of confidentiality agreements. For the Japanese lessons, disclosure permissions were obtained after the fact. The TIMSS videotape kit also includes a preliminary analysis of the taped lessons[8] that follows the procedures used in the actual study. In addition, the TIMSS project produced a CD-ROM with the same classroom excerpts.[9]

What the Video Excerpts Show

The video excerpts, it turns out, provide indispensable insights that complement the more widely cited studies. They are the primary source for the following analysis, which compares the assessments and conclusions of the many studies with the actual classroom events as documented on tape.

Geometry

The tape shows the Japanese geometry lesson beginning with the teacher asking what was studied the previous day. After working to extract a somewhat meaningful answer from the class, he himself gives a summary: Any two triangles with a common base (such as *AB* in Figure 5.1) and with opposing vertices that lie on a line parallel to the base (such as the line through *C*, *D*, and *P*) have the same area because the lengths of their bases are equal, and[10] their altitudes are equal.

The teacher states this principle and uses his computer graphics system to demonstrate its potential application by moving vertex *P* along the line *CD*. The demonstration shows how to deform triangle *ABP* in a way that preserves its area. Next, he explains that this principle or method is to be the *foundation*[11] for the forthcoming problem, which he then presents. It is the following:

> Eda and Azusa each own a piece of land that lies between the same pair of lines. Their common boundary is formed by a bent line segment as shown. The problem is to change the bent line into a straight line segment that still divides the region into two pieces, each with the same area as before.

FIGURE 5.1   (letters *A* and *B* enhanced)

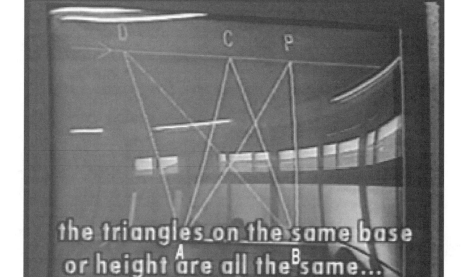

FIGURE 5.2

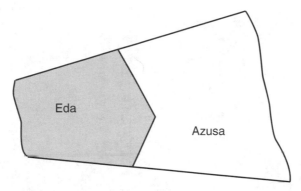

Despite the previous review, the problem is still going to be a challenge for eighth-graders, and it is fair to infer that the teacher understands this. In geometry, one of the most difficult challenges in a construction or proof is determining where to put the auxiliary lines. These lines are needed to construct the angles, parallel lines, triangle(s), and so on that must be present before a geometry theorem or principle can be applied to solve the problem. For the exercise in Figure 5.2, the key step is to draw two crucial auxiliary lines. One defines the base of a triangle that must be transformed in a way that preserves its area. The other is parallel to this base and runs through its opposing vertex.

So what should a master instructor do? The answer is on the tape.

After explaining the problem, the teacher asks the students to estimate where the solution line should go and playfully places his pointer in various positions that begin in obviously incorrect locations and progress toward more plausible replacements for the bent line. Now here is the point. With the exception of two positionings over a duration of about one second (which come shortly after the frame shown in Figure 5.3), none of his trial placements approximate either of the two answers that are the only solutions any student will find.

Rather, they are all suggestive of the orientation for the auxiliary lines that must be drawn before the basic method can be

FIGURE 5.3

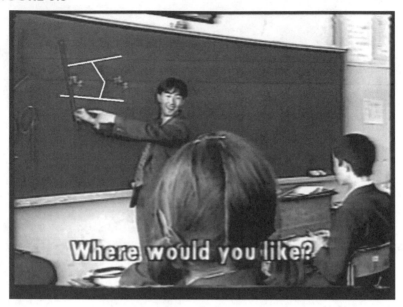

applied. He is giving subtle hints and calling the students' attention to the very geometric features that must be noticed before the problem can be solved. It is surely no accident that the teacher reaches two particular pointer placements more often than any other. One is shown in Figure 5.4. The other is parallel to this placement, but located at the vertex that forms the bend in the boundary between Eda and Azusa.

Only after this telling warm-up—the heads-up review of the solution technique necessary to get the answer and the seemingly casual discussion loaded with visual cues about what must be done—are the children allowed to tackle the problem.

But this is not the end of the lesson, and the students only get an announced and enforced three minutes to work individually in search of a solution.

As the children work, the teacher circulates among the students to provide hints, which are mostly in the form of leading questions, such as: "Would you make this the base? [The question is] that somewhere there are parallel lines, OK?"[12]

FIGURE 5.4

He then allocates an additional three minutes during which those who have figured out the solution discuss it with the other teacher. Weaker students are allowed to work in groups or use previously prepared hint cards. The tape does not show what happens next. The TIMSS documentation reports that students prepare explanations on the board (nine minutes).[13]

Then a student presents his solution. The construction is clearly correct, and he starts out with a correct explanation. However, when the time comes to find the solution, he gets lost and cannot see how to apply the area-preserving transformation that solves the problem. The teacher then tells him to use "the red triangle" as the target destination.

The advice turns out to be insufficient, and the teacher *steps in* (as shown in Figure 5.5) to redraw the triangle that solves the problem and calls the student's attention to it with the words "over here, over here." The student seems to understand and begins the explanation afresh. But he soon winds up saying, "Well, I don't know what I am saying, but . . . ." He then regains

FIGURE 5.5

The area is...

his confidence, and the presentation comes to an end. A number of students say that they do not understand. Then another student explains her answer, but the presentation is omitted from the tape. According to the Moderator's Guide,[14] these two student presentations take less than three minutes altogether.

FIGURE 5.6

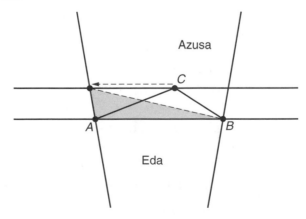

Azusa

Eda

FIGURE 5.7

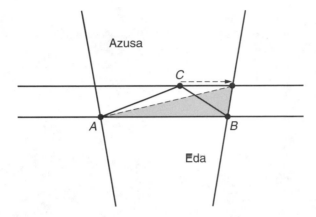

Next, the teacher explains how to solve the problem. There are two equivalent answers that correspond to moving vertex *C*, in the context of Figure 5.1, to the left or to the right. Both directions solve the problem, and he shows this. Such a duality should not be surprising, because the word problem is not described in a way that, in the context of Figures 5.1, 5.6, and 5.7, can distinguish left from right. For completeness, we show the two ways that the triangle transformation technique can be used to solve the problem. In order to make the connection between the review material and the follow-up Eda-Azusa exercise absolutely clear, the solution with its two versions have been rotated to present the same perspective as in Figure 5.1, which introduced this triangle transformation technique.

No one devised an alternative solution method.

The lesson continues with the teacher posing a new problem that can be solved with the same technique. This time the figure is a quadrilateral, and the exercise is to transform it into a triangle with the same area. At this point, the basic solution method should be evident because the previous problem, as the teacher pointed out, also concerned the elimination or straightening of a corner in an area-preserving way.[15] However, added difficulty comes from the need to recognize that two consecutive sides of the quadrilateral should be viewed as representing the bent line of

FIGURE 5.8

Figure 5.2. Notice, by the way, that if each of the other two neighboring sides is extended as an auxiliary line, then the resulting figure is changed into a version of the Eda-Azusa problem. (See Figure 5.9.) Evidently, this exercise is well chosen.

The basic line-straightening method can be applied so that any one of the four vertices can serve as the point where the line bends, and this designated vertex can be shifted in either of two

FIGURE 5.9

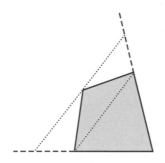

directions to merge one of its two connecting sides with one of the auxiliary lines. The students again work individually for three minutes, then are allowed to work in groups, use hint cards, or ask the teacher.

The TIMSS documentation indicates that this joint phase lasts for twenty minutes and includes students presenting their answers. There are apparently eight such presentations, which were selected to illustrate all eight ways the basic method can be applied: There are four vertices that each can be moved two ways. Then the teacher analyzes these eight ways in greater depth and explains how they all use the same idea. All students remain seated during this portion of the lesson, and the teacher controls the discussion carefully and does almost all of the speaking.

An Analysis of the Teaching and Its Content

This lesson is nothing less than a masterpiece of teaching, and the management of classroom time was remarkable. Although many students did not solve the first problem of the day, the assignment certainly succeeded in engaging everyone's attention. The second problem was no giveaway, but it afforded students the chance to walk in the teacher's footsteps by applying the same ideas to turn a quadrilateral into a triangle. The teacher-led study of all possible solutions masked direct instruction and repetitive practice in an interesting and enlightening problem space.

Evidently, no student ever developed a new mathematical method or principle that differed from the technique introduced at the beginning of the lesson. In all, the teacher showed ten times how to apply the method. The lesson is an excellent example of how to teach problem solving because each successive problem required an ever deeper understanding of the basic proof technique. For homework, the teacher asked the students to transform a five-sided polygon into a triangle with the same area.[16]

Notice that this lovely problem variation hints at the use of induction: The way to solve it is to transform a five-sided figure into a quadrilateral, which can then be transformed into a triangle. The basic corner elimination scheme can now be seen to work for any (convex) polygon so that any such n-sided polygon can be transformed into one with $n - 1$ sides and the same area, for $n > 3$.

It is also worth pointing out that the solution technique, which is a specific application of measure-preserving transformations, has additional uses. It appears, for example, in Euclid's proof of the Pythagorean Theorem (cf. Book I Prop. 47 of Euclid's *Elements*).[17] More advanced exercises of this type appear on national middle school mathematics competitions in China and regional high school entrance examinations in Japan. And it is not much of a stretch to suggest that measure-preserving transformations lie at the heart of those mysterious changes of variables in the study of integral calculus. All in all, the lesson is a wonderful example of the importance of a deep understanding of mathematics and its more difficult aspects.

Algebra

The Japanese algebra lesson begins with student-presented answers for each of the previous day's six homework problems.[18] These activities, along with the accompanying classroom discussion, are omitted from the excerpts.

Then the teacher presents a more challenging problem. It uses the same basic calculation method that the students have been studying, but needs one commonsense extension. The problem is this:

> There are two kinds of cake for sale. They must be bought in integer multiples; you cannot buy a fraction of a cake. The most delicious cake costs 230 yen, and a less tasty one is available for 200 yen. You wish to purchase ten cakes but only have 2,100 yen. The problem is to buy ten cakes and have as many of the expensive cakes as possible while spending no more than 2,100 yen.

It is clear that the students had already studied versions of the problem that would permit fractional units of cakes to be purchased. The reproduction of the six homework exercises as shown in the TIMSS Moderator's Guide confirms that the class was already experienced with the technical mechanics necessary to solve problems with inequalities.[19] It is also evident that they had been studying word problems and the translation of word problems into equations and inequalities that can then be solved. Indeed, the teacher introduces the problem with the remarks, "Today will be the final part of the sentence problems."[20] Thus, it is fair to infer that the only difference between the cake problem and the material they had just reviewed is the requirement that the solution must comprise integer multiples of each cake.

After making sure that the students understand the problem, he asks them to devise a way to solve it. They get an announced and enforced three minutes.

Next, the teacher solicits solution approaches from the students. A student volunteers that she tried all possibilities. Her approach was to try ten cheap cakes, then nine cheap ones and one expensive one, and so on, until she had the best answer. However, she was unable to finish in the three minutes that the teacher allocated for the problem. The teacher emphasizes the point, and it will soon become clear that part of the lesson is to show that this unstructured approach is unsound.

He then briefly discusses another way to solve the problem. The approach, which is quite inventive, uses a notion of marginal cost. If we buy ten of the most expensive cakes, we exceed our budget by 200 yen. Trading in an expensive cake for a cheaper cake gives a net savings of 30 yen. Obviously, seven cakes have to be traded in, which shows that the answer is three expensive cakes and seven cheaper ones. As the teacher expected,[21] no student solved the problem this way.

Then he calls on another student, who explains how she set up the problem as an inequality, solved it as an equality, then rounded the number of expensive cakes down to the nearest lesser integer. As she explains the equation, he writes it on the board. Only a few students understand the explanation, and he asks for another explanation of the same process. In subsequent activities that are only summarized on the tape and in the Moderator's Guide, the teacher passes out a worksheet and works through a detailed analysis of the solution for the class.

After the detailed presentation, another problem of the same type was assigned, but with larger numbers. The teacher's words are telling:

> If you count one by one, you will be in an incredibly terrible situation. *In the same way that we just did the cake situation, set up an inequality equation by yourself* and find out . . . [the answer]. Because finding the answers one by one is hard, I wonder if you see the numerous good points of setting up inequality equations . . . .

The students work on the problem individually. After eleven minutes, the teacher went over the problem with the class. The video excerpts contain no group-based problem solving in this algebra lesson, and the Moderator's Guide confirms that none of the class time included problem solving in groups.

Each class ended with the teacher summarizing the solution technique that constituted the lesson of the day.

An Analysis of the Teaching and Its Content

Students never developed new solution methods. In the algebra class, the students were given the opportunity to learn firsthand why amorphous trial-and-error approaches (which seem to be encouraged by some of the latest reform programs) do not work. While the tape does not explicitly show how many students were able to solve the original cake problem in the allotted time, the student responses suggest that no more than four or five could possibly have succeeded. But the three minutes of struggle might well have served to make the lesson more purposeful.

From a mathematical perspective, the cake problem was designed to require a deep understanding of inequality problems and their solution. Mathematicians would say that when we solve a problem, we find all of the answers. If the cake problem had allowed fractional purchases and had simply required that altogether any mix of ten cakes be purchased for at most 2,100 yen, then the algebraic formulation would read

$$230x + 200(10 - x) \le 2100$$

where x is the number of expensive cakes purchased and $10 - x$ is the number of the inexpensive ones. The problem would also require that x be nonnegative because you cannot buy negative quantities of cake. A little algebraic manipulation gives the solution as the interval

$$0 \leq x \leq \tfrac{10}{3}$$

Now, every x in this interval is a solution to the simplified problem, and every solution to the problem is in this interval. So if we want a special answer, the interval $[0, \tfrac{10}{3}]$ is the place to look. If we want the largest x, it is $\tfrac{10}{3}$. If we want the largest integer x, it is 3. And if we wanted the largest even integer, for example, we would look nowhere else than into $[0, \tfrac{10}{3}]$ to conclude that this answer is $x = 2$. Incidentally, a complete answer must also observe that the number of inexpensive items is nonnegative (which is to say that $x \leq 10$).

So this problem variant is more than a matter of common sense; it exposes students to a deep understanding of solutions to inequalities and the implications of real-world constraints. Moreover, the problem illustrates the idea of decomposing a complex exercise into a more basic problem whose solution can then be adapted to achieve the original objective.

In summary, the video excerpts feature challenge problems that cover fundamental principles, techniques, and methods of systematic thought that lie at the heart of mathematics and problem solving. As such, they ought to provide experiences that build a powerful foundation of intuition and understanding for more advanced material yet to come. As a derivative benefit, these problems are so rich they can be readily transformed into follow-up exercises for use as reinforcement problems in class and as homework.

Defining Terms: Discovery and Invented Methods

Many publications claim that the Japanese lessons teach students to invent solutions, develop methods, and discover new principles. For example, this view is expressed in the Glenn

Commission report[22] and is endorsed by the Videotape Study as well: "[In Japan, the] problem . . . comes first [and] . . . the student has . . . to invent his or her own solutions."[23] In fact, the Videotape Study reports that the fifty Japanese lessons averaged 1.7 student-presented alternative solution methods per class.[24] Yet the excerpts exhibit no signs of such activity. They contain just one student-devised solution alternative, and it failed to produce an answer.

These differences are fundamental, and they should be reconciled. Part of the difficulty is that students are unlikely to devise their own solutions when the time is limited, and the problems are so difficult that hints are needed. Moreover, the exercises seem to be designed to teach the value and use of specific techniques. Students would presumably have a better chance of finding alternative solution methods for less challenging exercises. And they would have an even better chance with problems that can be solved by a variety of methods that have already been taught. Examples might include geometry problems in which different basic theorems can be used and studies of auxiliary lines in which the exercises are designed so that different auxiliary lines build different structures that have already been studied. The Videotape Study illustrates alternative solution methods with the U.S. assignment to solve $x^2 + 43x - 43 = 0$ by completing the square and by applying the quadratic formula.[25] Of course, this problem directed students to use different methods they already knew. The example contains no hint of any discovery.

So the questions remain: Where are the alternative solution methods, and when do they demonstrate signs of student discovery?

The answers are in the Videotape Study. It presents actual examples that were used to train the data analysts who counted the "Student Generated Alternative Solution Methods" (SGSM1, SGSM2, . . .) in each lesson. These examples, it turns out, come from the geometry lesson in the video excerpts: The two student presentations for the Eda-Azusa problem are coded as SGSM1 and SGSM2.[26] Similarly, the second problem, in which each of four vertices could be moved in two directions, has the codings SGSM1-SGSM8. *Altogether, this lesson is counted as having ten student-generated alternative solution methods, even though it contains no student-discovered methods whatsoever.* And the failed try-all-possibilities approach in algebra excerpts is counted as yet another student-discovered solution method.[27]

The Videotape Study also contains a partial explanation for the source of these judgments. It reports that the data coding and interpretation procedures were developed by four doctoral students—none of whom were in mathematics programs.[28] Moreover, the Videotape Study states that the project's supporting mathematicians only saw code-generated lesson tables and were denied access to the actual tapes.[29] It seems reasonable to infer, therefore, that they did not participate in the design of these coding practices. As for the question of invention, the Videotape Study explains: "When seatwork is followed by students sharing alternative solution methods, this generally indicates that students were to invent their own solutions to the problem."[30] There appears to have been a sequence of interpretations based on student presentations being very generously counted as student-generated alternative solution methods and, ultimately, as some kind of invented discoveries that might even depend on new principles the students had not yet learned.[31]

On the other hand, the contributions by the Japanese teachers received much less generous recognition. Yet in the defining examples of student discovery, the teachers—not the students—manage the ideas and lead the education process.

Additional Statistics from the TIMSS Projects

It is worth reiterating that in the Japanese lesson excerpts, each of the four exercises began with students working individually to solve the problem. Similarly, the Stigler-Hiebert analysis states, "Students rarely work in small groups to solve problems until they have worked first by themselves."[32] The detailed TIMSS Videotape Classroom Study contains no comparable statement and even implies otherwise: "[After the problem is posed, the Japanese] students are then asked to work on the problem . . . sometimes individually and sometimes in groups."[33] However, not one of its eighty-six figures and bar charts documents instances where problems began with students working in groups. Chart 41 indicates that of the seatwork time spent on problem solving, 67.2 percent of the time comprised individual effort and 32.8 percent of the time was spent in group work.[34]

Another TIMSS study addressed this issue by collecting statistics for carefully balanced samples of eighth-graders. For each country, the sample base comprised approximately 4,000 students. Their teachers were queried about their classroom organization and whether most of the lessons had students working in small groups, individually, and/or as a class. Teachers also were asked if they assisted students in the classroom assignments. The results, which were weighted by the number of students in each responding teacher's class, are reproduced below (Figure 5.10) for the United States and Japan.[35]

The results show that Japanese lessons do not have significant numbers of small-group activities. In fact, American classes evidently contain four to six times as many such lessons. Of course, it should be noted that the data is based on questionnaires and depends, therefore, on the judgment of each respondent. The meaning of "most or every lesson" might have cultural biases, as might the definitions of "small groups" and "teacher assistance."

FIGURE 5.10

Country	Organizational Approach "Most of Every Lesson"				
	Work Together as a Class with Teacher Teaching the Whole Class	Work Individually with Assistance from Teacher	Work Individually without Assistance from Teacher	Work in Pairs or Small Groups with Assistance from Teacher	Work in Pairs or Small Groups without Assistance from Teacher
Japan	22	78	27	15	1
United States	r 22	r 49	r 50	r 19	r 12

An "r" indicates teacher response data available for 70–84% of students.

Still, these TIMSS statistics support the notion that the Japanese style of teaching is substantially different from many of the U.S. reform practices.

The Matter of Pedagogy

One such reform approach relies on discovery-based learning, which aims to have the students themselves discover mathematical principles and techniques. At first blush, the idea of discovery-based learning seems attractive. After all, we are more likely to recall what we discover for ourselves, and even if we forget such a fact, we should be able to rediscover it at a later date. According to Cobb and colleagues, "It is possible for students to construct for themselves the mathematical practices that, historically, took several thousand years to evolve."[36]

However, as with any idealized theory, the real issues are in the implementation practices.

- Judgments must determine how much classroom time should be allocated for students to discover the mathematics and must resolve the necessary tradeoffs among allocated time for guided discovery, for direct instruction, for reinforcement exercises, and for review.

- There must be detection and correction mechanisms for incorrect and incomplete "discoveries."

- There must be allowances for the fact that in even the best of circumstances, only a handful of students have any likelihood of discovering nontrivial mathematical principles.

The videotaped lessons from Japan show fundamental decisions that are startling and quite different from the reform practices in the United States. In the Japanese classes, the time allotted for the first round of grappling with problems was remarkably modest. Consequently, the remaining time was sufficient for student presentations to help identify conceptual weaknesses, for teacher-managed assistance and summations, and for follow-up problems designed to solidify understanding. However, because of the time limitations and the difficulty of the problems, most students were learning via a model of "grappling and telling." That is, students would typically struggle with a tough problem in class, but not find a solution. They would then learn by being told how to solve it and would benefit from the opportunity to contrast unsuccessful approaches against methods that work.[37] There is no question that preliminarily grappling with a problem is both motivational and educational.[38] Similarly, discussion about why some approaches fail and why a solution might be incomplete, along with the exploration of alternative problem-solving techniques are all highly beneficial investments of time. But the use of grappling and telling creates yet another implementation issue, which is: Who should do the telling?

In some teaching practices, the theory of discovery-based learning is extended to include the notion of cooperative learning, which holds that the students should teach one another because they "understand" each other. However, both the TIMSS videotape and the data in Figure 5.10 show that the Japanese style of teaching is by no means purely or principally based on cooperative learning. Although students get a substantial amount of time to explain their solutions, the video excerpts show that Japanese teachers are by no means passive participants. Student explanations frequently need—and get—supervision, and students can be remarkably incoherent (cf. Figure 5.5) even when their solutions are absolutely perfect. When all is said and done, the teachers do the teaching—and the most important telling— but in an interactive style that is highly engaging and remarkably skillful.

According to Stigler and Hiebert, some lessons feature considerably more direct instruction or extended demonstrations while yet others demand that the students memorize basic facts.[39] Students might even be asked to memorize a mandate to think logically.[40] Evidently, the lessons do not follow a rigid pattern. If any theme is common to these approaches, perhaps it is that although the lessons vary depending on the nature of the mathematical content, they always engage the students in an effort to foster thinking and understanding.

Placing Japanese Teaching in the Context of U.S. Reform

The video excerpts show Japanese lessons with a far richer content than the corresponding offerings from the United States and Germany. According to the Videotape Study, the Japanese, German, and U.S. eighth-grade classes covered material at the respective grade levels 9.1, 8.7, and 7.4 by international standards.[41] Evidently, the interactive nature of the Japanese teaching style and the use of challenging problems are managed so well that the content is actually enhanced. We believe that a key reason for this high performance level is the efficient use of grappling and telling coupled with the benefits of disguised reinforcement exercises.

Additional analysis shows that 53 percent of the Japanese lessons used proof-based reasoning, whereas the comparable statistic for the U.S. lessons—which included both traditional and reform programs—stood at zero.[42] And in terms of the development of concepts and their depth and applicability as well as in terms of the coherence of the material, the quality assessments were much the same.[43] By all evidence, the use of proof-based reasoning as reported in Japan is not at all representative of the reform programs in the United States, and the use of such remarkably challenging problems seems beyond the scope of any U.S. program past or present.

When comparing U.S. reform practices and Japanese teaching methods, the Videotape Study offers somewhat guarded conclusions that are sometimes difficult to interpret. The report reads:

> Japanese teachers, in certain respects, come closer to implementing the spirit of current ideas advanced by U.S. reformers than do U.S. teachers. For example, Japanese lessons include high-level mathematics, a clear focus on thinking and problem solving, and an emphasis on students deriving alternative solution methods and explaining their thinking. In other respects, though, Japanese lessons do not follow such reform guidelines. They include more lecturing and demonstration than even the more traditional U.S. lessons [a practice frowned upon by reformers], and [contrary to specific recommendations made in the NCTM Professional Standards for Teaching Mathematics,[44]] we never observed calculators being used in a Japanese classroom.[45]

Subsequent elaboration on the similarities between U.S. reform and Japanese pedagogy recapitulates these ideas in the context of various reform goals, but again offers no statistical evidence to compare with the data accumulated from the analysis of Japanese teaching practices.[46] Consequently, it is difficult—absent additional context—to compare these reform notions in terms of mathematical coherence, depth, international grade level, or the preparation of students for more advanced studies and challenging problems. Not surprisingly, "the spirit of current reform ideas" seems difficult to measure. Similarly, the Japanese and U.S. reform pedagogies appear incomparable in their management of classroom time, their use of proof-based reasoning, their tradeoffs between student discovery and the use of grappling and telling, as well as their use of individual and small-group activities.

These distinctions notwithstanding, the notion that Japanese teaching might be comparable with U.S. reforms is given even greater emphasis in a major government report, which flatly declares: "Japanese teachers widely practice what the U.S. mathematics reform recommends, while U.S. teachers do so infrequently."[47]

This report on best teaching practices worldwide makes no mention of any differences between the U.S. reforms and Japanese teaching styles. Evidently, its perspective differs from that of its source of primary information, which is the more cautiously worded TIMSS Videotape Study.[48] Moreover, even the differences identified in the Videotape Study—which concern direct instruction, calculators, and teacher-managed demonstrations—are all matters of contention in the U.S. debate over classroom reform.

Lastly, it is significant (but seldom reported) that the Videotape Study makes a distinction between the idealized goals as prescribed in the NCTM Professional Standards for Teaching Mathematics and as embodied in actual classroom practices of some reform programs. In particular, the study discusses two reform-style lessons. One involves playing a game that happens to be devoid of mathematical content. The teacher claims this lesson is in accord with NCTM teaching standards. Stigler et al. disagree: "It is clear to us that the features this teacher uses to define high-quality instruction can occur in the absence of deep mathematical engagement on the part of the students."[49] The other lesson was deemed to be compliant with the spirit of NCTM reforms. It began with the teacher whirling an airplane around on a string. The class then spent the period in groups exploring how to determine the speed of the plane and coming to realize that the key issues were the number of revolutions per second and the circumference of the plane's circular trajectory. The homework was a writing assignment: The students were asked to summarize their group's approach and to write about the role they played in the group's work. The study did not evaluate the content by grade level nor compare the lesson against the qualities that seem representative of Japanese teaching practices.

The Videotape Study reported that there was, apart from some minor differences, "little quantitative evidence that reform teachers in the United States differ much from those who claim not to be reformers. Most of the comparisons were not significant."[50] However, it is not evident how effective the study's comparison categories were at quantifying the key differences in various teaching practices.

Other Characterizations of Japanese Classroom Practices

Studies that use human interaction as a primary source of data must rely on large numbers of interpretations to transform raw, complex, occasionally ambiguous, and even seemingly inconsistent behavior into meaningful evidence. Given the complexity of the lessons, it is not surprising that different interpretations should arise. The Videotape Study—to its credit—documents an overview of these decision procedures, although their specific applications were far too numerous to publish in detail. Moreover, the study actually contains a wide diversity of observations, ideas, and conclusions, which sometimes get just occasional mention and are necessarily excluded from the Executive Summary. Understandably, this commentary—along with any supporting context—is also missing from the one-sentence to one-paragraph condensations in derivative policy papers.[51] Perhaps the seventh and eighth words in the opening line of the study's Executive Summary explain this issue as succinctly as possible: "preliminary findings."[52] It is now appropriate to explore these larger-picture observations and to place them within the context of actual lessons.

The Videotape Study even offers a couple of sentences that support our own observations:

> [Japanese] students are given support and direction through the class discussion of the problem when it is posed (figure 50), through the summary explanations by the teacher (figure 47) after methods have been presented, through comments by the teacher that connect the current task with what students have studied in previous lessons or earlier in the same lesson (figure 80), and through the availability of a variety of mathematical materials and tools (figure 53).[53]

Unfortunately, these insights are located far from the referenced figures and the explanations that accompany them. The words are effectively lost among the suggestions to the contrary that dominate the report. It is also fair to suggest that the wording and context are too vague to offer any inkling of how powerful the "support and direction through class discussion" really was, and likewise, the value of the connections to previous lessons is left unexplored. This discussion does not even reveal if these connections were made before students were assigned to work on the challenge problems or after. For these questions, the video excerpts provide resounding answers: The students received masterful instruction.

The Videotape Study's Math Content Group analyzed thirty classroom lesson tables that were selected to be representative of the curriculum. Their assessments, as sampled in the study, agree with our overall observations, apart from the use of hints, which were mostly omitted from the lesson tables. Unfortunately, the analyses are highly stylized with abstract representations for use in statistical processing and were, presumably, not intended to be a reference for the actual teaching.[54]

Another sentence in the study begins with the potentially enlightening observation that:

The teacher takes an active role in posing problems and helping students examine the advantages of different solution methods, *[however, rather than elaborating on how this takes place, the sentence changes direction with the words]* but the students are expected to struggle with the mathematical problems and invent their own methods.[55]

This interpretation of student work as inventive discovery appears throughout the TIMSS Videotape Study. In its analysis of the excerpted Japanese geometry lesson, the study categorizes the teacher's review of the basic solution method (shown in Figure 5.1) as "Applying Concepts in New Situation,"[56] but inexplicably switches tracks to count the student applications as invented student-generated alternative solution methods. Another such instance reads, "Students will struggle because they have not already acquired a procedure to solve the problem."[57] Similarly, the study never explains how teachers participate in the problem solving by teaching the use of methods and by supplying hints. Its only discussion about hinting is to acknowledge the offer of previously prepared hint cards.[58] And by the time the Glenn Commission finished its brief encapsulation of student progress, even the struggle had disappeared along with proper mention of extensive teacher-based assistance.

Searching for Answers

Let there be no doubt: The fact that we found no evidence of widespread inventiveness or student discovery should not be interpreted as a condemnation of exploration by students. Rather, it suggests a need for balance based on a realistic recognition of what can and cannot be done in classrooms.

Creativity and independent mathematical thought should be fostered, and alternative solution methods should be encouraged and studied. Students need to know that problems can be solved in different ways. They should learn to step back from a problem and think about plausible solution methods. And they need experience in selecting the best strategies for plans of first attack.[59] Similarly, students should learn firsthand how problems are adapted to fit the method and how methods can accommodate new problems.

The Japanese lessons illustrate master instruction designed to foster this higher-level reasoning. When combined with modeling, these activities comprise the essence of problem solving.

However, despite the wealth of hints, the careful reviews of the necessary material, and the presumptive benefits accumulated from years of exposure to these teaching practices, the students discovered no new principles, theorems, or solution methods. And despite extensive assistance, many students did not conquer the first challenge problem of the day. These are sobering facts, and their implications for mathematics education should not be overlooked.

Just imagine: If the application of principles already learned and just reviewed is so difficult, consider how hard it must be to devise new principles. Ask mathematicians what they can do with three minutes of original thought. Chances are your answer will be no more than a quizzical look. New principles do not come cheap; research mathematics—even when there is strong evidence to suggest what might be true—requires enormous amounts of time. And eighth-graders will find the concepts and principles underlying eighth-grade-level math just about as difficult to develop. In short, there is a fundamental difference between problem solving and developing new principles. There are world-class mathematicians who are mediocre problem solvers and vice versa.[60] Few mathematical researchers would ever confuse the art of problem solving with the development of new mathematics. The implications for K–12 education and mathematics pedagogy are clear. Before we can understand what teachers and students should be doing in daily lessons, we must have a deep understanding of what they are doing as well as of what they can and cannot do. These distinctions—profound but sometimes subtle—lie at the heart of why modern mathematics developed over a period of two centuries or so and why arithmetic and elementary mathematics took even longer.

Conclusions

Large-scale video studies must rely on data coding and all kinds of preliminary judgments and filterings to encapsulate raw data. To cut through these sources of potential information loss and possible confusion, this study did something that the others did not. We supported our observations with a combination of the actual video images, a meticulous analysis of the mathematics lessons, and detailed citations together with a careful presentation of the context for each reference. Similarly, we sought to include relevant information regardless of whether or not it supported our conclusions. And whenever inconsistencies surfaced, we endeavored to reconcile the differences.

Of course, we must avoid extrapolating from a few "representative" tapings to draw conclusions about a much larger set of lessons, much less about the national characteristics of classroom teaching in the United States, Germany, and Japan. But with 229 lessons unavailable, and just six representative classes in view, there is little choice but to analyze the evidence that is in the public domain. Accordingly, this study should be viewed as a cautionary warning about widely cited opinions that might in fact be erroneous.

In summary:

- The videotapes of Japanese lessons document the teaching of mathematical content in a style that is deep and rich.

- The excerpts do not support the suggestion that in Japan, "[the] problem . . . comes first [and] . . . the student has . . . to invent his or her own solutions."[61]

- The evidence does suggest that in Japan, "students rarely work in small groups to solve problems until they have worked first by themselves."[62]

- Similarly, the evidence gives little weight to the notion that "Japanese teachers, in certain respects, come closer to implementing the spirit of current ideas advanced by U.S. reformers than do U.S. teachers."

- The evidence does confirm that "in other respects, Japanese lessons do not follow such reform guidelines. They include more lecturing and demonstration than even the more traditional U.S. lessons . . . ."[63]

- The excerpts show Japanese classes featuring a finely timed series of minilessons that alternate between grappling-motivated instruction on how to apply solution methods and well-chosen challenge exercises designed to instill a deep understanding of the solution methods just reviewed. No other interpretation is possible.

- Some official U.S. government reports overemphasize unsubstantiated claims about Japanese pedagogy while omitting all mention of the remarkably high-quality *instruction* that is characteristic of Japanese lessons.

- Studies of problem solving in the classroom should include statistical analyses of as large a variety of practices and interactions as possible, including the use of grappling and telling, in-progress hints and mentoring, and preparatory discussion with hints and applicable content. Similarly, the roles of teacher assistance in presentations of all kinds ought to be better understood.

- Research projects in mathematics education should strive to maintain open data to support independent analyses. In addition, great care should be exercised to ensure that the encodings and analyses incur no loss of mathematical content or pedagogy.

It is perhaps fitting to close with a few words that strip away the citations, figures, tables, and video images that characterize the preceding analysis and to express some observations in more human terms.

Everyone understands that students must learn how to reason mathematically. The heart of the matter, therefore, is how—not whether—to teach problem solving and mathematical investigation. We must not be so desperate for the teaching of problem solving that we acclaim all such efforts to be one and the same and, therefore, equally promising. The video excerpts document exemplary instances of master teachers instructing students in the art of adapting fundamental principles to solve problems. In each sample excerpt, the class had already learned the basic method necessary to solve the challenge problems of the day. However, students had to possess a solid understanding of the method before it could be applied successfully.

This form of teaching requires a deep understanding of the underlying mathematics and its difficulty. Students must be properly prepared so that they can master the content at an adequate pace. Whenever hints are necessary, the teacher must be sensitive to these needs and stand ready to offer whatever assistance is appropriate to open the eyes of each individual learner. More often than not, most students will be unable to apply fundamental principles in new settings until they see step-by-step examples completed by the teacher. In these cases, the students should then get the opportunity to walk in the teacher's footsteps by applying the approach to a new problem that is designed to have the same challenges in a slightly different context.

These are the lessons that must be learned from the videotape of Japanese teaching. As the excerpts demonstrate, a master teacher can present every step of a solution without divulging the answer and can, by so doing, help students learn to think deeply. In such circumstances, the notion that students might have discovered the ideas on their own becomes an enticing mix of illusion intertwined with threads of truth. Unfortunately, such misunderstanding risks serious consequences if it escalates to a level that influences classroom practice and education policy. In retrospect, it seems appropriate to offer one last cautionary recommendation: Unless lesson studies include a comprehensive analysis of the mathematics content and the full range of teaching techniques, their conclusions will perforce be incomplete and, as a consequence, vulnerable to misconceptions about the very practices that best enhance student learning.

Notes

1. Cf. J. W. Stigler et al., *The TIMSS Videotape Classroom Study: Methods and Findings from an Exploratory Research Project on Eighth-Grade Mathematics Instruction in Germany, Japan, and the United States* (National Center for Education Statistics, 1999), 134.

2. J. Glenn et al., *Before It's Too Late: A Report to the Nation from the National Commission on Mathematics and Science Teaching for the 21st Century,* Report EE0449P (Education Publications Center, U.S. Department of Education, September 27, 2000), 16.

3. M. O. Martin et al., *School Contexts for Learning and Instruction: IEA's Third International Mathematics and Science Study* (TIMSS International Study Center [ISC], 1999).

4. I. V. S. Mullis et al., *TIMSS 1999 International Mathematics Report, Findings from the IEA's Repeat of the Third International Mathematics and Science Study at the Eighth Grade* (TIMSS ISC, Dec. 2000).

5. J. W. Stigler et al., *TIMSS Videotape Classroom Study.*

6. J. W. Stigler and J. Hiebert, *The Teaching Gap: Best Ideas from the World's Teachers for Improving Education in the Classroom* (Free Press, 1999).

7. *Eighth-Grade Mathematics Lessons: United States, Japan, and Germany* (Videotape, NCES, 1997).

8. *Moderator's Guide to Eighth-Grade Mathematics Lessons: United States, Japan, and Germany* (NCES, 1997).

9. *Video Examples from the TIMSS Videotape Classroom Study: Eighth-Grade Mathematics in Germany, Japan, and the United States* (CD ROM, NCES, 1998).

10. In Figure 5.1, the translation shows an "or" instead of an "and." This mathematical error is due to a mistranslation of the spoken Japanese.

11. *Moderator's Guide,* 136.

12. Ibid., 140.

13. Ibid.

14. Ibid., 139–41.

15. Ibid., 141.

16. The assignment probably should be restricted to convex figures; otherwise it includes irregular cases that are difficult to formalize. On the other hand, this concern is just a minor technicality that has no effect on the pedagogical value of the problem.

17. In fact, the technique is central to Euclid's development of area in general, which is based on transforming any polygon into a square with the same area. And the nat-

ural extension of this problem became a question for the ages: how to square the circle.

18. *Moderator's Guide*, 114.

19. Ibid.

20. Ibid., 159.

21. Ibid., 164.

22. J. Glenn et al., *Before It's Too Late*, 4.

23. J. W. Stigler et al., *TIMSS Videotape Classroom Study*, vi.

24. Ibid., 55.

25. Ibid., 97.

26. Ibid., 26–27.

27. In particular, the *Moderator's Guide* (pages 161–63) discusses this one unsuccessful approach as the entirety of the section titled "Students Presenting Solution Methods."

28. J. W. Stigler et al., *TIMSS Videotape Classroom Study*, 24.

29. Ibid., 31.

30. Ibid., 100.

31. Cf. J. W. Stigler et al., *TIMSS Videotape Classroom Study*, vi; L. Peak et al., *Pursuing Excellence: A Study of U.S. Eighth-Grade Mathematics and Science Teaching, Learning, Curriculum, and Achievement in International Context* (NCES, 1996), 9; and J. Glenn et al., *Before It's Too Late*, 16.

32. J. W. Stigler and J. Hiebert, *The Teaching Gap*, 79.

33. J. W. Stigler et al., *TIMSS Videotape Classroom Study*, 134.

34. Ibid., 78.

35. A. E. Beaton et al., *Mathematics Achievement in the Middle School Years: IEA's Third International Mathematics and Science Study* (TIMSS ISC, 1996), 154–55.

36. P. Cobb, E. Yackel, and T. Wood, "A Constructivist Alternative to the Representational View of Mind in Mathematics Education," *Journal for Research in Mathematics Education* 23 (1992): 28.

37. D. L. Schwartz and J. D. Bransford, "A Time for Telling," *Cognition and Instruction* 16 no. 4, (1998): 475–522.

38. Cf. D. L. Schwartz and J. D. Bransford, "A Time for Telling," and J. D. Bransford et al., *How People Learn: Brain, Mind, Experience, and School* (National Research Council, National Academy Press, 2000), 11.

39. J. W. Stigler and J. Hiebert, *The Teaching Gap*, 48–51.

40. Ibid., 49.

41. J. W. Stigler et al., *TIMSS Videotape Classroom Study*, 44.

42. Ibid., vii.

43. J. W. Stigler and J. Hiebert, *The Teaching Gap*, 59.

44. The bracketed additions are elaborations from page 123 of the *Videotape Study*, where the discussion of calculator usage is reworded and thereby avoids the grammatical misconstruction we have caused with the unedited in-place insertion.

45. J. W. Stigler et al., *TIMSS Videotape Classroom Study*, vii.

46. Ibid., 122–24.

47. L. Peak et al., *Pursuing Excellence*, 9. See also pages 41 and 43.

48. J. W. Stigler et al., *TIMSS Videotape Classroom Study*.

49. Ibid., 129.

50. Ibid., 125.

51. Cf. L. Peak et al., *Pursuing Excellence*, and J. Glenn et al., *Before It's Too Late*.

52. J. W. Stigler et al., *TIMSS Videotape Classroom Study*, v.

53. Ibid., 134.

54. Ibid., 58–69. For example, the analysis of the excerpted geometry lesson consists of a directed graph with three nodes, two links, and nine attributes. The first node represents the basic principle (attribute PPD) for the presentation illustrated in Figure 5.1. The node's link has the attributes NR (Necessary Result) and C+ (Increased Complexity). It points to a node representing the Eda-Azusa challenge exercise. The representations were used to get a statistical sense of various broadbrush characteristics of the lessons.

55. Ibid., 136.

56. Ibid., Figure 63, 101.

57. Ibid., 35.

58. Ibid., 26–30.

59. It is worth noting that the German algebra lesson (unlike either of the U.S. lessons) also covered strategy. The excerpted lesson on two equations in two unknowns has a review of the three solution methods that had been already taught. Then a more difficult problem that has two additional features is introduced. First, it requires the collection of like terms. Second, the coefficients permit the solution methods to be applied to one of the variables more easily than the other. This second issue seems to have been missed by the entire class and is revealed by the teacher only after the class has worked (too hard) to solve the problem. There is also some discussion about the advantages and disadvantages of each solution method.

60. Of course, problem solving is one component of research mathematics, but it can have a remarkably minor role in the very complex art of formalizing and establishing mathematical frameworks and fundamental principles.

61. Cf. J. W. Stigler et al., *TIMSS Videotape Classroom Study*, vi.

62. J. W. Stigler and J. Hiebert, *The Teaching Gap*, 79.

63. J. W. Stigler et al., *TIMSS Videotape Classroom Study*, vii.

Part Three

Constructive Tests for Accountability

Chapter 6

Portfolio Assessment and Education Reform

Brian Stecher

Educational policy makers in a substantial number of states are looking toward assessment to accomplish the dual goals of increasing educational accountability and changing instructional practice. Portfolios have gained favor with many of these individuals because of the belief that portfolios better model the kinds of activities students should engage in while providing scores that are valid for accountability purposes. If you believe that "what you test is what you get," then portfolios may be the form of testing that provides the optimum benefit.[1]

This chapter reviews the evidence on the effectiveness of large-scale portfolio assessment in the United States, including state assessment systems in Vermont and Kentucky, portfolio experiments in Pittsburgh, Pennsylvania, and California, and the experiences of the National Assessment of Educational Progress (NAEP). The evidence indicates that portfolio assessments are relatively weak as tools for educational accountability (in comparison with other assessment methods), but they are relatively strong in influencing educational practice (again, in comparison with other assessment methods). Even here their promise is limited because they are also costly, both in terms of the cost of scoring and in terms of teacher and student time.

We begin with a discussion of the definition of portfolio assessment and the purposes this form of assessment might serve. Then we review the research on portfolio assessments, including their technical quality, their effects on classroom practices, and the burden/costs they place on students and teachers.

Portfolio Assessment: What and Why

Portfolio assessment of academic subjects draws its inspiration from the world of art. An artist's portfolio contains a purposeful collection of his or her own work. Such a portfolio is highly personal; it can include fully realized images, preliminary sketches, multiple versions of the same piece, and so on. Its contents reveal the skills of the artist as well as the choices the artist makes in assembling the work.

An academic assessment portfolio is a collection of student work that reflects the skills the student has mastered in a particular subject domain. However, as in the case of the artist, the portfolio format permits considerable variation in emphasis. Portfolio assessment guidelines can be designed to capture different aspects of student work. For example, portfolio assessments can be designed to emphasize development of expertise over time by requiring students to collect drafts, revisions, and final work at the beginning, middle, and end of the year. Alternatively, portfolio assessments can be designed to document optimum performance. Vermont students were required to collect five to seven of their "best pieces" in their mathematics portfolios.[2] A portfolio assessment could also be designed to emphasize breadth of understanding. In Kentucky, students were instructed to include particular types of writing in their writing assessment portfolios, including a poem, a persuasive letter, and so on.[3] Thus, the notion of a portfolio assessment is quite broad, and without some further stipulation, portfolio assessments may differ from place to place.

Differences may also arise because portfolio assessments can serve multiple purposes, and the choice of purpose will affect the way the portfolio assessment is structured and implemented. Educators cite at least four purposes for using portfolio assessments. First, portfolios can encourage student reflection and self-evaluation. Reviewing a portfolio of his or her own work can make a student more self-aware, can build a student's understanding of the cumulative nature of learning and the interrelationships among the skills he or she has acquired, and can enhance a student's ability to evaluate his or her own work. Second, portfolios can be used to help teachers monitor student learning, diagnose their strengths and weaknesses, and plan better instruction. By focusing the teacher's attention on student work rather than test scores, the portfolio permits more refined judgments of skill acquisition and contributes to more thoughtful planning for remediation or enrichment. Third, portfolios can encourage curriculum change. Administrators may choose to mandate portfolio assessments to encourage teachers to change the nature of instruction. For example, the implementation of a writing portfolio assessment will force teachers to spend time on extended writing assignments; mathematics portfolio assessments often necessitate more classroom emphasis on mathematical problem solving. Finally, portfolio assessments can be used as a basis for systemwide accountability. Many educators believe portfolio assessments provide more valid information about important student outcomes than do multiple-choice tests. They believe that portfolios focus attention on complex, fully realized products of student activity, whereas standardized, on-demand, multiple-choice tests focus attention on separable facts and disaggregated procedures.

With all this variation in structure and purpose, one must be cautious in making statements about portfolio assessments in general. Not only may portfolio assessments differ substantially one from another, but small differences in implementation can have large differences in consequences. For example, J. R. Novak and colleagues found that small differences in scoring rubrics affected teachers' understanding of narrative writing.[4]

Fortunately, those jurisdictions whose portfolio assessment systems have been studied most thoroughly have implemented systems that share many common features. With slight variations, the portfolio assessments in these locations have the following characteristics:

- Constructed, not selected products. The portfolio contains work produced by students in response to classroom assignments, including such things as written essays, drawings, graphical representations, and so on. Most of the contents are produced by students working alone, but some clearly identified collaboration with other students may be allowed.

- Limited number of pieces. The portfolio contains a small number of examples of student work (roughly three to seven pieces) rather than a complete compendium of work for the year.

- "Embedded" in instruction. The work collected in a student's portfolio has been produced as part of ongoing classroom activities. One consequence of the embedded nature of portfolio assessments is that the contents of the portfolios can vary from teacher to teacher because assignments vary.

- Student choice. Each student selects the pieces to include in his or her portfolio (with varying degrees of input from the teacher). As a result, the pieces that are included in the portfolio will vary from student to student within a given class.

- Cumulative. Each portfolio is accumulated over an extended period of time, and is not created "on demand" like a standardized test.

- Introductory essay. The portfolio contains a description of the contents or a reflective essay in which the student explains his or her choices.

- Scoring system. There is a more or less objective procedure for reviewing the contents of each portfolio and assigning one or more scores to the student.

- Dual purposes. In the sites that have been studied most extensively, portfolios were implemented both to influence instruction and to provide valid scores for accountability purposes.

Evidence About Portfolio Assessment

The bulk of the research on portfolio assessment was conducted in a handful of jurisdictions. These programs and research efforts are summarized below.

The Vermont Portfolio Assessment Program

The Vermont Portfolio Assessment program was implemented in 1990–91 as the first centralized assessment system in the state's history.[5] As such, it received considerable attention within Vermont. Because of its novel use of portfolios it also received considerable attention nationwide. The program began on a pilot basis in 1990–91, and it was made operational the following year. The system assessed each student in fourth and eighth grade in two subjects, mathematics and writing.

The most important elements of the system were portfolios of student work in mathematics and writing. The mathematics portfolio consisted of five to seven "best pieces" selected by the student from all the work done during the year. Mathematics portfolios were scored on seven dimensions, four reflecting aspects of mathematical problem solving (understanding the task, approaches/procedures, decisions along the way, and outcomes of activities) and three reflecting aspects of mathematical communication (language, representation, and presentation). Each dimension was scored on its own four-point scale.

In writing, students selected a single "best piece" and included other writing of specified types, which were graded as a set. Writing portfolios were scored on five dimensions (purpose, organization, details, voice/tone, and usage/mechanics/grammar). Again, each dimension had its own four-point scale.

The goal of the portfolio assessment program was to report dimensional-level scores that would permit comparisons among schools. A random sample of portfolios from each class was sent for central scoring by teachers. The developers hoped that school-level dimensional scores derived from this sample of students would be valid for school-level accountability.

In addition to assessment portfolios, the Vermont system also included a common test, called the Uniform Test, which was taken by all students. The Uniform Test in mathematics included both multiple-choice and constructed-response components; the Uniform Test in writing consisted of a single writing prompt. Initially, the main purpose of this test was to validate the portfolio scores. Over time, the program has been revised to place greater emphasis on common components. As of 2000, the portfolios are still part of the formal assessment system in Vermont but their role relative to other components has diminished.

Most of the published research on the Vermont program was conducted between 1991 and 1994 by researchers from RAND.[6] These studies examined the technical quality of scores from the mathematics and writing portfolios. However, the researchers focused their investigation of changes in classroom practices on the mathematics portfolios, which were the most innovative part of the system.

Kentucky Instructional Results Information System (KIRIS)

In 1990, the Kentucky legislature enacted the Kentucky Educational Reform Act (KERA) in response to a court mandate to reform the education system in Kentucky. KERA was a comprehensive reform that changed school finance, teacher professional development, the organization of primary grade schooling, and the statewide curriculum. A prominent feature of KERA was a new accountability system for schools based primarily on performance-based assessments rather than multiple-choice tests. KIRIS was developed to comply with the assessment requirements of KERA. The system was initiated in 1990 and continued in operation through the 1997–98 school year.[7] In 1998–99, the system underwent a substantial redesign, and it is now known as the Commonwealth Accountability Testing System (CATS). The writing portfolios were retained, but not the mathematics portfolios.

The KIRIS testing program had a number of different components, including multiple-choice items, constructed-response items, performance events (with a collaborative component), on-demand writing prompts, and portfolios in writing and mathematics. The program covered seven subject areas, including mathematics, science, social studies, writing, reading, arts and humanities, and practical living/vocational studies. Initially, testing was done in grades four, eight, and twelve in all subjects, but the burden on these students and teachers became too great. After about four years, the elementary testing was divided between grades four and five and the middle-school testing between grades seven and eight. Later changes further divided high school testing among three grade levels.

Students were classified into four performance levels in each subject based on their scores on the relevant assessments. The levels were called Novice, Apprentice, Proficient, and Distinguished. Each school received an overall KIRIS accountability score based on the percentage of students achieving the Proficient level of performance in each subject. The accountability formula also gave credit for performance on a set of noncognitive indicators, including attendance and dropout rate (at the secondary level). Schools were expected to improve their performance annually with an eventual goal equivalent to all students reaching the Proficient level. Cash rewards were given to schools for making large gains. Schools that scored poorly and failed to make improvement were assigned Distinguished Educators to work with them to improve their scores. The rewards system operated in two-year cycles, so schools' performance in one biennium was compared with their performance in the previous biennium.

The structure of the portfolios in Kentucky was similar to that in Vermont. Students compiled their assessment portfolios by selecting pieces from a working portfolio they collected all year. Assessment portfolios in writing consisted of six pieces, including a personal narrative; a poem, play, or piece of fiction; a persuasive or informative piece; a piece from another subject area; a best piece; and a letter about growth as a writer. Portfolios were scored by classroom teachers, who assigned a single performance level to each student based on the whole portfolio. In assigning the score, raters considered six dimensions of performance in writing (purpose and approach, idea development, organization, sentences, wording, and surface features). Writing portfolio scores were the sole indicator of writing proficiency in KIRIS. Mathematics proficiency was measured by a combination of on-demand testing and portfolios. (The mathematics portfolios were collected every year, but the scores were included in the computation of the schools' accountability index during the second biennium only.)

The Kentucky Department of Education encouraged researchers to study the program and contribute to its improvement. In addition, KIRIS was the subject of much controversy in the state because of the more innovative components. As a result, there was considerable research on the technical quality of scores and the effects of KIRIS on classroom practice.[8]

Pittsburgh, Pennsylvaina

The Pittsburgh School District experimented with writing portfolios in grades six through twelve beginning in 1992. Students compiled working portfolios throughout the year, then selected four pieces to be included in their assessment portfolio at the end of the year. They were supposed to choose an important piece, a satisfying piece, an unsatisfying piece, and a free pick. All drafts as well as the final piece and a written reflection on each piece were to be included in the assessment portfolio. The portfolios also included a table of contents, a writing inventory, and a final reflection.

A stratified random sample of portfolios was selected for scoring by trained teachers. Each portfolio was scored as a whole on three six-point scales whose endpoints were "inadequate performance" and "outstanding performance." The scales reflected accomplishment in writing, use of process and strategies for writing, and growth, development, and engagement as a writer. These rubrics were developed during several years of discussions of writing conducted as part of the Arts PROPEL project in Pittsburgh. Two judges rated each portfolio, and if their scores differed by no more than a point, their scores were summed to produce the final score. If greater differences occurred, a third judge was used to arbitrate.

The Pittsburgh portfolio assessment was studied by researchers at the Educational Testing Service (ETS).[9]

National Assessment of Educational Progress (NAEP)

The NAEP conducted trial assessments using writing portfolios in fourth and eighth grades in 1990 and 1992. These were exploratory efforts to examine the feasibility of using writing portfolios on a larger scale in future assessments. The results were not reported, and there were no consequences for students or teachers. The 1990 trial was mounted somewhat late, and participation was not as complete as desired. Students contributed a single best piece, which was scored using a six-point scale. In 1992, the NAEP prepared participants better, and teachers collected three pieces from each student. The pieces were classified by genre and scored using six-point, genre-specific rubrics. The process was coordinated and studied by researchers at ETS who were responsible for the NAEP.[10]

California Learning Assessment System (CLAS)

Between 1992 and 1994, researchers from ETS worked with the California Department of Education to develop a portfolio assessment component for the CLAS testing program. The portfolio development process focused on mathematics and language arts, and the project was designed to emphasize performance that was consistent with state standards and curriculum frameworks. As part of the developmental effort, portfolios were collected in language arts and mathematics from a sample of students in grades four and eight. The language arts portfolios were scored on two dimensions: constructing meaning and composing and expressing ideas. The mathematics portfolios were scored on three dimensions: mathematical content, communicating mathematics, and putting mathematics to work. Scores were assigned to the portfolio as a whole, not to individual pieces, and students were classified into four performance levels based on their scores.

The levels were called Beginning, Developing, Accomplished, and Exemplary. There was also a classification for portfolios that had "not enough evidence to judge." The research has been reported by the Educational Testing Service.[11]

Findings

Although these five portfolio assessment programs are different in important ways, the research results paint a fairly consistent picture of the quality of scores derived from portfolios, the effects of portfolio assessments on classroom practices, and the burdens/costs of portfolios (in terms of teacher and student time). Portfolio assessments are relatively weak as accountability tools when compared with other forms of assessment. The scores appear to be less reliable and less valid than scores from standardized, multiple-choice tests. In contrast, portfolio assessments have relatively strong effects on practice. Evidence suggests that portfolio assessments lead to changes in classroom practices in the desired direction. However, this change comes at a relatively high price in terms of student and teacher time. The administrative burden on teachers is particularly high, and it does not appear to lessen over time. These findings are explored in the following sections.

Portfolio Assessment As an Accountability Tool

If portfolio scores are to be used for accountability purposes, it is essential that they have adequate technical quality. A careful analysis of the technical quality of portfolio scores should consider three things: the consistency of ratings of individual pieces (rater reliability), the consistency of student performance across pieces (score reliability), and the interpretability of scores (validity). The research reviewed here suggests that portfolio assessments are weak on all three counts. There are substantial differences between the scores assigned by two raters to a given piece of work. Student performance varies from piece to piece. And as a result of these two inconsistencies, it is difficult to interpret overall scores assigned to student portfolios. In addition, variations in the difficulty of tasks assigned by different teachers and in the conditions under which students prepare their pieces further clouds the interpretation of scores.

The most comprehensive evidence on reliability comes from Vermont and Kentucky, where portfolios were used on the largest scale for the longest periods of time. In both states, raters showed only moderate agreement on the scores they assigned to individual pieces of student work on the dimensions of interest. Koretz summarized the results of research in Vermont in 1993 (the second year of the portfolio assessment program), and these figures are displayed in Table 6.1.[22] The first row reflects the agreement between two raters on individual pieces from the mathematics portfolio and on the "best piece" or the rest of the writing portfolio. Each piece in the mathematics portfolio was rated on seven dimensions, and each component of the writing portfolio was rated on six dimensions. Table 6.1 displays the average value of the correlation between two raters on each dimension. The results are quite low (0.50 or less). (A correlation of 1.0 means that higher scores from one set of raters are always associated with higher scores from the other set of raters and lower scores are always associated with lower scores. A correlation of 0.50 means that scores from one set of raters predict only 25 percent of variance in scores from the other set of raters.)

The results in the second row indicate the degree to which raters agreed with each other about a student's performance on a dimension after combining ratings across all the pieces in the portfolio. These values are higher than the first row, particularly in mathematics, which may have to do with the number of pieces

TABLE 6.1 Average Inter-reader Correlations on Vermont Portfolio Assessments in Mathematics and Writing, 1993

	Writing	*Mathematics*
One piece, one dimension	.45	.50
All pieces, one dimension	.52	.65
All pieces, all dimensions	.63	.79

(five to seven in math; only "best" and "rest" in reading). Nevertheless, the correlations are still too low to permit reporting of dimension-level scores, which was the goal of the portfolio assessment program. The inability to achieve this goal was a great blow to the program's developers. In the end, they reported only total scores combining all pieces and all dimensions. The third row of the table shows the correlation between raters on total scores. Even these values are relatively low and do not offer great confidence in the accuracy of the overall rating process.

Over time, the consistency of ratings in Vermont improved, particularly in math. Table 6.2 presents similar results for total scores (summed across all pieces and all dimensions) over the four-year period from 1991 to 1995. With training and improvement in rubrics, total math scores reached acceptable levels of reliability, but this was never the case for dimension-level scores, and it was not true in writing.

Table 6.3 contains similar results for writing portfolio assessments conducted in Kentucky and Pittsburgh. In Kentucky, inter-rater correlations on total writing scores across pieces and dimensions were similar to those achieved in later years of the Vermont program. Koretz computed the comparable statistics for Pittsburgh.[13] He reported correlations at the dimension level that were of similar magnitude. Results from the NAEP were similar.

TABLE 6.2　Inter-rater Correlations on Total Scores on Vermont Portfolio Assessments in Mathematics and Writing, 1991–1995

	1991–92	1992–93	1993–94	1994–95
Writing				
Grade 4	.49	.56	.74	.64
Grade 8	.60	.63	.69	.66
Mathematics				
Grade 4	.60	.72	.76	.80
Grade 8	.53	.79	.83	.89

Rater agreement during the second year of the NAEP trial writing assessment was marginally lower than the values reported in Table 6.3. Inter-rater correlations on narrative, informative, persuasive, and overall writing scores in grades four and eight on the NAEP fell in the range of .59 to .68.

An additional source of inconsistency in portfolio assessment scores comes from differences in the performance of students across pieces within a portfolio. This was demonstrated in mathematics (more than writing) in Vermont in 1992. An analysis of dimension-level scores in grades four and eight found a substantial student-by-piece interaction, which means that students performed relatively differently from one piece to the next.[14]

Given the inconsistencies in scoring reported above, it is not surprising that portfolio assessment scores cannot be interpreted in the intended manner. Another way to say this is that the scores lack validity for the intended interpretation. The best way to judge the validity of portfolio assessments is to compare the scores with other measures of similar and dissimilar performance. Scores should converge with measures of similar domains and diverge with measures of different domains. For example, one would expect a new test of math to correlate more highly with another test of math than with a test of social studies. If this does not occur, it calls into question the meaning of the new test score.

There are two instances in which portfolio assessment scores can be analyzed in this manner. In Vermont, researchers compared scores on uniform tests of math and writing with scores on

TABLE 6.3   Mean Inter-reader Correlations on Writing Portfolio Assessments, Kentucky 1993–94 and Pittsburgh 1992

	Total Writing Score *(Kentucky)*	*Writing Dimensions[a]* *(Pittsburgh)*
Grade 4	.67	
Grade 8/Middle school	.70	.60 – .67
High school		.71 – .77

a. As reported by Koretz, 1998.

math portfolios, and they did not find the expected pattern of results. Table 6.4 shows the correlations of mathematics portfolio total scores with Uniform Test scores in mathematics and writing (both organization and usage). Surprisingly, the correlations between math portfolios and math Uniform Tests were no greater than correlations with writing Uniform Tests.[15] This raises serious questions about the meaning of scores from the mathematics portfolio assessment.

Similar questions are raised by results from the NAEP writing portfolio trial. The correspondence between scores from the writing portfolios and scores on the on-demand NAEP writing sample was no better than chance.[16] In fact, the correlation between scores was only 0.15.[17] Although these two assessments are trying to tap somewhat different aspects of writing, this level of similarity seems unconvincing. In Kentucky, an expert panel that convened to evaluate KIRIS found inadequate evidence to support the use of the scores for their intended purpose. The convergent and divergent patterns of scores from the various testing components of KIRIS was not convincing.[18]

Finally, it is difficult to use portfolio assessments for comparative purposes when the conditions under which pieces are produced are not standardized. In Vermont, 44 percent of eighth-grade teachers and 65 percent of fourth-grade teachers placed limits on the kind of assistance they provided to students completing pieces; the remainder of teachers did not. One-fourth of the teachers said students' pieces were not revised at all, whereas at the other extreme, 10 percent reported that the average piece was revised three times. Similar discrepancies in the

TABLE 6.4   Average Correlations[a] Between Mathematics Portfolio Total Score and Vermont Uniform Test (UT), 1993

	Writing UT: Organization	*Writing UT: Usage*	*Math UT*
Grade 4	.33	.33	.35
Grade 8	.35	.38	.31

a. Disattenuated for unreliability of raters.

conditions under which portfolio pieces were produced were found in Kentucky.[19]

There are a number of factors that may explain the low reliability of scores from portfolio assessments. First, the uniqueness of each portfolio (which advocates cite as one of the strengths of the approach) forces developers to create very generalized scoring rules. Because each portfolio will contain different pieces of work, scoring rubrics have to be quite generic. As a result, they may not provide enough guidance to raters to insure comparability of ratings. Second, portfolios can include very complex and elaborate assignments (another of their strengths). However, student performance may vary greatly between complex tasks. Such variation reduces the consistency of scores. Third, complex tasks take a long time to complete as well as a long time to score, so most portfolio assessments limit the contents to a relatively few pieces. This exacerbates the problems created by variation in student performance because there are fewer performances to judge.

The low reliability of portfolio assessment scores automatically limits their validity. If the scores themselves are not accurate, they are unlikely to be consistent with other measures. Moreover, most portfolio assessments are implemented as part of efforts to reform curriculum. They are designed to measure constructs that are not well measured by existing tests. Under these circumstances it can be difficult to specify in advance what pattern of relationships among measures is anticipated. If there are no clear expectations to begin with, it can be difficult to determine whether the pattern of results is consistent with expectations.

Portfolio Assessment As a Curriculum Reform Tool

Evidence suggests that portfolio assessments encourage changes in curriculum and instruction. In Vermont and Kentucky, where these changes have been studied most thoroughly, the introduction of portfolio assessment has led to changes that were consistent with the goals of the accompanying reform effort. These reforms, like those in Pittsburgh and California, emphasized "authentic" curriculum (for example, writing with purpose and audience in mind, mathematical problem solving). Most also emphasized changes in instructional practices to make classroom interactions more "student-centered," that is, giving students more responsibility for structuring and monitoring their own work and encouraging teachers to act more as facilitators. The evidence about changes in curriculum associated with portfolio assessments is the strongest, but there is also evidence about changes in instruction.

The Vermont mathematics portfolio assessment was designed to emphasize problem solving and mathematical communication rather than algorithms and computation, and teachers reported changing their curriculum accordingly. There were widespread increases in the time spent on problem solving and mathematical communication.[20] Approximately three-quarters of teachers said students spent more time making charts, graphs, and diagrams (70 percent), writing reports about mathematics (70 percent), and applying mathematical knowledge to new situations (75 percent). One-half of the teachers in Vermont reported that their classes devoted more time to exploring mathematical patterns.

Researchers in Kentucky found similar curriculum changes in mathematics and language arts, which were consistent with the goals of KERA.[21] In mathematics, teachers reported spending more class time on problem solving and communication and less on number facts. In language arts, teachers indicated that more class time was devoted to writing for a variety of purposes and on analysis of texts and less time to spelling, punctuation, and grammar.

Instructional practices are somewhat harder to measure than curriculum, but researchers reported changes in teaching associated with portfolio assessments in Vermont, Kentucky, Pittsburgh, and California.[22] The reported effects included:

- instructional changes (California).
- increases in the amount of time that learning occurs in pairs or small groups (Vermont).
- more innovative lesson planning (Vermont).
- increases in instruction leading to complex thinking and problem solving (Vermont).

- greater use of open-ended questions (Kentucky).

- increases in student choice of ideas for writing (Kentucky).

- curriculum and instruction changes in writing (Pittsburgh).

Researchers have also identified some negative effects that may be attributable to portfolio assessments in a high-stakes context. Kentucky teachers shifted curriculum in questionable ways in reaction to the grade-specific accountability system used by KIRIS.[23] Many fourth-grade teachers increased the time that students spent studying subjects tested in fourth grade (writing, reading, and science), whereas many fifth-grade teachers increased the time students spent studying subjects tested in fifth grade (mathematics, arts and humanities, social studies, and practical living/vocational studies). This curriculum shift is understandable given the high-stakes testing environment created by KIRIS; however, it is also troubling. Annual changes in the balance among subjects are not part of the Kentucky reform plan, and their long-term impact on student achievement is unknown. Researchers in Vermont reported a subtle form of curriculum narrowing as a result of the scoring rubrics used with the high-stakes portfolio assessment. They found that teachers focused instruction on the aspect of portfolios that scored well rather than the broader domain of knowledge the portfolios were supposed to reflect.[24] They called the phenomenon "rubric-driven instruction," and suggested that in Vermont, rather than "what you test is what you get," they were finding that "what you score is what you get."

The Costs and Burdens of Portfolio Assessment

Portfolio assessments also generate added costs and burdens. This form of assessment is more costly to develop and to operate than standardized tests, and it places greater demands on teachers and students. There are few good estimates of actual costs, but the additional demands placed on teachers have been well documented. These added burdens include additional preparation time, more classroom time for completing tasks and for managing portfolios, and added scoring time. Moreover, these burdens did not diminish during the first couple of years that portfolio assessment was operational. However, both principals and teachers felt the benefits outweighed the burdens, at least in the early years of the program.

Some of the additional costs and burdens associated with portfolios are easy to quantify, whereas others are quite difficult to measure. The operational costs are borne primarily by the jurisdiction responsible for the assessment. They include the cost of designing the system, specifying the type of student work desired, developing scoring guides, training teachers to understand the assessment, and organizing scoring and reporting. At present there are no comprehensive estimates of the total cost of operating portfolio assessments in any of the jurisdictions that have been studied. However, there are some reports that illuminate the cost of selected components. For example, researchers reported that every teacher in Vermont attended two days of paid professional development each summer for the first two years of the program, but they did not estimate the cost of this training. Kentucky developed a statewide system of professional development centers to support KERA and KIRIS. Although the total cost of these centers was millions of dollars, no one has estimated the cost associated specifically with KIRIS. The Vermont Department of Education paid teachers to come together during the summer to score a random sample of portfolios from across the state. Researchers estimated that the costs associated with this scoring were at least $13 per portfolio, which is more than twice the cost of scoring and reporting services for most standardized multiple-choice tests.[25]

The responsibility for implementing portfolio assessments falls most heavily on teachers. Table 6.5 shows the average number of hours per month that teachers in Vermont and Kentucky devoted to three types of activities in support of the mathematics portfolios.[26] The greatest demands related to preparation, and these ranged from ten to twelve hours per month on average. Teachers participated in professional development workshops to learn about the assessment, and they had to prepare lessons and activities to generate appropriate student work. Vermont teachers reported that they spent additional preparation time on the following activities (in order of frequency): preparing portfolio lessons, finding appropriate tasks or materials, attending professional development workshops, and discussing portfolios with colleagues.

The portfolio assessment also placed substantial demands on classroom time. Teachers in the two states reported that students spent ten to fourteen hours per month in class working on mathematics portfolio pieces. Vermont teachers reported that classroom time was devoted to completing tasks for the first time, revising tasks, and organizing portfolio materials, in that order. In Kentucky, the classroom time associated with portfolios was devoted to teaching the skills needed to prepare students, doing pieces for the first time, revising/rewriting, and organizing/managing, in that order. Although the bulk of these activities are certainly associated with learning, this still represents a substantial shift in instructional emphasis. Teachers reported that they were taking the time from other instructional activities to devote to portfolio projects. In fact, almost all teachers said it was difficult to cover the curriculum because of the demands of the portfolios. For the most part, teachers reported reducing the time they spent on the mechanical aspects of mathematics, such as computation.

And finally, Table 6.5 shows that teachers spent a great deal of time outside of class scoring student portfolios. In Vermont, researchers reported the average scoring time for a typical month; in Kentucky, scoring was concentrated during a specific period in the spring, and researchers reported total scoring time during this

TABLE 6.5 Average Weekly Teacher Time Devoted to Mathematics Portfolio Activities, Vermont (fourth and eighth grade) and Kentucky (eighth grade)

	Vermont	Kentucky
Preparation	12	10
Class time	14	10
Scoring	5	20[a]

[a] Total hours during the scoring period.

period. Teachers in both states felt that scoring was much too time-consuming. It is worth noting that the desire for more accurate scores may lead to even greater demands on time. The Pittsburgh experience suggests that scoring is improved by in-depth, extended, thoughtful discussions to develop shared interpretive frameworks.[27]

Because most of this research was conducted early in the life of the portfolio assessment program, one might expect that demands on teacher and student time would decrease. However, any decrease that did occur during the period investigated by these researchers was quite small. For example, during the first year of the portfolio assessment, 60 percent of the Vermont teachers said they lacked adequate time to prepare. More than two-thirds of the teachers surveyed the next year said the burden had not decreased. Similarly, in the third year of the Vermont program, 80 percent of teachers said scoring was still too time-consuming.

Although the demands of portfolio assessments were great and principals and teachers complained about the amount of time they devoted to the portfolios, on balance, both groups were enthusiastic about the reforms. Researchers characterized the Vermont portfolio assessment as a "worthwhile burden" in the minds of Vermont teachers and principals. In addition, a substantial proportion of Vermont principals said they were going to expand the use of portfolios to other, nontested grades. This is a relatively strong endorsement given their criticism of the additional demands created by the portfolios. What is unclear is how long this endorsement will continue if the portfolios fail to achieve greater reliability and validity and if the burdens do not decline.

Summary

Although the number of jurisdictions using portfolio assessments is small, they have been implemented and studied in enough locations to warrant initial conclusions about their utility. The evidence supports the conclusion that flexible portfolios that reflect differences in teachers' instructional emphases and students' choice of pieces have not achieved sufficient reliability or validity to be used for the purposes of accountability. The shortcomings derive in large part from the difficulty of developing scoring rubrics that are general enough to apply to widely different pieces, but specific enough to produce agreement among raters. This weakness, coupled with the wide variation in individual performance, leads to scores that do not appear to reflect the constructs the portfolios were designed to measure.

Nevertheless, portfolio assessments have some advantages over other types of assessment. They appear to be strong levers for change in curriculum and instruction. There is ample evidence that portfolio assessments encourage changes in curriculum that are consistent with related reforms—for example, mathematical problem solving and writing for specific audiences. They also promote changes in instruction.

However, these changes come at a price. Portfolio assessments are more expensive to develop and maintain than multiple-choice testing programs. Scoring, in particular, is costly. More important, portfolio assessments impose substantial burdens on teachers, in terms of preparation, classroom activities, and scoring. These burdens do not appear to diminish substantially during the first couple of years of implementation. Perhaps the best role for portfolio assessment is not as an accountability measure, but as a classroom-based assessment tool to help students and teachers improve diagnosis and instruction. This use may maximize the positive aspects of portfolios while minimizing their negative effects.

Notes

1. L. B. Resnick and D. P. Resnick, "Assessing the Thinking Curriculum: New Tools for Educational Reform," in *Future Assessments: Changing Views of Aptitude, Achievement, and Instruction,* ed. B. Gifford and M. C. O'Connor (Boston, Mass.: Kluwer, 1992).

2. Vermont Department of Education, *Looking Beyond 'The Answer': Vermont's Mathematics Portfolio Assessment Program* (Montpelier, Vt.: Vermont Department of Education, 1991).

3. Kentucky Department of Education, *Kentucky Instructional Results Information System: 1991–92 Technical Report* (Frankfort, Ky.: Kentucky Department of Education, 1993). Kentucky Department of Education, *Kentucky Instructional Results Information System: 1992–93 Technical Report* (Frankfort, Ky.: Kentucky Department of Education, 1994).

4. J. R. Novak, J. L. Herman, and M. Gearhart, "Issues in Portfolio Assessment: The Scorability of Narrative Collections" (CSE Technical Report No. 410, Los Angeles, Calif.: CRESST/UCLA, May 1996).

5. Vermont Department of Education, *Looking Beyond 'The Answer'*; R. P. Mills and W. R. Brewer, *Working Together to Show Results: An Approach to School Accountability in Vermont* (Montpelier, Vt.: Vermont Department of Education, October 18/November 10, 1988).

6. D. Koretz, B. Stecher, and E. Deibert, "The Vermont Portfolio Assessment Program: Interim Report on Implementation and Impact, 1991–92 School Year" (CSE Technical Report No. 350, Los Angeles, Calif.: CRESST/UCLA, August 1992). D. Koretz, B. Stecher, S. Klein, D. McCaffrey, and E. Deibert, "Can Portfolios Assess Student Performance and Influence Instruction? The 1991–92 Vermont Experience" (CSE Technical Report No. 371, Los Angeles, Calif.: CRESST/UCLA, December 1993); D. Koretz, B. Stecher, S. Klein, and D. McCaffrey, "The Evolution of a Portfolio Program: The Impact and Quality of the Vermont Program in Its Second Year (1992–93)" (CSE Technical Report No. 385, Los Angeles, Calif.: CRESST/UCLA, July 1994a); D. Koretz, B. Stecher, S. Klein, and D. McCaffrey, "The Vermont Portfolio Assessment Program: Findings and Implications," *Educational Measurement: Issues and Practices* 13, no. 3 (fall 1994b): 5–16; B. Stecher, "Implementation and Impact of the Vermont Portfolio Assessment Program" (paper presented at the annual meeting of the National Council on Measurement in Education, Atlanta, Ga., April 1993). B. Stecher and E. Hamilton, "Portfolio Assessment in Vermont, 1992–93: The Teachers' Perspective on Implementation and Impact" (paper presented at the annual meeting of the National Council on Measurement in Education, New Orleans, La., April 1994); B. Stecher and K. Mitchell, "Portfolio-Driven Reform: Vermont Teachers' Understanding of Mathematical Problem Solving" (CSE Technical Report No. 400, Los Angeles, Calif.: CRESST/UCLA, 1995).

7. Kentucky Department of Education, *Kentucky Instructional Results Information System: 1991–92 Technical Report;* Kentucky Department of Education, *Kentucky Instructional Results Information System 1992–93 Technical Report.*

8. Kentucky Department of Education, *Kentucky Instructional Results Information System 1992–93 Technical Report.* R. K. Hambleton, R. M. Jaeger, D. Koretz, R. L. Linn, J. Millman, and S. E. Phillips, *Review of the Measurement Quality of the Kentucky Instructional Results Information System, 1991–1994* (Frankfort, Ky.: Kentucky General Assembly, 1995). E. Kifer, "Perceptions, Attitudes, and Beliefs About the Kentucky Education Reform Act (KERA)," in *A Review of Research on the Kentucky Education Reform Act (KERA),* ed. Kentucky Institute for Education Research (Frankfort, Ky.: Kentucky Institute for Education Research, 1994); D. Koretz, S. Barron, K. Mitchell, and B. Stecher, *Perceived Effects of the Kentucky Instructional Results Information System (KIRIS)* (Santa Monica, Calif.: RAND, 1996); R. Pankratz, *Summary of Research Related to KERA* (Frankfort, Ky.: Kentucky Institute for Education Research, 1995); B. Stecher, S. Barron, T. Kaganoff, and J. Goodwin, "The Effects of Standards-Based Assessment on Classroom Practice: Results of the 1996–97 RAND Survey of Kentucky Teachers of Mathematics and Writing" (CSE Technical Report No. 482, Los Angeles, Calif.: CRESST/UCLA, 1998).

9. P. G. LeMahieu, D. H. Gitomer, and J. T. Eresh, "Portfolios Beyond the Classroom: Data Quality and Qualities" (manuscript no. 94-01, Princeton, N.J.: Educational Testing Service, 1995).

10. C. A. Gentile, J. Martin-Rehrmann, and J. H. Kennedy, "Windows into the Classroom: NAEP's 1992 Writing Portfolio Study" (report no. 23-FR-06, Washington, D.C.: U.S. Department of Education, National Center for Education Statistics, 1995).

11. W. H. Thomas, B. A. Storms, K. Sheingold, J. I. Heller, S. T. Paulukonis, A. M. Nunez, and J. Y Wing, "Portfolio Assessment Research and Development Project: Final Report" (Princeton, N.J.: Educational Testing Service, Center for Performance Assessment, December 1993).

12. D. Koretz, "Large-Scale Portfolio Assessments in the U.S.: Evidence Pertaining to the Quality of Measurement," *Assessment in Education* 5, no. 3 (1998).

13. Ibid.

14. Koretz, Stecher, et al. "Can Portfolios Assess Student Performance?"

15. Koretz, Stecher, et al., "Evolution of a Portfolio Program."

16. D. Koretz, "Large-Scale Portfolio Assessments in the U.S."

17. Gentile, Martin-Rehrmann, and Kennedy, "Windows into the Classroom."

18. Hambleton, Jaeger, et al., *Review of the Measurement Quality of the Kentucky Instructional Results Information System, 1991–94.*

19. Koretz, Barron, et al., *Perceived Effects.*

20. Koretz, Stecher, et al., "Can Portfolios Assess Student Performance?"

21. Koretz, Barron, et al., *Perceived Effects;* Stecher, Barron, et al., "Effects of Standards-Based Assessment on Classroom Practice."

22. Koretz, Barron, et al., *Perceived Effects;* Stecher, Barron, et al., "Effects of Standards-Based Assessment on Classroom Practice"; LeMahieu, Gitomer, and Eresh, "Portfolios Beyond the Classroom"; Thomas, Storms, et al., "Portfolio Assessment Research and Development Project."

23. Stecher, Barron, et al., "Effects of Standards-Based Assessment on Classroom Practice."

24. Stecher and Mitchell, "Portfolio-Driven Reform."

25. Koretz, Stecher, et al., "The Vermont Portfolio Assessment Program."

26. Koretz, Stecher, et al., "Evolution of a Portfolio Program"; Koretz, Barron, et al., *Perceived Effects.*

27. LeMahieu, Gitomer, and Eresh, "Portfolios Beyond the Classroom."

Chapter 7

Using Performance Assessment for Accountability Purposes

William A. Mehrens

Why is there such great interest in performance assessment? Are large-scale performance assessments administratively feasible, professionally credible, publicly acceptable, legally defensible, and economically affordable?

Performance assessment is currently a hot topic in education, and it is easy to be impressed with the enthusiasm, energy, and optimism displayed by those doing research on performance assessment. However, as with any hot topic, there are those who have put on their advocacy hats before the data support it. It is my hope to bring a reasoned discussion to the issue of performance assessment for accountability purposes.

A simple statement of my position is that I am in favor of performance assessment by individual teachers who integrate their assessments with their instruction; I am in favor of performance

This chapter originally appeared in *Educational Measurement: Issues and Practice* (Spring 1992). It has been slightly revised and updated.

assessment as a supplement to more traditional examinations for licensure decisions;[1] and I am in favor of some *limited, experimental* tryouts of performance assessment for other accountability purposes. Many questions must be answered and problems overcome before it should be used on a wide-scale basis.

The title and thrust of this article are on the use of performance assessment in accountability programs. Yet most of the research and rhetoric regarding the advantages of performance assessment have been in the realm of individual pupil diagnosis. When one switches from local classroom assessment for individual purposes to mandated assessment for accountability purposes, different issues arise. If performance assessment is used for high-stakes accountability purposes, many of the same kinds of problems that have occurred with multiple-choice tests will exist. For example, there will be the potential problem of focusing instruction toward the particular sample of the domain that is being assessed. This will neither be beneficial to instruction nor result in accurate inferences about the domain.

Any assessment used for accountability faces higher criteria than assessment used for individual pupil assistance within the classroom. Any assessment to be used for accountability purposes has to be administratively feasible, professionally credible, publicly acceptable, legally defensible, and economically affordable.[2] In my view, performance assessment will have more trouble meeting several of these criteria than do multiple-choice tests.

As Fitzpatrick and Morrison pointed out in 1971, "There is no absolute distinction between performance tests and other classes of tests."[3] The distinction is the degree to which the criterion situation is simulated. Typically, what users of the term mean is that the assessment will require the examinee to construct an original response. Some people seem to call short-answer questions or fill-in-the-blank questions performance assessments. However, it is more common in performance assessment for the examiner to observe the process of the construction; thus, there is heavy reliance on observation and professional judgment in the evaluation of the response.

The first point that should be stressed is that performance assessment really is not new. It was employed when the Gilead guards challenged the fugitives from Ephraim who tried to cross the Jordan River:

> "Are you a member of the tribe of Ephraim?" they asked. If the man replied that he was not, then they demanded, "Say Shibboleth." But if he could not pronounce the "sh" and said "Sibboleth" instead of "Shibboleth" he was dragged away and killed. As a result, 42,000 people of Ephraim died there at that time.
>
> (Judges 12: 5–6)

That obviously was a performance examination. I point it out because I heard a speaker at a recent professional meeting say that "performance tests have only been around a couple of years." Even a reading of the 1971 Fitzpatrick and Morrison chapter in the second edition of *Educational Measurement*[4] could have prevented such an inaccurate statement. However, it is true that the popularity of talking about performance assessment as the latest solution to our educational problems is a new phenomenon.

Factors Supporting Performance Assessment

Like all "new" developments, performance assessment is backed by a very large number of people for a variety of reasons. Several of the major reasons are as follows: (a) the old (but largely inaccurate) criticisms of multiple-choice tests; (b) the belief of cognitive psychologists that assessment of procedural knowledge requires formats other than multiple-choice questions; (c) the increased concern that multiple-choice tests delimit the domains we should be assessing; (d) the wide publicity of the Lake Wobegon effect of teaching too closely to multiple-choice tests; and, finally, (e) claims that there are deleterious instructional/learning effects of teaching to multiple-choice test formats. Certainly these five points are related and overlapping, but they will be discussed separately.

Traditional (But Largely Incorrect) Criticisms of Multiple-Choice Tests

There have been three main criticisms of objective paper/pencil tests: They are biased, they measure irrelevant content, and the format demands only the ability to recognize an answer—not to actually work problems. Of course, any of these criticisms can be true, but they are not necessary concomitants of the multiple-choice format.

Bias

This article is not the place to discuss the bias charge, but much research has been published about that issue. Publishers of high-stakes multiple-choice tests know a great deal about what test construction/analyses steps to take to prevent and/or detect bias. Well-constructed multiple-choice tests generally fare well under psychometrically accepted definitions of test bias.

Irrelevant Content

The issue of content relevance is related in part to the issue of whether the multiple-choice format can only be used for a limited number of educational objectives/goals. But the issues are separable. To give you a flavor of the criticism, consider the following quote: "We're spending hundreds of millions of dollars on tests that don't tell us anything about what kids know or know how to do."[5] While this quote was directed more at existing commercial standardized tests than the objective format per se, the rhetoric stems at least in part from incorrect beliefs about what multiple-choice tests can measure. In addition to the incorrect concern about irrelevant content, there is concern about the lack of total inclusiveness of the content and its lack of perfect match with the curriculum.[6]

There will never be universal agreement about the goals/objectives of education. However, one must keep in mind that standardized multiple-choice achievement test domains are based upon very thorough reviews of existing curricula guides and textbooks. These, one would assume, have been developed and/or adopted because they have some match to the goals of the local schools. Most parents do want their children to learn the content domains sampled by multiple-choice standardized achievement tests.

Measurement of Recognition Only

The criticism that multiple-choice tests measure only recognition is reflected in the following statements:

Standardized multiple-choice tests have drawn increasing fire as too simplistic, measuring the ability to recognize knowledge rather than the ability to think and solve problems, an important skill in today's jobs.[7]

It's testing for the TV generation—superficial and passive. We don't ask if students can synthesize information, solve problems or think independently. We measure what they can recognize.[8]

The notion that multiple-choice items cannot measure higher-order thinking skills is unfortunate and incorrect. Over the years, Forsyth has given any number of talks illustrating that multiple-choice achievement test items can tap higher-order thinking skills.[9] If his examples have not convinced the doubtful, they simply are not open-minded—or perhaps they do not think at a high enough level. Look at the sample multiple-choice questions sent to students who register for the SAT. You could not possibly answer those questions without engaging in some problem solving and/or higher-order thinking.

Cognitive Psychologists' Influence

Cognitive psychologists distinguish between declarative and procedural knowledge (or content knowledge and process knowledge). As Snow and Lohman[10] point out, all cognitive tasks require both types of knowledge, but different tasks differ in the relative demands they place on the two. It is generally accepted that some types of procedural knowledge are *not* amenable to multiple-choice types of assessment. The increased (and in my view correct) push for procedural knowledge goals has led to an increase in the attempts to engage in performance assessment. (However, this should not result in a *replacement* of objective tests.)

Over the past decade or so, many individuals have been hypothesizing on "what cognitive psychology seems to offer to improve educational measurement."[11] Snow and Lohman suggest that the implications of cognitive psychology are largely for measurement *research* and that "cognitive psychology has no ready answers for the educational measurement problems of yesterday, today, or tomorrow."[12] Other researchers generally seem to agree with this assessment.[13] None of these researchers suggest wide adoption of their exploratory research.

Based on his research, Siegler warns us "that even seemingly well-documented cognitive psychological models may be drastically incorrect, and that diagnoses of individuals based on these models could only be equally incorrect . . . the time does not seem ripe to advocate their use in the classrooms."[14]

In spite of the somewhat cautionary tone used above, I am convinced that cognitive psychologists do have something to offer those of us in measurement. However, I, like Snow and Lohman,[15] think that it is primarily in terms of helping measurement specialists to develop new and better theories. We should not jump on any "performance assessment for accountability" bandwagon before those theories are understood much more thoroughly.

Delimited Domain

Partly as a result of cognitive psychologists' influence, there has been increased concern that multiple-choice tests cannot assess all the important domains of educational goals/objectives. Across the decades, measurement specialists have agreed that objective tests cannot adequately cover all objectives. For example, no one believes they are a good way to measure perceptual motor skills. However, as measurement-driven instruction has increased, the concern about the delimitation of the measured domains has increased.

Many important areas can be efficiently assessed via multiple-choice questions. As Weinstein and Meyer make clear in their chapter on the implications of cognitive psychology for testing, many different educational tasks require simple recall, particularly tasks in the lower grades and in introductory courses. Further, experts differ from novices in their knowledge base, and research suggests "that domain knowledge is a necessary but insufficient condition for acquiring strategies and expertise."[16]

Collis and Romberg, advocates of performance assessment in mathematics, admit that multiple-choice items provide "an efficient and economical means of assessing knowledge of and ability in routine calculations, procedures, and algorithms. *All* [italics added] seem to agree that these skills are still an important part of mathematics education."[17]

In spite of my belief in the importance of procedural knowledge and the importance of doing some assessing by other than multiple-choice testing, I remain puzzled by some of the writings regarding this "new" performance testing. Some suggest that multiple-choice tests are indirect and what we need are more direct measures of achievement. But cognitive psychologists focus on processes (such as metacognitions) that are *not* amenable to direct measurement.[18] Some think the problem is that multiple-choice tests do not cover a broad enough domain.[19] But performance tests will access narrower domains—perhaps in more depth.[20] Some are concerned with the curriculum-test mismatch and the efforts of educators to change the curriculum to increase the match—these people generally see measurement-driven instruction as a bad thing. Others are interested in using new assessment procedures to reform the curriculum and they hope there is teaching to the assessment. All of this confusion is compounded by those who refuse to separate the issues of test content and test form (which are related, but not identical, issues).

Lake Wobegon Effects

High-stakes tests can lead to teachers' teaching too closely to the test, thus raising scores without raising the inferred achievement. Some advocates of performance assessment suggest that it is appropriate to teach directly to that type of assessment because the instructors will be teaching appropriate material in ways they ought to be teaching it. Consider the following quotes:

> Teaching to these [California Assessment Program] tests is what we want because the tests are 100 percent connected with real-world on-the-job performance.[21]

> If schools spend three or four weeks a year teaching to a performance-based test, at least they'll be teaching things they ought to be teaching in ways they ought to be teaching it.[22]

However, those who feel that performance assessment is the solution to teaching to the test are sadly mistaken. Their reasoning misses the point about inappropriate test preparation. They basically ignore the domain/sample problem that is exacerbated when one delimits the sample as one must in a performance assessment.

Deleterious Instruction

Tied to all the above issues is the apparent belief by some that if one tests via a multiple-choice test and teaches so that students do well on the multiple-choice test, the instruction must be deleterious, but if one assesses via performance measures, the instruction will be beneficial.

It is true that the format of the assessment will have some effect on instructional practices, that this effect will be greater if the assessment is for high-stakes accountability decisions, that answering multiple-choice questions is not a task that is done a lot outside of school, and that excessive instruction tied too closely to an unrealistic form of assessment is a poor instructional strategy. Nevertheless, it is not true that performance assessment will necessarily lead to high-quality instruction. The Honig and Shavelson ideas quoted above are not necessarily true. The California Assessment Program's five performance items in math[23] are certainly not "100 percent connected with real-world on-the-job performance." Further, teachers could spend time teaching correct answers to these questions without "teaching in ways they ought to be teaching it."

Again, I have perhaps sounded too cautionary. Writing assessment has probably increased the instruction of writing and that is a good thing. I suspect performance assessment of safety procedures in the science laboratories might increase the efforts of teachers to teach safety procedures, and that would be a good thing. But it is important to keep in mind Linn's admonition that we need to do more than just assume that the alternatives to multiple-choice items will have no bad side effects of their own.[24] We must be prudent in our charges regarding the ills of multiple-choice test and in our claims about the wonders of performance assessment for instruction.

Problems with Performance Assessment for Accountability

Like other forms of assessment, the particular problems that are likely to be faced with performance assessment vary somewhat depending on a variety of dimensions, such as (a) secure vs. nonsecure assessments, (b) matrix sampling vs. every pupil assessment, and (c) accountability vs. instruction.

Secure vs. Nonsecure Instruments

One disadvantage of performance assessment is that with only a few questions, there is no way to keep the exact content of the exam secure. Once performance assessments have been used, they cannot be reused to test the same higher-order thinking process. One can memorize an answer to a higher-order question just as well as one can memorize an answer to a basic skills question. Thus, performance assessments have to be new each year—adding to the developmental costs and making across-year comparisons of growth very difficult.

Baker and colleagues took a different approach by suggesting that "only if the tasks and scoring criteria are made public . . . can teachers guide students to meet such standards, and then only if the same tasks are used."[25] Although I grant that this may be done without corrupting the inference for some physical performance tests (for example, diving), performance assessment tasks that have a metacognitive component do not allow for such release and reuse of the tasks.

Matrix Sampling vs. Every Pupil Testing

Different cost issues arise with these two methods. Assessments that would be cost prohibitive for every pupil testing may be reasonable in a matrix sampling approach. However, if individual student scores are not reported, this makes the assessments much less useful to individual teachers, and a lack of student motivation makes the results suspect. Further, some high-stakes tasks, such as those used for licensure and high school graduation requirements, demand every pupil testing.

Accountability vs. Instruction

As mentioned earlier, high-stakes tests used for accountability purposes need to meet what Baratz-Snowden[26] has referred to as the five "apple" criteria: administratively feasible, professionally credible, publicly acceptable, legally defensible, and economically affordable.[27] I maintain that performance assessment is likely to have difficulty meeting many of these standards. Currently, it appears to meet the professionally credible and publicly acceptable criteria, but that could be because it is in the fad stage. More careful scrutiny may change that.

Administratively Feasible/Economically Affordable

Because resources are always limited, the costs of performance assessment must be of great concern. The Educational Testing Service has reported that "one state with a strong commitment to educational assessment found that redesigning its state program around performance tasks would increase by tenfold the cost of the existing state assessment program."[28] Given my belief that most performance exercises are not reusable without distorting the inference, there are some very real questions about the developmental costs in performance assessment for accountability.

Even after performance assessments have been developed, the costs of administering and scoring them are high. Frequently special equipment is needed for administration, and it is not feasible to have enough copies for simultaneous administration. Consider, for example, the four components planned for an assessment of teachers' laboratory skills:[29] a preobservation questionnaire, a preobservation conference, an observation, and a postobservation conference. The observation lasts thirty to forty-five minutes, and observers in the pilot study were trained for three days. All this is certainly expensive. This is not to suggest we should not do performance assessments, but cost-benefit ratios must be considered.

Publicly Acceptable

So far the performance assessment advocates have done a good job with public relations. But, as with multiple-choice tests, once performance assessments have been used awhile for accountability purposes and the teachers complain about their lack of validity for accountability inferences, there may be a reduction in public acceptability. Once the public understands that the costs will be substantially higher, one might expect some loss of acceptance of the process.

Legally Defensible

"Legally, performance assessment is considered a test."[30] Whether this is how all courts would decide the issue, prudent individuals developing performance assessments for high-stakes decisions would be wise to act as if this were the case.[31] Psychometric experts for plaintiffs generally attack tests based on whether the *Standards for Educational and Psychological Testing*[32] have been followed. One would expect them to do the same for performance assessments. That performance assessments will meet the various psychometric standards of reliability, validity, and so on, has not been adequately demonstrated. Other legal concerns also need to be considered. For example, if there is any disparate impact on protected groups, how might one deal with the fact that observers (graders) may be aware of the group status of the students? If there is debate about the scoring process, will there be documentation of the performance so rescoring can occur?

Professionally Credible

Professional credibility pertains at least to three overlapping groups: teachers, those involved in teacher education, and psychometricians. Because of effective public relations efforts and face validity, performance assessment probably has more credibility than multiple-choice testing for the first two groups. It is impossible to know if that will continue if performance assessment becomes widely used for accountability. Wide use will result in more scrutiny than such assessments have currently been given, and the whole movement could implode following such scrutiny. Psychometricians will probably place or withhold their stamps of approval based on evidence regarding the psychometric properties of the assessments. This may place them on the credibility continuum at a point different from those individuals who minimize the importance of psychometric properties.

Validity

Generally, psychometricians believe it is important to validate new approaches to testing before any wide implementation.[33] Performance assessments have face validity—or what Popham[34] says can be more pedantically described as verisimilitude. Face validity helps in the acceptance of an assessment procedure, and some level of face validity is essential for public credibility. But, as psychometricians know, face validity "is not validity in the technical sense; it refers not to what the test *actually* [italics added] measures, but to what it *appears superficially* [italics added] to measure."[35] It does not take the place of real validity and is simply not sufficient. To date, there is little evidence on the validity of performance assessments.

In studying the validity of performance assessments, one should think carefully about whether the right domains are being assessed, whether they are well defined, whether they are well sampled, whether—even if well sampled—one can infer to the domain, and what diagnostically one can infer if the performance is not acceptably high.

A wish to assess the different domains was a major reason for implementing performance assessment, and in a general sense, I am in favor of what cognitive psychologists and reform educators are stressing. Nevertheless, the appropriateness of performance domains is as subject to debate as are those domains assessed via multiple-choice tests. In general, performance assessment measures a narrower domain than multiple-choice testing, but assesses it in more depth. Is this good? There should probably be more discussion regarding just which narrow domains need to be assessed in depth.

If one is satisfied that the right domains are being assessed, one should still consider whether they are defined tightly enough. Critics of standardized tests have suggested that the domains are not well enough defined in those tests. My general observation is that the domains of multiple-choice achievement tests that have been used for accountability purposes have been more tightly defined than many performance assessment domains.

The major problems for valid performance assessment relate to the limited sampling and the lack of generalizability from the limited sample to any identifiable domain. One of the generally accepted advantages of multiple-choice testing is that one can sample a domain very thoroughly. Because performance assessment takes more time, fewer tasks (questions) can be presented. Thus, the sampling of the domain is less dense. For example, in California there were only five mathematics items on the state performance assessment.[36] One would be hard-pressed to generalize to any curricular domain from such a limited sample.

Even if sampling is adequate, there is the question of whether one can generalize from the sample to a larger domain. This is dependent upon the intercorrelations between the portions of the domain in the sample and those portions not in the sample. Certainly research has indicated that higher-order thinking skills and problem solving are specific to relatively narrow areas of expertise, and there appears to be little transfer from one subject matter to another on these constructs.[37]

But even *within* a subject matter area, generalizability is "iffy." As Herman has pointed out, "Research in performance testing demonstrates how fragile is the generalizability of performance."[38] She gives as one example the research that indicates writing skill does not generalize across genres. The teacher's guide for the *Writing* supplement of the *Iowa Test of Basic Skills* reports correlations between essays in different *modes* of discourse that average .36.[39]

Or consider the generalizability of performance in a science laboratory assessment. Some research has been conducted in California on the development of a science laboratory assessment for new teachers. In their 1990 final report, Wheeler and Page wisely state that they do not know if their prototypic exercises will generalize

across different science laboratory situations—grades K–12; earth, life, and physical sciences; various types of lab activities; different groups of students; and different lab setting, including field trips. . . .

Conclusions about the generalizability of the assessment should be based on a large-scale field testing that includes many more types of situations.[40]

At this point, we simply do not have enough data indicating the degree to which we can generalize from most of the performance assessments that are being conducted. Much of the evidence we do have suggests that generalizability is extremely limited.

Even if the domain is the correct one, it is well defined, the sample is adequate, and generalizability is possible, validity problems remain. As mentioned earlier, if the assessment is not secure, students will be taught how to do that particular task. This not only makes the inference to the domain inappropriate, it means one may make an incorrect inference about the sample performance. For anything other than a completely physical skill (for example, diving), one is typically making an inference about the cognitive processes used. But one can memorize reasons as well as facts. Anytime one wishes to infer something like a metacognition, it is important that the assessment be secure.

And finally, a threat to validity that deserves mention is the impossibility of making a precise inference from a poor score on a performance assessment. If, for example, one accepts Anderson's theory of skill development, there are three stages: the declarative stage, the knowledge compilation stage, and the procedural stage.[41] At which stage is an individual whose skill development is inadequate? Multiple-choice tests could assess the first two levels.

Reliability

There are several threats to reliability in performance assessment. One has to do with the small number of independent observations (the sampling problem discussed above). A second has to do with the subjectivity of the scoring process. A third has to do with a lack of internal consistency that influences generalizability (discussed above).

Reliability refers to random error in a measurement, and if random error is too great, any perceived relevance of the assessment is illusory because nothing is being measured.[42] Thus, one cannot possibly make any valid inference from the data.

The only performance assessment area that has reported much evidence on reliability has been writing assessment. There, the major evidence reported is rater reliability. It generally runs in the low .80s, although it can be substantially lower or higher. For example, the average inter-rater reliabilities for the *Writing* supplement to the *Iowa Test of Basic Skills* was .95.[43] Welch obtained inter-rater reliability estimates of .75 to .77.[44] Dunbar and colleagues report on nine different studies where the rater reliabilities range from .33 to .91.[45] To obtain the higher levels of rater reliability is costly. It requires careful selection and extensive training of the raters, precise scoring guidelines, and periodic rechecking of rater performance.

Score reliabilities are reported less often, but, when reported, are quite a bit lower. The *Writing* supplement to the *Iowa Test of Basic Skills* had an average score reliability (two essay samples using the *same mode* of discourse) of .48.[46] The score reliabilities reported in the Dunbar article ranged from .26 to .60. As they stated, these values are "extremely low relative to common standards for high-stakes tests."

Given that writing assessment is the most developed and researched mode of performance assessment, it seems safe to conclude that there are serious problems with the reliability of many performance assessments.

Many issues arise concerning scoring, scaling, equating, and aggregating data:

1. It is obvious that there is subjectivity in assigning the scores to a performance. This means that *who* does the scoring is very important for any test used for accountability. Some telling data regarding scoring by anyone having a vested interest in the results come from the judgments of teacher performance by principals. State after state has obtained very negatively skewed distributions when principals score teacher performance. When assessing for *accountability* purposes, it is imperative to have performances scored by those who do *not* have a vested interest in the outcome. Having teachers score their own students' performances will

not work. Further, if the school building or school district is being held accountable for the scores on performance assessments, the scores must come from outside the district.

The issue of *what* is to be scored is also of considerable importance. Typically, "an examinee response is complex and multifaceted, comprising multiple, interrelated parts."[47] One can use either componential or holistic scoring. As Millman and Greene pointed out, in either case, to develop the scoring criteria requires a clear understanding of what it means to be proficient in the relevant domain (which, in turn, assumes there is a good definition of the domain). Most advocates of performance assessment probably will opt for developing scoring profiles.[48] The *Standards* require that the reliabilities of the subscores are reported. Further, if the data are going to be used for individual diagnostic purposes, one should report the reliability of the difference scores in the profile. These will obviously be lower than the individual score reliabilities. The profiles for students' performances may well be so unreliable that they are useless.

2. Determining how to scale the data from performance assessments is another challenge. In his article on the NAEP Proficiency Scales, Forsyth[49] convincingly argues that those scales do *not* yield valid criterion-referenced interpretation. Large-scale performance assessments will likely be equally difficult to scale.

3. Because performance assessments yield fewer independent pieces of data and because specific assessments should not be reused, the equating problems are formidable. For longitudinal comparisons and fairness in accountability, the scores on different forms of performance assessments must be equated so that they represent the same level of achievement regardless of when the performance is assessed, which tasks are given, or which raters score the performance.

4. Decisions about the unit of reporting will be difficult to make. Certainly for those performance assessments that are

based on group activities, the unit cannot be the individual.[50] However, other types of assessment may lend themselves to individual reporting.

Ethnic Group Differences

One of the reasons for moving to performance assessments is that some individuals are hopeful that performance assessments will show smaller ethnic group differences than do multiple-choice tests. The results are not yet all in with respect to this hope, but evidence on writing assessments across the nation do not show smaller differences between black and white performers than are obtained from multiple-choice tests.[51] Further, the data will be more complicated to interpret due to the subjective scoring processes and the potential opportunity (where performance is observed) for scorers to allow ethnicity to influence their scores.

Conclusions/Implications

As measurement specialists have known for decades, multiple-choice tests measure some things very well and very efficiently. Nevertheless, they do not measure everything, and their use can be overemphasized. Performance assessments have the potential to measure important objectives that cannot be easily measured by multiple-choice tests.

Some exciting research has been conducted regarding performance assessment, but much more research is needed. Like Wolf and colleagues, I would call for "mindfulness"[52] in the performance assessment research and hope that the researchers would "be as tough-minded in designing new options as [they] are in critiquing available testing."[53] Evidence regarding psychometric characteristics must be gathered. One cannot "pursue these new modes of assessment . . . on the mere conviction that they are better."[54] And finally, I agree with Wolf and colleagues that researchers should be "standing on the shoulders rather than the faces of another generation."[55]

While continuing the research, performance advocates should not be overselling what performance assessment can do. Wiggins has suggested, "It's wrong to say [performance assessments] were oversold; they were overbought."[56] I do not see it that way. I think they have been both oversold and overbought.

Most large-scale assessments have added performance assessments to their existing array of efficient multiple-choice tests, not replaced them. There is no question but that the multiple-choice format is the format of choice for many assessments—especially for measuring declarative knowledge.

From at least one point of view, performance assessment is a good thing for measurement specialists and education in general. It has resulted in more money and more resources being devoted to assessment. This has opened up a whole new assessment industry. It should result in more research regarding the effects of testing on teaching and learning. Nevertheless, I agree with Haney and Madaus who suggest that "the search for alternatives [to multiple-choice tests] is somewhat shortsighted."[57] We also need to keep in mind a statement Lennon made more than two decades ago:

> To encourage the innocent to root around in the rubble of discredited modes of study of human behavior, in search of some overlooked assessment "jewels," is to dispatch a new band of Argonauts in quest of a nonexistent Golden Fleece.[58]

Finally, we should heed the wisdom of Boring: "The seats on the train of progress all face backwards; you can see the past but only guess about the future."[59]

Notes

1. This is because of the high costs of false positives in licensure.
2. J. Baratz-Snowden, ed., *RFP-National Board for Professional Teaching Standards* (Washington, D.C.: National Board for Professional Teaching Standards, 1990).
3. R. Fitzpatrick and E. J. Morrison, "Performance and Product Evaluation," in *Educational Measurement,* 2d ed., ed. E. L. Thorndike (Washington, D.C.: American Council on Education, 1971): 238.

4. Ibid., 237–70.

5. Albert Shanker, cited in G. Putka, "New Kid in School: Alternate Exams," *Wall Street Journal* (November 16, 1989): B1.

6. See E. L. Baker, M. Freeman, and S. Clayton, "Cognitive Assessment of History for Large-Scale Testing" in *Testing and Cognition,* ed. M. C. Wittrock and E. L. Baker (Englewood Cliffs, N.J.: Prentice Hall, 1991), 131–53.

7. E. R. Fiske, "But Is the Child Learning: Schools Trying New Tests," *New York Times,* 31 January 1990, B1–B2.

8. Linda Darling-Hammond as quoted in Fiske, "But Is the Child Learning," B8.

9. See, for example, R. A. Forsyth, "Measuring Higher-Order Thinking Skills" (presentation at the meeting of the Institute for School Executives, Iowa City, Iowa, 1990).

10. R. E. Snow and D. F. Lohman, "Implications of Cognitive Psychology for Educational Measurement" in *Educational Measurement,* 3d ed., ed. R. L. Linn (New York: American Council on Education and Macmillan Publishing Company, 1989), 263–331.

11. Ibid., 263.

12. Ibid., 320.

13. See S. Ohlsson, "Trace Analysis and Spatial Reasoning: An Example of Intensive Cognitive Diagnosis and Its Implications for Testing," 251–96; A. Lesgold et al., "Applying Cognitive Task Analysis and Research Methods to Assessment," 325–50; and R. L. Linn, "Diagnostic Testing," 489–98, all in N. Frederiksen et al., *Diagnostic Monitoring of Skill and Knowledge Acquisition* (Hillsdale, N.J.: Lawrence Erlbaum Associates, 1990).

14. R. S. Siegler, "Strategy, Diversity and Cognitive Assessment," in *Educational Researcher* 18, no. 9 (1989): 15–20.

15. Snow and Lohman, "Implications of Cognitive Psychology for Educational Measurement."

16. C. E. Weinstein and D. K. Meyer, "Implications of Cognitive Psychology for Testing: Contributions from Work in Learning Strategies," in *Testing and Cognition,* ed. Wittrock and Baker, 42.

17. K. Collis and T. A. Romberg, "Assessment of Mathematical Performance: An Analysis of Open-Ended Test Items," in *Testing and Cognition,* ed. Wittrock and Baker, 102.

18. Weinstein and Meyer, "Implications of Cognitive Psychology for Testing," in *Testing and Cognition,* ed. Wittrock and Baker.

19. E. L. Baker, M. Freeman, and S. Clayton, "Cognitive Assessment of History for Large-scale Testing," in *Testing and Cognition,* ed. Wittrock and Baker, 131–53.

20. Actually, the evidence regarding whether multiple-choice tests and other assessments cover the same domains is quite mixed. Some research suggests the same domains/constructs are being measured; other research suggests that there are some differences. See T. A. Ackerman and P. L. Smith, "A Comparison of the Information Provided by Essay, Multiple-Choice, and Free-Response Writing Tests," *Applied Psychological Measurement* 12, no. 2 (1988): 117–28; R. E. Bennett, D. A. Rock, and M. W. Wang, "Equivalence of Free-Response and Multiple-Choice Items," *Journal of Educational Measurement* 28, no. 1 (1991): 77–92; M. Birenbaum and K. K. Tatsuoka, "Open-Ended Versus Multiple-Choice Response Formats—It Does Make a Difference for Diagnostic Purposes," *Applied Psychological Measurement* 11, no. 4 (1987): 385–96; R. Farr, R. Pritchard, and B. Smitten, "A Description of What Happens When an Examinee Takes a Multiple-Choice Reading Comprehension Test," *Journal of Educational Measurement* 27, no. 3 (1990): 209–26; M. E. Martinez, "A Comparison of Multiple-Choice and Constructed Figural Response Items" (paper presented at the annual meeting of the American Educational Research Association, Boston, Mass., April 1990); R. E. Traub and C. W. Fisher, "On the Equivalence of Constructed-Response and Multiple-Choice Tests," *Applied Psychological Measurement* 1, no. 3 (1977): 355–70; R. E. Traub and K. MacRury, "Multiple-Choice Versus Free-Response in the Testing of Scholastic Achievement," in *Tests and Trends 8: Jahrbuch der Padagogischen Diagnostik,* ed. K. Ingencamp and R. S. Jager (Weinheim & Basel, Switzerland: Beltz Berlag, 1990): 128–59; W. C. Ward, "A Comparison of Free-Response and Multiple-Choice Forms of Verbal Aptitude Tests," *Applied Psychological Measurement* 6, no. 1 (1982): 1–12; W. C. Ward, N. Frederiksen, and S. B. Carlson, "Construct Validity of Free-Response and Machine-Scorable Forms of a Test," *Journal of Educational Measurement* 17, no. 1 (1980): 11–30.

21. Honig, cited in C. Pipho, "Stateline," *Phi Delta Kappan* 71, no. 4 (1989): 262–63.

22. Richard Shavelson, cited in R. Rothman, "States Turn to Student Performance As New Measure of School Quality," *Education Week* 9, no. 10 (1989): 1, 12–13.

23. California State Department of Education, *A Question of Thinking: A First Look at Students' Performance on Open-Ended Questions in Mathematics* (Sacramento, Calif.: California State Department of Education, 1989).

24. S. Moses, "Assessors Seek Test That Teaches," *APA Monitor* 21, no. 11 (1990): 36–37.

25. Baker et al., "Cognitive Assessment of History for Large-Scale Testing," in *Testing and Cognition,* ed. Wittrock and Baker, 137.

26. Baratz-Snowden, *RFP-National Board for Professional Teaching Standards.*

27. Admittedly, her writing pertained to licensure tests, but I believe the generaliza-

tion of the criteria to accountability assessment is reasonable.

28. Educational Testing Service, *Annual Report* (Princeton, N.J.: Educational Testing Service, 1990), 6.

29. P. Wheeler, "Assessment of Laboratory Skills of Science Teachers via a Multi-Methods Approach" (paper presented in the symposium on Innovative Assessment Prototypes for the California New Teacher Project at the annual meeting of the American Educational Research Association and the National Council on Measurement in Education, Boston, Mass., April 1990).

30. B. R. Nathan and W. F. Cascio, "Introduction: Technical and Legal Standards" in *Performance Assessment: Methods and Applications* (Baltimore, Md.: The Johns Hopkins University Press, 1986), 1.

31. See *Watson v. Fort Worth Bank and Trust*, 1988, for a discussion of this issue in employment testing.

32. AERA, APA, and NCME, *Standards for Educational and Psychological Testing* (Washington, D.C.: American Psychological Association, 1985).

33. See R. S. Nickerson, "New Directions in Educational Assessment," *Educational Researcher* 18, no. 9 (1989): 3–7.

34. See W. J. Popham, "Face Validity: Siren Song for Teacher-Testers," in *Assessment of Teaching: Purposes, Practices, and Implications for the Profession*, ed. J. V. Mitchell Jr., S. L. Wise, and B. S. Plake (Hillsdale, N.J.: Lawrence Erlbaum Associates, 1990), 1–14.

35. A. Anastasi, *Psychological Testing*, 6th ed. (New York: Macmillan, 1988), 144.

36. California State Department of Education, *A Question of Thinking*.

37. See S. P. Norris, "Can We Test Validly for Critical Thinking?" *Educational Researcher* 18, no. 9 (1989): 15–20, for a discussion of both epistemological and psychological generalizability of critical thinking.

38. J. Herman, "Research in Cognition and Learning: Implications for Achievement Testing Practice," in *Testing and Cognition*, ed. Wittrock and Baker, 157.

39. A. N. Hieronymus et al., *Writing Supplement Teacher's Guide: Iowa Tests of Basic Skills* (Chicago: Riverside Publishing Co., 1987), 28.

40. P. Wheeler and J. Page, *Development of a Science Laboratory Assessment for New Teachers, Grades K–12*, Final Report (Mountain View, Calif.: RMC Research Corporation, 1990), 60–61.

41. J. R. Anderson, *The Architecture of Cognition* (Cambridge, Mass.: Harvard University Press, 1983).

42. Fitzpatrick and Morrison, "Performance and Product Evaluation."

43. Hieronymus et al., *Writing Supplement Teacher's Guide*.

44. C. Welch, "Estimating the Reliability of a Direct Measure of Writing Through

Generalizability Theory" (paper presented at the annual meeting of the American Educational Research Association, Chicago, April 1991).

45. S. B. Dunbar, D. M. Koretz, and H. D. Hoover, "Quality Control in the Development and Use of Performance Assessments," *Applied Measurement in Education* 4, no. 4 (1991): 289–303.

46. Hieronymus et al., *Writing Supplement Teacher's Guide.*

47. J. Millman and J. Greene, "The Specification and Development of Tests of Achievement and Ability" in *Educational Measurement,* R. L. Linn, ed., 344.

48. D. Wolf et al., "To Use Their Minds Well: Investigating New Forms of Student Assessment," in *Review of Research in Education,* ed. G. Grant (Washington, D.C.: American Educational Research Association, 1991), 31–74.

49. R. A. Forsyth, "Do NAEP Scales Yield Valid Criterion-Referenced Interpretations?" *Educational Measurement: Issues and Practice* 10, no. 3 (1991): 3–9.

50. See, for example, the prototype math exercises for the Maryland State Department of Education, in Maryland State Department of Education, *Maryland School Performance Assessment Program: Prototype Mathematics Task* (Maryland State Department of Education, 1990).

51. S. B. Dunbar, "Comparability of Indirect Measures of Writing Skill As Predictors of Writing Performance Across Demographic Groups" (paper presented at the annual meeting of the American Educational Research Association, Washington, D.C., April 1987); L. Feinberg, "Multiple Choice and Its Critics," *The College Board Review,* no. 157 (1990); R. L. Linn, E. L. Baker, and S. B. Dunbar, "Complex Performance-Based Assessments: Expectations and Validation Criteria," *Educational Researcher* 20, no. 8 (1991): 15–21.

52. Wolf et al., "To Use Their Minds Well," 33.

53. Ibid., 60.

54. Ibid., 62.

55. Ibid., 36.

56. Cited in R. Rothman, "New Tests Based on Performance Raise Questions," *Education Week* 10, no. 2 (1990): 1, 10, 12.

57. W. Haney and G. Madaus, "Searching for Alternatives to Standardized Tests: Whys, Whats, and Whithers," *Phi Delta Kappan* 70, no. 9 (1989): 683.

58. R. T. Lennon, "A Time for Faith" (presidential address at the annual meeting of the National Council on Measurement in Education, Los Angeles, Calif., April 1981), 3–4.

59. E. G. Boring, *History, Psychology and Science* (New York: Wiley, 1963), 5.

Part Four

State Testing Policies

Chapter 8

Learning from Kentucky's Failed Accountability System

George K. Cunningham

The law that mandated educational reform in Kentucky is called the Kentucky Education Reform Act (KERA), and it was originally implemented as a response to a decision rendered by Judge Ray Corns of the Franklin Circuit Court in the *Rose vs. Council for Better Education.*[1] Judge Corns ruled that the Kentucky General Assembly had failed to provide an efficient system of common schools as required by the state constitution. In his ruling, Kentucky's entire legal framework for education was ruled unconstitutional. He also ruled that the system of school financing was inefficient and discriminatory. He did not restrict himself to these matters alone. His ruling included these additional requirements:

> Lest there be any doubt, the result of our decisions is that Kentucky's *entire system* of common schools is unconstitutional. There is no allegation that only part of the common school system is invalid, and we find no such circumstance. This decision applies to the entire sweep of the system—all its parts and parcels. This decision applies to all

the statutes creating, implementing, and financing the system and to all regulation, etc., pertaining thereto. This decision covers the creation of local school districts, school boards, and the Kentucky Department of Education to the Minimum Foundation Program and Power Equalization Program. It covers school construction and maintenance, teacher certification—the whole gamut of the common school system in Kentucky. (215)

As is true in every state, there are many in Kentucky who conclude that public schools have failed to deliver an appropriate education to its students. There has been a long series of attempts to reform the state's education system. The most obvious problem in Kentucky has been the low proportion of students who graduate from high school. Of course, if the rate of high school graduation is low, so also will be the proportion of students obtaining college degrees. Kentucky has always been one of the poorest performers in these two categories and remains so today.

Although Kentucky has never lacked for ambitious plans for improving education, it has always lacked the political will and money to implement them. Judge Corns' ruling changed all of that. Some of what would later become KERA was already in the form of proposed legislation, including such provisions as higher standards, alternative assessment, and cash incentives. This legislation passed in the state senate but failed in the house largely because of the $75 million in costs and skepticism about whether an acceptable assessment could be found. With the groundwork completed for the most part, the state supreme court decisions ensured the implementation of these programs. Ironically, while the legislature balked at a $75 million price tag, KERA has now already cost billions of dollars. The cost of the Kentucky Instructional Results Information System (KIRIS) alone, for the 1995–96 school year, has been estimated by Lawrence Picus[2] to be somewhere between $120 million and $254 million.

With the requirement in Judge Corns's rulings mandating a complete rewriting of all statutes referring to Kentucky's schools, the governor and legislature had an unprecedented opportunity to improve the quality of the state's schools. The question that had to be faced was how to go about accomplishing this goal. What they did not do was seek a legislative consensus for the many parts of KERA. This caused problems at the time, and it continues to plague the system today.

According to Paul Blanchard, a political science professor at Eastern Kentucky University, in passing the KERA legislation, the representatives of Governor Wilkinson and the legislative leaders followed a nondeliberative process.[3] Decisions were made privately and anyone who called for public debate soon found himself or herself suppressed. The legislation was passed with a large number of road improvements and pet projects for legislators included. Although one of the stated purposes of KERA was the elimination of patronage, it was passed with a series of arm twists, threats, and rewards for compliant legislators. The result was a quick passage, but little real commitment of legislators to the educational goals of KERA other than the political support that their party leaders demanded.

David Hornbeck, Governor Wallace Wilkinson, his assistant Jack Foster, and the Democratic leadership of the house and senate created KERA. This group became the membership of the Task Force on Education Reform appointed by the general assembly in July 1989. The final report of the task force was adopted on March 7, 1990. This final report became the Kentucky Education Reform Act (KRS 158.6451).

KERA makes sweeping changes in the state's educational structure. The justification for these changes was the belief that Kentucky languished near the bottom of all states in most categories of educational performance. For example, the task force cited the fact that the percentage of Kentucky citizens with a bachelor's degree was among the lowest of any state. In 1998, Kentucky still ranked forty-eighth in this category, hardly an improvement. Kentucky's ACT scores remained flat throughout the 1990s during the period of KERA implementation. In the meantime, the national averages went up slightly. In 2002, the average ACT scores in Kentucky declined. This pushed Kentucky's performance even further below the national average than it was in 1992.

In most categories, National Assessment of Educational Progress (NAEP) scores in Kentucky have increased slightly, but not as much as other states, and as a result, Kentucky has fallen even further behind other states since 1992. The only bright spot in Kentucky's NAEP scores comes from an increase in 1998 fourth-grade reading scores. Although this increase has been repeatedly cited as an indication of the success of KERA, these increases can more reasonably be attributed to a higher rate of exemptions from the NAEP assessment. Students with individual educational plans (IEPs) that contain restrictive accommodations for testing are not allowed to participate in the NAEP assessment. Because the Kentucky assessment focuses only on school accountability, it has extremely generous rules for accommodations. For this reason, school principals try to maximize the number of students eligible for special education services. This classification makes them eligible for accommodations that lead to higher scores. This also makes them ineligible for participation in the NAEP assessment. In 1998, 10 percent of students were excluded from NAEP participation. Only 4 percent were exempted during the previous testing. The increased number of these exemptions best explains the increases in fourth-grade reading performance between 1994 and 1998.

The implementation of KERA led to changes in nearly every facet of the Kentucky educational system. Numerous additional programs were mandated by legislation, many at great expense. These included a more equitable distribution of funds for school districts, the requirement that the first three years of primary school not be differentiated by grades, the implementation of school-based decision making, expanded preschool programs, a reorganized department of education, extended school services, and several others. The most expensive of these innovations and the one that has had the greatest impact on instruction in the classroom is the accountability system, formerly called KIRIS (the Kentucky Instructional Results Information System), now renamed the Commonwealth Assessment Test System (CATS).

The Kentucky Instructional Results Information System (KIRIS)

KIRIS was developed in the early 1990s, at a time when there was considerable excitement about new ways of assessing students or new ways of using old techniques. These new ideas chiefly involved the replacement of multiple-choice items with performance assessments (also called authentic testing). The original legislation required that KIRIS be entirely performance-based by 1996. For the purposes of the legislation, portfolios were considered a performance assessment. The Kentucky Department of Education (KDE) and the legislators who were supporting this assessment methodology understood that it would not be practical to make the initial forms of the test entirely performance-based because the appropriate testing technology had not been developed. The earliest version of the school index was based on constructed response items, portfolios, and Performance Events. The Performance Events were an initial attempt at performance assessment, and they were expected to eventually replace the constructed response items. The school accountability indexes also included a nonacademic score based on dropout and attendance statistics. Multiple-choice items were administered and scored, but they were not included in the school indexes. Because they were not being used, the KDE eventually stopped administering them in the mid-1990s, only to be forced by the legislature to reintroduce them in 1998. The math portfolios and the Performance Events were eliminated in 1996.

Legislative Changes in Kentucky's Accountability System in 1998

The Kentucky General Assembly met in the spring of 1998 amidst expectations that they were going to make major alterations in or actually eliminate the Kentucky accountability system. Teachers across the state, who were in a position to be keenly aware of the deficiencies in the assessment, supported legislation that would have eliminated KIRIS. The fight started in the senate, and its members, particularly those on the Education Committee, were inundated with telephone calls, most of them from teachers, urging them to fix or eliminate the system. The committee reported out a bill (SB 243) to the full senate that would have greatly scaled back KIRIS. It passed with just one dissenting vote. The house of representatives, on the other hand, passed a bill that demanded far fewer changes (HB 627). In the ensuing conference committee meetings, a compromise bill (HB 53) was crafted based on HB 627 and SB 243. This bill was approved by the legislature and signed into law by the governor. HB 53 mandated only a few changes but did provide a mechanism for a more ambitious restructuring of the accountability system.

The most obvious change and one that represented a victory of style over substance was the change in the name of the accountability system, from the Kentucky Instructional Results Information System (KIRIS) to the Commonwealth Assessment Test System (CATS). The new name was unveiled in front of posters celebrating the University of Kentucky Wildcats' winning the NCAA basketball championship. The signs said simply, "Go CATS."

The authority for deciding whether the test should change was given to the Kentucky Board of Education (KBE). Board members were to be advised by three committees: the Education Assessment and Accountability Review Subcommittee (EAARS), made up of eight members of the general assembly; a School Curriculum Assessment and Accountability Council (SCAAC); and a National Technical Advisory Panel on Assessment and Accountability (NTAP). In addition to its advisory role, the EAARS was responsible for reviewing regulations. The NTAP was given the responsibility for determining whether the CATS tests were of a sufficient level of reliability and validity to permit scores to be reported on transcripts.

During acrimonious debates about whether to change, eliminate, or leave KIRIS untouched, the staff of the KDE and the KBE led the opposition to changes. They were supported by the two major state newspapers, the *Louisville Courier Journal* and the *Lexington Herald Leader*, and the Pritchard Committee, a private foundation devoted to the promotion of educational reform in Kentucky. The SCAAC was given the leadership role in determining the direction of the changes. Since it included the commissioner of Education, the chair of the state school board, and the director of the Pritchard Committee—all opponents of the movement to change KIRIS—it should come as no surprise that this committee did not recommend many substantive changes in the KIRIS tests. The changes that have been implemented as KIRIS made the transition from KIRIS to CATS are not apparent to parents, students, and teachers. Students continue to answer constructed-response and multiple-choice questions and submit writing portfolios as they did with the previous assessment system.

The CATS assessment is administered to fourth- and fifth-grade students in elementary school, seventh- and eighth-graders in middle school, and tenth-, eleventh-, and twelfth-graders in high school. It assesses reading, mathematics, science, social studies, arts and humanities, and practical living and vocational skills. The primary item format since the inception of KIRIS has been constructed-response questions. Written expression has always been assessed with writing portfolios. Multiple-choice items, which have been extensively piloted in the past but never counted in the school index, now contribute 33 percent to each subject matter index. Furthermore, HB 53 requires that the results from the Comprehensive Test of Basic Skills (CTBS-5), a standardized achievement test, be included in the computation of the school index. The KBE and the KDE were reluctant to do this. In order to fulfill the legal requirement that CTBS scores be included, they assigned it a weight of 5 percent. A small proportion of a school's score is based on graduation, rates, and retention. This input, called the nonacademic index, is weighted 5 percent for elementary schools and 10 percent for middle and high schools. It actually adds almost nothing to the variability in schools' accountability index because almost every school already receives nearly all of the 100 points allocated to it.

Instead of being evaluated as right or wrong, students' responses to the constructed-response items and the on-demand writing prompts and their performance on portfolios are placed in one of four categories: Novice, Apprentice, Proficient, and Distinguished. These are collectively referred to as the NAPD scale. With KIRIS, the points associated with each of these categories were as follows: 0 points for Novice, 40 points for

Apprentice, 100 points for Proficient, and 140 points for Distinguished. Student scores were translated into school accountability scores that could range from zero to 133.6. It is 133.6 rather than 140 because the nonacademic score can be no higher than 100.

One of the problems that the CATS revision was intended to address was the wide range in performance encompassed by the Novice and Apprentice categories. Most students fell into one of these two categories, with few considered Proficient and almost none Distinguished. In order to provide finer discriminations, the Novice and Apprentice categories were further divided. The Novice category was divided into Medium Novice (13 points) and High Novice (26 points). The Apprentice category was divided into Low Apprentice (40 points), Medium Apprentice (60 points), and High Apprentice (80 points). Students rated Proficient are awarded 100 points as before, and a Distinguished rating was still assigned 140 points. The effect of these changes was to increase ratings on the school accountability index.

A high level of academic achievement in Kentucky is operationally defined as an average score of proficient on KIRIS, which is equivalent to an accountability score of 100. All schools were originally supposed to achieve this score by 2012. The timeline has now been extended to 2014.

Because of the vast differences in student populations, consequences were not based on the absolute level of student performance. It was felt that this would have been unfair because of differences in school populations. Some schools would have been expected to do well because of the high educational and economic level of their parents, whereas others, because of deficiencies in these same areas, could be expected to perform poorly. KIRIS was designed to correct for that tendency by rewarding or punishing schools based on improvement rather than absolute performance. This was accomplished by establishing baselines for each school and goals that had to be achieved each two years (a biennium) that were called "thresholds." There were many problems with this system. For example, mathematical errors built into its design meant schools that successfully reached their assigned threshold every year would not come close to a score of 100. Expected performance was based on performance in the previous two years, and consequences were determined by performance in relation to that expectation. As a result, good performance in a biennium would lead to high thresholds and inevitably to poor performance in the next biennium. Conversely, poor performance in a biennium would lower the goals and make it easy for a school to be rewarded the following biennium. Schools designated as being "in crisis" were not schools with a history of poor performance. They were instead schools that performed exceptionally well in one biennium and thereby were saddled with an impossible goal for the next biennium. The schools most likely to be rewarded were those that had easy improvement goals because of bad performance the previous biennium.

With the revision of KIRIS into CATS, new thresholds are no longer recomputed every two years. Instead, a straight-line model is being employed. The average from 1999 and 2000 school years are used as a baseline. A separate chart is created for each school with a line drawn from the school's baseline score in 2000 to a score of 100 in 2014. This is the Meeting Goal line because schools at or above this line receive cash rewards at the end of each two-year period. A second line, called the Assistance line, is drawn from the baseline to a score of 80 in 2014. Schools that score below the Assistance line must undergo a Scholastic Audit. Schools with scores between these two lines are considered to be Progressing and they do not get rewards or an audit. Schools are expected to increase their performance in equal increments in each two-year biennium at a rate that will lead to their attainment of a score of 100 by 2014. As long as a school's accountability score does not fall a standard error below the Assistance line, it is considered to be making appropriate progress. The purpose of the straight-line model was to eliminate the seesaw effect that occurred when a school was highly successful one year, leading to an unachievable goal for the next year and likely unsatisfactory performance. By going to a straight-line system, they eliminated that problem but introduced a new one. The new problem is one that the old KIRIS design was intended to eliminate. Under the KIRIS system, schools were expected to show the greatest improvement when they were furthest from 100 and lesser improvement as they approached their goal. It was assumed that it would be easiest for a school to show large improvement when they were far from their goal and increasingly difficult as they approached the goal of 100. With CATS, the same amount of improvement is required in each two-year period regardless of a school's position in relation to 100.

When KIRIS was implemented in the early 1990s, it differed from the standards-based reform found in other states by imposing high rewards for successful schools and severe consequences for schools with poor performance. Teachers in Reward schools received cash bonuses of up to $2,500. Unsuccessful schools were labeled as being In Crisis and they faced severe sanctions. The staff in In Crisis schools was placed on probation and a Distinguished Educator assigned to supervise reclamation of the school. These Distinguished Educators were given sweeping powers. They could order teachers to change the way they were teaching, and if the teachers did not comply, they could be fired. Although the power was rarely invoked, the mere threat had a chilling effect on staff members. Teachers were often afraid to question any suggestions made by the Distinguished Educator. The poisoned climate led to an increased rate of resignations in the affected schools. Parents of students in In Crisis schools had to be notified by mail that their school was a failure, and they were to be given the opportunity to transfer. With the change to CATS, the designation of In Crisis and the consequences to the teacher were eliminated. Although the threatened consequences were understandably unpopular with teachers and they advocated their elimination, during the eight years this rule was in effect, only nine schools were ever labeled In Crisis. Most of these schools were guilty of no more than doing too well the previous cycle and therefore being cursed with an impossible-to-achieve threshold. No teachers were ever dismissed based on the recommendation of a Distinguished Educator.

The primary effect of HB 53 on the consequences was to eviscerate them. Schools that reach their goals get reward money, and the amount can be sizable. The school council decides how the money is to be used, and they can distribute it to the faculty if they choose. The sanctions for schools that fail to reach their goals have been greatly weakened. To be identified as a school that is below their Assistance line can certainly be embarrassing, but it is a lot better than being labeled In Crisis and maybe closed. A school performing below its Assistance line is required to undergo a Scholastic Audit to determine whether the school needs Commonwealth Improvement Funds or the assistance of a Highly Skilled Educator. It can be anticipated that most principals will conclude that the funds will be more useful than the advice of a consultant. The accountability system has been ameliorated in another way. Although schools are supposed to have reached an accountability index of 100 by 2014, the way CATS is structured, a school could be a standard error below at 80 and still be considered to be making satisfactory progress. A school could be rewarded by having its students obtain an average score of High Apprentice with none achieving a score of Proficient, the supposed goal of Kentucky's accountability plan.

Conspicuous by its absence in HB 53 is any mention of performance assessments. The KBE and the KDE finally realized that the performance assessments in past iterations of KIRIS did not work, and they were eliminated. They also recognized that labeling a constructed-response formatted test a *performance assessment* was dishonest. On the other hand, writing portfolios, which have proved to be the least reliable of any of the previously used measures, continue to be included as part of a school's accountability score.

Combining the results of multiple-choice tests with those from constructed-response items poses another challenging technical problem. Although the contractor, McGraw-Hill, has considerable experience and expertise in this area, the publisher concedes that the assumptions upon which this scaling methodology is based are wildly implausible.

One of the principal complaints about KIRIS voiced by teachers was that schools were being evaluated based on cohorts of students from different years. Since KERA was first implemented, teachers have asserted that these cohorts can differ dramatically. Eighth-graders in one year might contain many high-achieving students, whereas in the following year the students may be much weaker. Teachers have urged the adoption of longitudinal comparisons because these differences between cohorts have made comparisons between years unfair. HB 53 mandated the use of longitudinal comparisons. This legislation also required the inclusion of credit for successful student performance in sanctioned events with an established protocol of adjudication, such as band contests. The committees given responsibility for the design of CATS were given considerable latitude in the structure of CATS, and they decided that it would be too difficult to include either band contests or longitudinal results in a school's accountability index. Information about school performance in band contests appears only on the school report card.

Restandardizing CATS

Setting cut-points, the score that differentiates between passing and failing, is the most difficult aspect of standards-based assessment. The task becomes more difficult as the number of cut-points that must be set increases. With KIRIS, distinctions had to be made among the four categories of Novice, Apprentice, Proficient, and Distinguished. In their training, scorers are given verbal descriptions and examples of what the various standards are supposed to mean, and they make the ultimate decisions about each student response. The number of distinctions increased with CATS because different levels were designated within the Novice and Apprentice categories. Efforts are made to "moderate" the grader's standards for scoring student answers to make them more consistent. The scores are also adjusted statistically to correct for differences in difficulty among items.

In spring 2001, the KBE decided to change the way the grading standards for CATS were set. The scoring system had always used absolute standards because KERA demanded a high level of academic achievement for all Kentucky students regardless of how the typical students were performing at the time. It had always been recognized that Kentucky students had a long way to go before they reached the high levels expected of them, but KERA was supposed to bring students up to the point that they were Proficient by 2014.

During the first six years of KIRIS, the scores of elementary schools increased about 15 points, middle schools about 6, and high schools about 11. As shown in Table 8.1, by 1998, this brought elementary schools up to a little less than 50, high schools to a point a little above 50 and middle schools to 44.

An examination of the results of KIRIS over the years revealed that the improvement that had been achieved in the first six years resulted primarily from having students move from the Novice to the Apprentice category, not to the Proficient category, the stated goal of KERA. Much of the improvement from Novice to Apprentice came from inducing students who were leaving their answer sheets blank and being labeled Novice, to write something down. Graders are allotted only seconds to grade each answer, so filling up a page, even if the content was not very good, could bring some of these Novice scores up to the Apprentice level. The most dramatic change in Table 8.1 is the large increase in performance in 1999 and 2000. These increases do not represent any real improvement in student performance. They are instead the result of changes in scoring that occurred with the introduction of CATS.

TABLE 8.1   Average KIRIS Accountability Scores Across Levels

Year	Elementary	Middle School	High School
1992	33.4	37.5	40.0
1993	35.7	37.4	34.9
1994	40.9	41.8	43.3
1995	47.1	44.5	44.6
1996	45.2	41.0	43.3
1997	49.0	45.6	50.4
1998	48.8	43.9	51.3
1999	60.0	50.0	60.0
2000	61.0	51.0	61.0

Although the modified scoring associated with CATS provided an initial boost, it was not sufficient to bring students up to the KIRIS goal of 100 points or even to the 80 points that were defined as the goal under CATS. It had become obvious that having students in a school average 80 points was unrealistic. The solution was to turn CATS into a norm-referenced assessment. With the standards-based system upon which the KERA assessment was originally based, students are not compared with one another; they must reach an externally established standard. There is no guarantee that students will reach the desired high level of performance. Norm-referenced scaling presumes a normal distribution of student achievement in which half of all students will be above and half below the mean. The adoption of norm-referenced scaling made it possible to redefine Proficient as statistically average. The statistical goals of KERA are much more easily achieved using this system, and furthermore, no actual increase in student achievement is required.

To use norm-referenced interpretations of test performance properly, test items need to have a level of difficulty that ensures that student scores are spread across the distribution with some students at the top and some at the bottom. CATS is a difficult test on which almost all students are in the lower half of the possible distribution of scores. In some subject matter areas and grade levels, only a few students perform above the Apprentice level. If norm-referenced assessment was to be adopted, the difficulty of the items should have been adjusted so that student performance would be closer to a normal distribution. The changes in scaling were done behind the scenes with little public discussion, and it is unlikely that many educators, much less the public, understand the scaling issues. Making the difficulty of the items appropriate to the scale would have signaled an important change in CATS, and this is something that the KDE and the KBE were not anxious to do. As a result, a norm-referenced scaling scheme has been imposed on a very difficult test intended to measure absolute standards. The result is an assessment that has far worse psychometric characteristics than it would have had it been properly constructed. It is also an assessment for which a student's answer can be considered Distinguished even if it is incorrect.

Changing the standards on an accountability system employing constructed responses graded on a four-point scale (a polytomously scored test) is much more complex than doing so with a multiple-choice-based system in which items are scored as either right or wrong (dichotomously scored). With this latter system, to make it easier for students to pass without changing the items, all that needs to be done is set the cut-scores lower. With a polytomously scored, predominantly constructed-response test such as CATS, the definitions of Novice, Apprentice, Proficient, and Distinguished need to be changed to make them more easily attainable.

When the KBE decided to set new performance standards for CATS, they had to select a method. The Angoff method is the most widely used. It is implemented by having judges examine each item and decide what the probability is that a minimally competent student would get the item correct. It sets absolute standards, and for this reason, it would not solve the problem that the KBE needed to solve, which was that Kentucky students did not show improvement when compared with these sorts of standards. Furthermore, the Angoff method is appropriate for use only with dichotomously scored tests.

The KBE decided to pilot-test three methods of standard setting. The resulting study was a large-scale, complex, expensive study. It was their intention to select the best method or combination of methods from among the three. The CTB Bookmark, the Jaeger-Mills, and Contrasting Groups methods were compared. The CTB Bookmark method developed by McGraw-Hill, the contractor for the Kentucky assessments, is the most widely used of the three and has the advantage of being appropriate for use with both dichotomous and polytomous items. To implement the CTB Bookmark method, the contractor placed all of the items, including both constructed-response and multiple-choice, on a continuum, according to their difficulty. Each constructed-response item appeared four times to represent the four types of responses that corresponded with the NAPD scale. Judges, teachers, and other educators were asked to decide where on the continuum the cut-point between each NAPD level should be made. With the Jaeger-Mills method, judges reviewed each student response (content/grade specific) associated with a spring 2000 scale score. The median scale score of the responses judged to be at the dividing point between each level was used to determine each cut-point. The Contrasting Groups method used teachers to identify students they considered to be in each of the NAPD levels. The student's actual performance was then related back to these teacher appraisals. The result from each of the three methods was given to a committee established to sift through the results and provide the KBE with a number of options for setting the cut-scores. The CTB Bookmark method worked best and seemed to comport with what the panel expected. The Jaeger-Mills method was awkward and difficult to interpret, and the Contrasting Groups method yielded wildly high scores.

Although the panel was only supposed to provide a set of options to the KBE from which they were to choose, they went ahead and actually set the standards. Their recommendations were allowed to stand, and the standards were applied to the 2000 results and disseminated. This proved embarrassing because the KDE had already posted the results of the 1999 and 2000 administration using the original scaling methods. The contrasts were dramatic. This release of results undercut the claims of the KDE and the KBE that the new standards were adopted because the old standards could not be applied to CATS.

Table 8.2 shows the percentage of students in either the Proficient or the Distinguished category for each of the subject areas assessed in the elementary schools. Table 8.3 shows the same for middle school students, and Table 8.4 for high school students. As can be seen, there was no real progress in moving students into the higher categories in 1999 and 2000 when the old standards were used. When these new standards were applied retrospectively to the 2000 data, in some subjects there are only modest changes, whereas in others the differences are dramatic.

At one time, it seemed unlikely that Kentucky schools would ever reach the goal of 100 by 2012 or even the more modest,

TABLE 8.2 Percentage of Elementary Students in the Proficient or Distinguished Categories

Content Areas	1993	1994	1995	1996	1997	1998	1999	2000	2000*
Reading	8	11	30	31	41	33	32	32	57.0
Math			18	14	19	20	21	25	34.0
Science	2	2	5	3	6	6	5	5	37.0
Social Studies	8	13	18	13	13	15	13	14	42.0
Arts and Humanities	1	1	1	2	3	3	5	5	15.6
Practical Living and Vocational Studies	2	3	3	3	4	6	6	7	50.0
Writing on Demand			3	3	3	5	2	5	
Writing Portfolio			16	13	16	17	22	23	

*Percentage of students in Proficient and Distinguished categories using the new revised standards.

TABLE 8.3 Percentage of Middle School Students in the Proficient or Distinguished Categories

Content Areas	1993	1994	1995	1996	1997	1998	1999	2000	2000*
Reading	11	19	13	13	18	15	13	12	53
Math			30	28	34	29	33	37	28
Science	2	1	2	1	1	1	1	1	37
Social Studies	10	16	21	13	15	12	10	12	31
Arts and Humanities	6	8	7	6	8	6	7	8	37
Pracactical Living and Vocational Studies	4	5	5	4	6	7	8	7	40
Writing on Demand			4	2	4	7	6	8	
Writing Portfolio			15	11	14	13	10	11	

*Percentage of students in Proficient and Distinguished categories using the new revised standards.

TABLE 8.4 Percentage of High School Students in the Proficient or Distinguished Categories

Content Areas	1993	1994	1995	1996	1997	1998	1999	2000	2000*
Reading	4	12	11	9	32	28	29	33	30
Math			16	23	28	27	33	33	29
Science	4	9	12	10	14	13	12	14	28
Social Studies	6	19	19	13	23	29	30	31	26
Arts and Humanities	2	4	1	2	1	4	4	5	21
Practical Living and Vocational Studies	2	4	4	2	7	6	7	7	53
Writing on Demand			2	1	5	23	9	13	
Writing Portfolio			19	20	21	22	24	24	

*Percentage of students in Proficient and Distinguished categories using the new revised standards.

redefined goal of 80 by 2014. Although there has been no real change in student achievement, by adding additional levels within Novice and Apprentice and adopting norm-referenced scaling, these goals are now attainable, at least for some schools.

Philosophy

In order to judge the effectiveness of educational reform in Kentucky, it is necessary to consider its purpose. KIRIS/CATS is not based on a consistent philosophy. It is instead the product of several conflicting philosophies. These philosophical disagreements reflect the deep divisions among educators across the nation.

At the same time that Kentucky courts were demanding changes in the state's educational system to make them more financially equitable, the business community began pressuring the governor and legislature to do something about the poor quality of the job applicants they were encountering. To politicians and business leaders, the solution to this problem could be found in the use of accountability based on testing. They were unaware of the controversies surrounding different instructional philosophies. The staff of the KDE had a deep commitment to the principles of progressive education, and they were willing to strike a bargain with the political and business advocates of education reform. They would implement a form of assessment to be used for accountability as long as they controlled the format of the assessment and the type of instruction that would be supported. Business and political leaders know little about instructional methods and are willing to accept the proposition that old and ineffective methods are actually new and promising. Student-centered instructional methods were not widely employed in Kentucky before the implementation of KERA, and it is not easy to see how progressive education beliefs can be made compatible with standards-based reform. It is unfair to require teachers to implement methods that are known to be ineffective in increasing student achievement, and then evaluate the teachers based on their students' performance.

Historically, the purpose of instruction in this country has been increasing student academic achievement. This is not the purpose of progressive education, which prefers to be judged by standards other than student academic performance. The Kentucky reform presents a paradox, a system structured to require increasing levels of academic performance while supporting a set of instructional methods that are hostile to the idea of increased academic performance.

Evaluating the Technical Qualities of KIRIS

Describing the technical characteristics of the Kentucky assessment systems in a compendious form is quite difficult. First, both KIRIS and CATS are incredibly complex. They have many parts, some of which have received almost no publicity. There are aspects of these systems about which only a handful of people in the state have any knowledge. Some of these aspects play a critical role in determining which schools are labeled successful and which are to be called failures. In designing this assessment program, numerous implementation decisions had to be made, and the wisdom of each of these requires consideration. A complete elaboration of these issues would require at least a book and perhaps more than one volume.

When the system was being designed in 1990, the Kentucky Department of Education and Advanced Systems for Measurement and Evaluation (ASME) were under enormous pressure to have the system up and running quickly. They had to assemble the system expeditiously without the luxury of time to consider alternatives. Their decisions were strongly influenced by distrust for conventional measurement doctrine, and they were under pressure to embrace the popular alternative assessment techniques of the day. They also believed that the first priority of the system was improving instruction. Its technical qualities were relegated to a secondary role.

Formal criticisms of the technical qualities of KIRIS have been documented in four reports, each written by nationally recognized experts with impeccable credentials. Each concluded that there were serious problems with KIRIS. No formal studies of the technical qualities of CATS have been published as of yet.

The first report was released on February 16, 1995. It was con-
ducted under the auspices of the Kentucky Institute for
Educational Research (KIER), which contracted with the
Evaluation Center at Western Michigan University in
Kalamazoo, Michigan.[4] The report is titled *Evaluation of the
Development and Implementation of KIRIS Through December
1994*. The director of the Evaluation Center was Daniel
Stufflebeam, one of the nation's leading experts on evaluation.
This report is commonly known as the *KIER Report*. The second
report was released on June 20, 1995, and was prepared for the
Office of Educational Accountability (OEA) of the Kentucky
General Assembly. This report is referred to as the *OEA Report*.[5]
The panel that prepared the report included Ronald Hambleton
from the University of Massachusetts, Richard Jaeger from the
University of North Carolina at Greensboro, Daniel Koretz from
the Urban Institute, Robert Linn from the University of
Colorado at Boulder, Jason Millman from Cornell University,
and Susan Phillips from Michigan State University. The *OEA
Report* concluded that KIRIS was so fatally flawed that it could
not legitimately be used for making any decisions. The third
report is called the *Catterall Report* and is titled *Kentucky
Instructional Results Information System: A Technical Review*.[6] The
Legislative Review Committee of the Kentucky legislature com-
missioned this report. It was intended to provide a basis for legislation that was expected to implement changes in KIRIS during
the 1998 legislative session. The *Catterall Report* echoes the serious concerns voiced in the previous two reports. A fourth report
written by Daniel M. Koretz and Sheila I. Barron was published
in the fall of 1998. It focuses on the validity of the KIRIS
accountability scores. It was produced by RAND and is titled *The
Validity of Gains in Scores on the Kentucky Instructional Results
Information System*.[7]

Reliability

The computation of the reliability of conventional achievement
and aptitude tests is relatively simple, and most of the technical
manuals that accompany standardized tests are overflowing with

these coefficients. An examination of Buros's *Mental Measurement Handbooks*, which provides technical information and critical reviews of all major aptitude and achievement tests, includes few that have weaknesses in this area. Reliability is the *sine qua non* of test construction, and it is not difficult to create highly reliable tests.

Whereas reliability is usually established for the scores of individual students, for the KIRIS/CATS assessment, it must be based on school scores. It is much more difficult to establish reliability for school scores than for individual scores. A test is reliable to the extent that it is characterized by only small amounts of error. There is a multiplicity of different sources of error variance associated with Kentucky's tests. Not only is there variability in students across items, but there also is variability in students within schools. There is also the error associated with the use of graders to evaluate student responses and error caused by the use of the twelve different test forms used with KIRIS and the six used with CATS.

Neither the KDE nor ASME has ever published properly computed reliability coefficients for either the individual student scores or the accountability index. The public has been told that the reliability of the school scores was acceptable but that the reliability of individual scores was not. For this reason, decisions about individual students cannot be made based on these scores. Reliability coefficients for the Accountability Scores assigned to schools have been reported, but they are based on an incorrect application of generalizability theory, which has resulted in inflated coefficients.[8]

The Reliability of Change Scores

The reliability of the accountability indexes would be important only if schools were evaluated based on the magnitude of these scores. With KIRIS/CATS, it is the difference between a school's accountability index and past scores that is used to assess schools, and it is the reliability of these differences that must be established. The difference between the two is called a "change score," and it is axiomatic in measurement that the reliability of change scores will always be lower than the reliability of the two scores upon which they are based. The KDE has always avoided any mention of problems with the reliability of change scores in their technical manual and other publications. Officials from the KDE have denied the significance of problems surrounding the reliability of change scores in several newspaper articles. The *OEA Report*[9] cites the *Standards for educational and psychological testing*[10] (1985) to confirm that the reliability of the KIRIS change scores can be expected to be lower than the reliability of the accountability indexes themselves.

Validity

The accountability scores from the KIRIS assessment have shown some increase over the years since its implementation. The average scores for each year across the three levels are provided in Table 8.1. The critical validity issue is whether these increases represent real improvement in academic achievement or reflect other factors, such as teachers preparing students for specific items, changes in test difficulty, or enhanced test-taking skills. These issues are addressed in all four of the external evaluations of KIRIS, and in each, it was concluded that the preponderance of evidence indicates that the increases do not reflect real improvement in overall academic achievement. Each year when the scores have been reported, the Kentucky Department of Education has announced with great fanfare that they provide proof that the reforms embodied in KERA have been successful in increasing student achievement. There is no evidence, other than testimonials and anecdotal reports, to support this position. The *OEA Report* responded to these periodic KDE announcements with the following analysis:

> . . . the reported gains in scores on KIRIS substantially overstate improvements in student achievement. Indeed, it is not clear whether any appreciable generalizable gains in achievement have been produced in some grades and subjects. The external evidence to which KIRIS scores can be compared fails to reflect the gains shown on KIRIS.[11]

The RAND report focuses on the question of whether the increases in the accountability scores represent improvement in overall student achievement.[12] RAND researchers compare student performance on KIRIS with reading and math performance on the NAEP test and eleventh- and twelfth-grade performance on the ACT test. They conclude that the increases in KIRIS accountability scores are not reflected in similar increases in scores on these external tests. In addition to the external evidence they cite, they collected internal evidence that they believe establishes that students perform better on reused items than on new items. They interpret this to mean that teachers are focusing their instruction on improving student performance on specific items rather than improving overall student knowledge. What they fail to emphasize is the degree to which increases in student performance across the years are mainly the result of three factors: (1) success in getting students to move from the Novice to the Apprentice levels; (2) the increase in the number of points awarded at the Novice and Apprentice levels; and (3) the rescaling of CATS.

The RAND report makes a number of suggestions for preventing the erosion of validity that RAND researchers have identified as having occurred with KIRIS. RAND researchers cite the likelihood that teachers and educators will do everything in their power to obtain higher scores when goals are overly ambitious and high stakes are based on student performance. They acknowledge that much of the inflation in state scores is unavoidable.

Lessons That Have Been Learned from Kentucky's Attempts to Establish Its Accountability System

All but one state has adopted statewide content standards and implemented an assessment program to determine whether students are achieving these goals. Kentucky was one of the first states to initiate a high-stakes accountability system, and from the beginning it showed a willingness to commit enormous resources to the reforming of its educational system. Some of the lessons that other states may be able to learn from Kentucky's experiences are described here.

1. Reexamine claims that all students can perform at the same high level.

An underlying assumption of KERA is that all students, including special education students with IEPs, can perform at the same high level. Other state reform programs make a similar claim. This marks a fundamental difference between traditionalism and progressive education. In the early twentieth century, when progressive education first gained influence, one of its major tenets was that students differed in their academic ability and could not all benefit from the traditional curriculum that was then in place. Progressives promoted the use of standardized tests to classify and track students. Traditionalists opposed the use of these tests and the tracking of students. They asserted that all students could learn at the same high level, which provides a contemporary justification for adopting the same high standards for all students.

To fully understand the policy, it is first necessary to parse the phrase "all students can learn at the same high level." If this phrase is intended to mean that all students can answer high-level questions equally well or all students can learn at the same rate, this assertion is false. Responding to high-level questions is a function of intelligence, and students differ in their possession of that trait. Students who are more intelligent also learn more quickly. This does not mean that all or at least most students cannot learn the same content, with the caveat that some academic content is beyond the ability of students at the low end of the intellectual continuum.

Kentucky and other states have gotten into trouble when they have gone too far with their assertion that all students can function at the same high level. Kentucky even requires this high level of performance from students diagnosed as requiring special education. States need to be realistic in their demands on students. Certainly, some states have overdone their tendency to excuse poor performance and give up on students too early. On the other hand, an assessment should not be structured in such a way that it repeatedly places students in circumstances where their failure is guaranteed.

2. Do not base state educational reform solely on the assessment of high-level thinking skills.

Many states, including Kentucky, have adopted policies that require their assessment to emphasize high-level thinking skills rather than mastery of the subject matter. This occurs for three reasons: (1) the content standards of many states are not sufficiently detailed to permit the measurement of actual achievement, (2) publishers prefer to include items assessing high-level thinking skills on standardized achievement tests, and (3) progressive educators prize process over content.

Quality of State Content Standards

Constructing high-quality content standards is difficult and expensive, and many states fall far short of the ideal. If a state's content standards are vague, cover only a select number of years, or do not provide adequate specificity, it will be difficult for the test publisher, with whom the state has contracted, to create a test that assesses content. Instead, test publishers can create the illusion of content validity by writing items that use content to assess high-level thinking skills. A bright student will be able to correctly answer the questions using reasoning skills even if he or she does not know the content well, but a student who does know the content and who is not blessed with great reasoning ability will get them wrong. The result is a test that appears to have content validity, but does not have construct validity because it is measuring higher-level thinking skills rather than achievement.

Test Construction Methods

Test publishers often rely on items that assess high-level thinking skills when faced with inadequate content standards as described above. There is a second reason why publishers like to include this sort of item on their tests. The psychometrists that create these tests generally believe that the most important characteristic of a test is internal consistency reliability as measured by Coefficient Alpha. They focus on this type of reliability because it is easy to compute and widely accepted, and tests with this quality are easily constructed. An examination of almost any technical manual for a standardized test will reveal that most of its pages are devoted to reporting Coefficient Alpha coefficients.

The highest Coefficient Alpha values are obtained when a single, internally consistent construct is measured. These conditions prevail for reading comprehension tests, for example. Other content, such as science and social studies, assessed on state tests is more multidimensional and tends to yield lower reliability coefficients. Since higher-level thinking skills represent a unitary construct, a test that includes many such items will be internally consistent. A social studies test constructed to focus on higher-level thinking will be more reliable than one that measures the mastery of social studies content. Tests also may end up with a lot of items measuring high-level thinking skills even if this was not the test publisher's intent. When the publisher conducts item analyses of its pilot tests, they use procedures that select items based on how much they contribute to reliability. Items measuring high-level thinking do this better than those that measure content and are therefore more likely to survive the item analysis process.

Progressive Education Philosophy

Progressive education philosophy tends to reject conventional assessment methods. When an assessment must be implemented, progressives tend to favor the assessment of higher-level thinking skills rather than requiring students to memorize or learn facts. They recognize that students with lower ability struggle with conventional tests, and they think tests that do not measure content and instead measure higher-level thinking skills will be fairer. In actuality, lower-ability students have even more trouble with such tests.

KERA and Higher-Level Thinking

The Kentucky Education Reform Act is predicated on the belief that all students and therefore all schools can perform at the same high level. This is not something that its creators wished were true; it is what they sincerely believed was true. This belief is incorporated into the structure of the assessment system in the strongest possible way. It is manifested in the original goal of having all schools achieve an accountability score of 100 by 2012 and the revised goal of 80 points by 2014.

The items used with KIRIS and now CATS are primarily constructed-response items. The items are quite difficult and generally require the application of higher-level thinking skills. In many cases, the items are far too difficult for students to even begin to make a response. This leads to a restricted range in student performance and a consequent diminution in reliability.

The futility of such an unrealistically high goal becomes evident when the released items from the test are examined. Some of the eleventh- and twelfth-grade items are so hard that students in graduate school would have a difficult time responding correctly to them. The idea that all high school students, including those who have been identified as needing special education accommodations, can eventually be brought up to a level of functioning where they can successfully answer these questions seems overly optimistic.

There is a strange disconnection between the designers and supporters of accountability systems such as those that have been implemented in Kentucky and the mainstream of cognitive science. In a letter to the editor that appeared in the *Louisville Courier* newspaper, Wilmer Cody, the former (1998) Commissioner of the Kentucky Department of Education, articulates the underlying assumptions of KERA as follows:

> Finally, a large body of research demonstrates that the most important factors governing how well children do in school have nothing to do with perceived differences in individual potential. On the contrary, children do well because of instructional leadership, a clear focus on academic achievement, high expectations, the quality of professional development, curriculum alignment, teacher skill, the effective use of learning time, and parental involvement.[13]

Although some of these factors are important and may play a role in how much students learn, it would be difficult to locate competent research that would demonstrate that these factors could overcome a student's lack of academic potential. There is extensive scientific evidence that contradicts the assertions made by Wilmer Cody.

3. Clearly delineate the content to be covered.

If teachers are to be held accountable for what their students have learned, they need to be given a clear description of exactly what students are supposed to learn. The logical sequence would be to adopt state content standards before developing the tests. Ideally, states need to go even further and specify the level at which students are to master the content. These content and performance standards provide the basis for a state's accountability system. In Kentucky, the process was reversed. The tests were developed first, and only later was the content defined.

When the KERA legislation was first implemented, six Learner Goals were specified. In addition, the KDE was supposed to create standards, which would identify what students should learn and determine the content to be included on the tests. At the same time, there was a sense of urgency about the need to get the testing program started. As a result, test items were written before standards were established. Since the program's inception, the standards have been chasing the tests. There have been six separate sets of standards published. These standards, in the order of their release, are the six Learner Goals, the Learner Outcomes, the Transformations, the Academic Expectations, the Content Guidelines, and the Core Content for Assessment. Each of these was intended to be the final word on what students were supposed to learn and the basis for the KIRIS assessment. These standards differ among themselves in terms of content and philosophy and provide minimal guidance for teachers endeavoring to prepare students for the KIRIS/CATS assessment. Throughout the implementation of KERA, the high standards implicit in the assessment have remained fixed in the test itself, but have never been clearly delineated in the published standards.

Kentucky assesses students three times in each subject, once in elementary school, once in middle school, and once in high school. Because of this schedule, the KDE decided to define only three sets of content standards. There is much that students need to learn in the grades between those being assessed, so the test authors are forced to make assumptions about what students should have learned in the years between those being assessed. They also must assume that students have mastered the lower-level skills, which is difficult to do if they are not spelled out. A more precise assessment of students will arise from a test that includes items that cover a range of difficulty, and this is hard to do if the content standards are restricted to just one year. Although it is a lot of trouble, states need to have content standards for every year. This allows them to construct properly sequenced tests.

The Kentucky content standards have another problem, one that is shared by many other states, particularly states with comprehensive and demanding content standards. The usual method of creating content standards is to put content specialists in charge. For example, the committee responsible for writing the math content standards might include specialists in math from the state department of education, math teachers from the public schools, school of education faculty, and math professors from arts and sciences units at state colleges and universities. All of these specialists share one important idea: A love of math, a recognition of its importance, and the belief that every educated person needs know a lot about this subject. As a result, they create content standards in math that are ambitious and require every student to be able to perform at a high level in math. Implicit in these content standards is the assertion that a considerable part of the school day should be devoted to instruction in this topic. The content standards for social studies, science, and arts and humanities are assembled with similar committees, as are the standards for the other subject areas. The authors of content standards in these content areas are no less committed to the field in which they specialize and the importance of its coverage in depth than those whose task it is to write the math standards. They would never agree that only a small proportion of the educational day should be devoted to their field in order to leave more time for math, science, or whatever. What this means, in practice, is that the content standards for each area are written in isolation, with each committee ensuring comprehensive coverage of their field. What is ignored are the limits imposed by the length of the school day. There is simply not enough time to include everything that these different specialists believe is important. This problem is exacerbated in Kentucky by the inclusion of arts and humanities and practical living/vocational studies in addition to the usual reading, math, science, and social studies. The leadership needed to tone down the requirements of some fields in order to have a reasonable range of content is just not there. The breadth of content listed in Kentucky's Core Content for Assessment, like the content standards of many other states, is so broad that it could never be covered.

4. Ensure that the instructional philosophy promoted by the department matches the instructional philosophy that underlies the state's educational reform.

The Kentucky Education Reform Act (KERA) was presented to the legislature as a conventional standards-based education reform, similar to the programs now adopted in forty-nine of fifty states. It was intended to define what students needed to know, to assess them to see if they had learned this content, and to hold principals and teachers accountable for their performance. The governor, the legislative leaders, and business leaders assumed that such a system would force students and teachers to work harder, which would lead to an improvement in student academic achievement. They strongly believed that a good school was one in which students demonstrated a high level of academic achievement. What they did not realize was that by placing control of Kentucky's educational reform in the hands of the KDE, they were empowering an administrative body infused with a progressive education philosophy that was the antithesis of the traditionalist philosophy of KERA.

Although a rejection of academic achievement as a criterion for judging the worth of schools may seem strange to noneducators, most of the established national organizations devoted to teacher training likewise reject academic achievement as an unworthy goal for public schools. For example, the state of Kentucky, like many other states, requires that teachers graduate from an education school that is accredited by the National Council for Accreditation of Teacher Education (NCATE). A careful reading of the NCATE standards and the voluminous supporting materials that accompany them will fail to identify any commitment to student achievement.

Kentucky has invested an enormous amount of money, along with teacher and student time, in a system that is devoted to increasing student achievement by imposing high-stakes standards. At the same time, it has handed control over the system to a department of education that is committed to the belief that academic achievement is not important. One of the most controversial aspects of the original KERA legislation was the requirement that the first three years of schools be ungraded. This meant that students who in most school systems would be separated into first, second, and third grade had to be grouped together in a primary class. This requirement was controversial and unpopular, and it was eventually modified to the point that it became an option rather than a mandate. Robert Slavin, in a review of the literature on nongraded elementary schools, co-authored with Roberto Guitterrez (1992), found inconsistencies in the achievement of students in nongraded classes.[14] They explained the inconsistency by attributing it to differences in instructional methods employed in successful and unsuccessful programs. Successful ungraded classes coupled direct instruction with effective methods of cross-age grouping. Those that were unsuccessful used student-centered instruction rather than direct instruction. The review asserts, "Individualized instruction, learning stations, learning activity packets, and other individualized or small group activities reduce direct instruction time with little corresponding increase in appropriateness of instruction to individual needs" (369). It also states that "to the degree that nongraded elementary schools came to resemble the open school, the research finding few achievement benefits to this approach takes on increased importance" (368). In the studies he reviewed, direct instruction methods were consistently favored over progressive education approaches. At about the same time that this review of literature was published, the Kentucky Department of Education distributed a manual to all elementary school principals titled *Best Practices in Ungraded Classrooms*. In this document, they listed what schools should and should not do when implementing the ungraded primary program. They urged schools to employ the instructional practices that Slavin found were ineffective and cautioned against adopting the practices that he recommended.

5. Avoid use of the term "criterion-referenced."

Criterion-referenced assessment (CRT) was first proposed for use with mastery learning by Robert Glaser.[15] At the time, mastery learning was considered a wonderful new instructional technique that would revolutionize education in the United States. This instructional method required that everything students were to learn be defined with behavioral objectives. Students were to learn these objectives in an empirically derived optimum sequence. Student progress was to be reported in terms of a listing of objectives mastered, an approach he labeled "criterion-referenced" testing. James Popham is credited with popularizing the term during this time.

It turned out that CRT was not easily adapted for use in schools. One problem, among many, was that defining instructional goals using behavioral objectives was difficult for any but the most concrete content such as math. Although the use of CRTs to explicitly describe what a student has learned declined, use of the term "criterion-referenced testing" continued. Its use continued because the public tends to view CRTs in a positive light while remaining skeptical about norm-referenced tests (NRTs). Apparently, CRT does well in focus groups. Politicians, departments of education, and publishers like to describe their assessment as "criterion-referenced testing" even though what they are doing bears no relationship to what Glaser and Popham meant by the term. The inconsistency between existing practice and the original definition of criterion-referenced testing was resolved by changing the definition. The ultimate authority regarding correct definitions in measurement is the *Standards for Educational and Psychological Testing (Joint Standards)* published by the American Psychological Association, the NCME, and the AERA.[16] Here is how a criterion-referenced test is defined in that publication: "A test that allows its users to make score interpretations in relation to a functional performance level, as distinguished from those interpretations that are made in relation to the performance of others. Examples of criterion-referenced interpretations include comparisons to cut scores" (174). What this definition purports to do is contrast CRTs with NRTs, but according to this definition, any test that sets a cut-score can be considered a criterion-referenced test. Since cut-scores can be appended to any test, an NRT is easily turned into a CRT. As a result, the distinction between a CRT and an NRT has been blurred. It is probably best at this point to view the use of the term "criterion-referenced" as a public relations strategy rather than a functional definition of an assessment procedure. Almost all state testing programs are called criterion-referenced, regardless of their format.

6. Use norm-referenced measurement for school comparisons and standards-based assessment for students.

In setting up a reform program, states have two choices. They can use a norm-referenced or a standards-based approach. An evaluation of student performance based on a determination of how students compare with each other is referred to as norm-referenced assessment. Norm-referenced scales have a characteristic bell-shaped curve and are calibrated using means and standard deviations. Each point on a norm-referenced scale can be associated with a fixed proportion of test takers. Cut-scores designate the percentage of students who will pass and the percentage who will fail. Points on a scale that are defined in terms of percentages of students are called percentiles. The main disadvantage to this approach is that passing or failing is unrelated to absolute levels of performance. No matter how well or how poorly the overall group performs, these proportions are maintained. The most important advantage to norm-referenced tests is that scales created in this way have properties that permit them to be treated mathematically. The science of assessment is based on norm-referenced assessments, and much more precise comparisons can be made using these methods. Item analysis techniques have been developed that adjust item difficulty in ways that push a distribution into the bell-shaped curve that maximizes reliability. The more sophisticated techniques of item-response theory require a norm-referenced approach.

Standards-based assessment interprets test scores by comparing them with absolute standards. Such comparisons can be more meaningful than merely comparing a student with other students. A determination of the desired level of student performance is designated ahead of time, and once this cut-score is established, passing or failing does not depend on how other students have performed. This means that the percentage of students who pass will not be known until the test is administered. Standards-based assessment is much more compatible with the underlying principles of standards-based reform than norm-referenced assessment. There are two primary disadvantages to the use of standards-based assessment: (1) tests developed in this way tend to have undesirable mathematical properties, and (2) setting cut-scores can be difficult.

Ideally, a standards-based test should consist of a set of items written at a difficulty level that assures that a student who is functioning at the appropriate academic level will get the items correct and the student who is not will get them wrong. A test constructed in this way will efficiently discriminate between those who have mastered and those who have not mastered the content. Standards-based assessment requires the implicit assumption that students can be divided into these two categories. It requires that the majority of students be at the extremes rather than in the center, as you would expect if the scores were normally distributed. Even if this assumption is satisfied, such a test will have dreadful psychometric qualities and scores from such a test should not be added together to create a school score. Kentucky, like many other states, creates elaborate school indexes based on this type of assessment. Because CATS has been changed to a norm-referenced test, there is no reason to maintain the item difficulty structure implemented when the test was standards-based, and there are even stronger reasons to change it. Other states have chosen a different path and performed extensive item analysis procedures on tests that are supposed to be standards-based. It is a mistake to use norm-referenced techniques to develop a standards-based test and wrong to use the assumptions of standards-based testing to create a norm-referenced test. When these sorts of mistakes are made, the quality of the test suffers, which usually means lower reliability. Although the standards-referenced approach has intuitive appeal, particularly in the evaluation of individual student performance, it provides a poor basis for comparing the performance of schools. It is better to use a norm-referenced approach to compare schools for accountability purposes.

7. Performance standards should have a rational basis.

Setting performance standards (assigning cut-points) is one of the most difficult problems in all of measurement. The job is even more of a challenge when there is a need for multiple cut-points, which is the case with CATS. Furthermore, CATS consists of a mixture of dichotomous and polytomous items, which makes the process of setting cut-scores even more difficult. Not only is there no accepted method of setting performance standards, there is serious doubt about whether a workable method for setting cut-scores even exists. The consensus expert on this topic was Richard M. Jaeger (now deceased). He was selected to write the chapter in the *Third Edition of the Educational Measurement Handbook*[17] (1989) that focused on standard setting. In reviewing the literature on standard setting, he cites the empirical research of

> . . . Poggio, Glasnapp, and Eros (1981),[18] showing that test standards depend heavily on the methods used to derive them, and results reported by Jaeger, Cole, Irwin and Pratto[19] (1980), showing that test standards vary markedly across types of judges used with a single standard-setting procedure. Linn et al. (1982)[20] conclude that thousands of students would be declared competent or incompetent in most statewide competency-testing programs on the basis of methodological decisions that have nothing to do with their abilities.

Both Glass (1978)[21] and Shepard (1979, 1980)[22] note that competence is by virtually all conceptions, a continuous variable. Setting a cutoff score that supposedly divides students into two distinct categories, the competent and the incompetent, is therefore unrealistic and illogical. Shepard argues strongly against the use of any single method of standard setting, and Glass would have us abandon competence testing altogether. (492)

Lest you note the dates associated with these conclusions and assume that better methods must be available by now, consider the 1999 report from National Research Council.[23] It explains that the National Assessment Governing Board (NAGB) has expended considerable resources studying how best to set the performance standards for the National Assessment of Educational Progress. Because NAEP scores are reported in terms of the achievement levels of "below basic," "basic," "proficient," and "advanced," the cut-points between them must be designated. There have been a series of reports criticizing the way these cut-points are set (Linn et al.[24] and Pellegrino et al.[25]). These reports have had as their particular focus NAGB's use of the Modified Angoff method. Although this method has been deemed inappropriate for setting the cut-points between achievement levels on the NAEP, no one has come up with a better way of doing it. The NAEP test is purely norm-referenced. Attaching cut-points to a norm-referenced test does not work well because its characteristic bell-shaped curve is not appropriate for this sort of standard setting. In 1978, Glass made what is still considered to be the definitive statement on standard setting, "To my knowledge, every attempt to derive a criterion measure [cut-scores] is either blatantly arbitrary or derives from a set of arbitrary premises" (258).[26]

Kentucky uses graders to place responses to constructed-response questions into the appropriate category. In doing this, they are making decisions about whether student performance is Novice, Apprentice, Proficient, or Distinguished. This approach does not work for multiple-choice items. For multiple-choice items, a decision must be made regarding the number of items that must be correctly answered in order to place a student into a particular category. McGraw-Hill has devised methods for combining constructed-response and multiple-choice items and placing them on the same scale. This method is called the CTB Bookmark method, and it is currently being used to scale the Kentucky assessment. Like other standard-setting methods, it requires judges to make arbitrary decisions about the cut-point between acceptable and unacceptable performance. Because it uses information about students' previous performance on the items, it is essentially a norm-referenced approach. Although it may seem ideal to be able to set absolute standards without reference to average performance, such a practice can lead to indefensible performance standards.

Advocates of standards-based reform are committed to the adoption of policies that will lead to higher academic performance. At the same time, it is important for states to set realistic standards. Ideally, standards should not be set so high that students cannot possibly meet them or so low that they become meaningless. Setting performance standards in this way is extraordinarily difficult. Standard setting is complex, and quite often, states end up with standards that were not what was intended. In most cases, this means cut-points are set too high.

While assigning cut-scores to tests constructed using norm-referenced methods may seem antithetical to standards-based reform, the use of standards-based assessment assumes that it is possible to make reasonable expectations of how students should perform prior to seeing the results of the student performance. Experience has shown this to be an implausible assumption. What tends to happen is that when reasonable people set minimal standards for what students need to know, they tend to overestimate acceptable student performance to a considerable degree. These overly ambitious performance standards stem from the same processes that lead to unrealistic content standards. Like content standards, performance standards tend to be set by subject matter specialists, either active teacher or university faculty. It is natural for them to believe that their own field is of utmost importance and to want students to aspire to the highest levels of performance in their areas. As is true with the setting of content goals, experts setting performance standards tend to narrowly focus on their own standards and ignore the time needed for other subject areas. When these standards are applied to student performance, the failure rate tends to be too high. When this occurs, the pressure from the community can be overwhelming, and as a result, the cut-scores are adjusted. The revised cut-scores end up being made on the basis of typical performance, which renders the decisions norm-referenced anyway.

8. Use a multiple-choice rather than a constructed-response/essay format.

Although the initial version of KIRIS, introduced in 1992, included multiple-choice items, performances on these items were not included in school accountability indexes. Eventually it was decided that the costs of having them written and scored, along with the amount of student time they required, could not be justified if they were not going to be used to compute school accountability indexes. The selection of performance assessments and constructed response items rather than a multiple-choice format was not based on sound measurement principles. It was based on hostility toward conventional assessment practices and a commitment to "cutting-edge" assessment methods. Multiple-choice items were viewed as an old-fashioned way of assessing students. This also was a time of great excitement about the potential of authentic testing, and it was the intention of the designers of KIRIS to have this assessment eventually be based only on performance assessments and portfolios.

When performance tests proved to be impractical, unreliable, and too expensive, the test had to depend almost entirely on constructed-response items. Although the problems associated with performance assessments also characterized the portfolios, the portfolios had such a strong constituency that their use has continued. In 1998, the Kentucky state legislature, in HB 53, mandated the use of multiple-choice items despite the objections of the KBE and the KDE. Multiple-choice items now contribute to a third of each content area score.

The most efficient, reliable, and economical way to make the sort of decisions that KIRIS was intended to make is with multiple-choice items. Multiple-choice and constructed-response items serve different purposes. Multiple-choice items are most useful for making comparative decisions about student and school levels of achievement. Constructed-response items are useful for communicating what students know and what they do not know. On the large-scale assessments administered in most states, including Kentucky, schools receive information only about student scores. The results of the spring administration are not released until the end of the following September, too late to be of much use to teachers. Ironically, the constructed-response format requires far more time (and expense), which makes their use in providing timely information about individual student performance impractical. Even if the results could be provided in a timely fashion, information about how each student performed on specific items is not provided, so the most important advantage to the constructed-response format is lost. For the purpose served by the Kentucky tests and those of most other states, multiple-choice items are far better.

The decision by the authors of KIRIS/CATS to use a constructed-response format rather than rely on the more commonly used multiple-choice format was not based on effectiveness or even pragmatic considerations. Instead, the decision was based on misinformation and/or distrust of conventional standardized testing. Some of the reasons given for not using multiple-choice items are as follows:

- They can only measure the recall of facts and isolated pieces of information.
- They cannot be used to assess higher-level thinking processes.
- They represent an old-fashioned method of assessment that has since been replaced by more modern assessment techniques.

- They do not provide a fair measure of the achievement of non-Asian minorities and economically deprived students.

None of these assertions can withstand careful analysis. Not only can multiple-choice items be used to assess facts, dates, names, and isolated ideas, but they also can provide an effective measure of high-level thinking skills. Although they are not appropriate measures of creativity and organizational ability, they can be used to measure virtually any other level of cognitive functioning. Because economically disenfranchised and minority students do poorly on standardized tests and standardized tests are made up of multiple-choice items, there is the mistaken belief that it is the item format that is the problem. The gap between the performance of minority and nonminority is actually greater for constructed-response than multiple-choice items.[27]

Multiple-choice items have several important advantages over constructed-response items. First, they are much less expensive and more reliable. They are more reliable because it is possible to include more items when multiple-choice items are used.

Item difficulty is a major headache in the implementation of standards-based systems. Even small deviations from the ideal can lead to tests that are either too easy or too hard. Inappropriate item difficulty can have an enormous impact on the number of students who pass or fail an assessment. The difficulty of items must be carefully controlled from year to year or no comparisons across years will be meaningful. When multiple-choice items are coupled with norm-referenced assessments, item difficulty presents few problems. The difficulty of multiple-choice items is easily manipulated by adjusting the similarities of the distracters to the correct answer. The more similar the distracter, the more difficult the item is, and the more different the distracters, the easier the item is. Because difficulty can be easily manipulated, it is possible to maximize variability and achieve high test-score reliability. Because students are being compared with each other and a different average is established each year, differences in test difficulty from year to year present few problems. On the other hand, problems with item difficulty are exacerbated when constructed-response items are used. The only way to control the difficulty of constructed-response questions is to change their content.

The most important type of validity associated with the large-scale assessments of achievement is content validity. This form of validity refers to the fidelity with which a test can assess instructional objectives. Tests made up of constructed-response items can contain only a limited number of items because each item requires a lengthy response. As a result, tests made up of constructed-response items will be less valid than those that utilize the multiple-choice format.

Multiple-choice and constructed-response items are compared in an article published in the *Journal of Educational Measurement*. The article was written by R. Lukhele, David Thissen, and Howard Wainer and titled "On the Relative Value of Multiple-Choice, Constructed-Response, and Examinee-Selected Items on Two Achievement Tests."[28]

The test they chose to study was the Advanced Placement (AP) testing program of the College Board. This test is a good choice because the training of the examiners and the sophistication of the scoring methods used with the constructed-response items are "state of the art." Whatever defects the study uncovers in the scoring of the constructed-response items cannot easily be attributed to flaws in the training of the examiners or the methods they employed.

The article begins by making two important points: Constructed-response items are expensive, and the information that can be obtained from these items is similar to what can be obtained from multiple-choice items. The authors state:

> Constructed-response items are expensive. They typically require a great deal of time from the examinee to answer, and they cost a lot to score. In the AP testing program it was found that a constructed-response test of equivalent reliability to a multiple-choice test takes from 4 to 40 times as long to administer and is typically hundreds of thousands of times more expensive to score. (234)

With respect to the uniqueness of the information provided by constructed-response items, they state:

The primary motivation for the use of constructed-response formats thus stems from the idea that they can measure traits that cannot be tapped by multiple-choice items—for example, assessing dynamic cognitive processes. (235)

Their conclusion was as follows:

Overall, the multiple-choice items provide more than twice the information than the constructed-response items do. Examining the entire test (and freely applying the Spearman-Brown prophesy formula), we found that a 75-minute multiple-choice test is as reliable as a 185-minute test built of constructed-response questions. Both kinds of items are measuring essentially the same construct, and the constructed-response items cost about 300 times more to score. It would appear, based on this limited sample of questions, that there is no good measurement reason for including constructed-response items. (240)

On the basis of the data examined, we are forced to conclude that constructed-response items provide less information in more time at greater cost than do multiple-choice items. This conclusion is surely discouraging to those who feel that constructed-response items are more authentic and hence, in some sense, more useful than multiple-choice items. It should be. (245)

When the purpose of a statewide accountability assessment is to make decisions about the effectiveness of schools, a multiple-choice item format is obviously preferable. From a technical, measurement perspective, there is really no choice. Of course, one option is to compromise and include both multiple-choice and constructed-response items. This is what Kentucky and several other states have chosen to do. The problem with using both item types is that it creates scaling problems because of the difficulties associated with combining the two item types. It is more difficult to do this with standards-based than norm-referenced assessment programs.

9. Do not use performance assessments in large-scale assessments.

The KERA legislation specifically mandated an assessment based on the use of performance assessments and portfolios, but at the time of the law's enactment, there was no established methodology for implementing such a program, and there were no other states that could serve as models. Instead of starting with an entirely performance- and portfolio-based assessment, the initial strategy was to create an assessment that depended primarily on constructed-response questions and portfolios, along with some Performance Events, which were a first step in the direction of performance assessment. As experience in the use of performance assessments increased, KIRIS was supposed to become more dependent on their use. The use of constructed-response and multiple-choice items was expected to decline until the test included only alternative forms of assessment.

The Performance Events had some of the properties of a performance assessment. Proctors were sent to each school to place students into groups. Each group was given one performance task, which could be in math, science, or social studies. In some cases, the task required the manipulation of concrete objects or the creation of a product, but usually the task was in the form of a conventional essay question. The Performance Event tasks were constrained by practical limitations. They had to take place in a room, usually the cafeteria, within a fixed amount of time, with all graded responses in the form of an individual essay. Only these individual responses were included in the accountability indexes of schools.

The Performance Events were expensive and presented many logistical headaches. Proctors and graders had to be hired and trained, schools were disrupted while the assessment took place, and the special equipment and/or supplies required for some items had to be assembled. The proctors could never be sure what supplies would be available at the schools. In some cases, even the expectation that hot water would be available proved overly optimistic.

Although one-tenth of the KIRIS budget was devoted to the Performances Events, their technical qualities were so dismal that they not only made no positive contribution to the reliability of the accountability scores, their inclusion actually lowered it. The biggest problem with using performance assessments in a standards-based accountability system, other than poor reliability, is the impossibility of equating forms longitudinally from year to year or horizontally with other forms of assessment. In Kentucky, because of the amount of time required, each student participated in only one performance assessment task. As a result, items could never be reused from year to year because of the likelihood that students would remember the tasks and their responses. This made equating almost impossible. Despite technical consultants devoting a great deal of attention to this problem and the use of several different equating schemes, no approach seemed to work.

An indication of the instability of the Performance Events scores can be seen in the eighth-grade Performance Events scores in math. On the 1992–93 test, the Performance Events score in math was 44.68; on the 1993–94 test, it was 40.69; and on the 1994–95 test, the score was 2.62. This is not a typo or error in computation. It is an indication of the incomparability of scores across years. The correlation between the math Performance Events scores and the math constructed-response scores for the years between 1993, 1994, and 1995 are .1882, .3991, and .3777 respectively, while the correlation between the math constructed-response scores and arts and humanities constructed-response scores are .6881, .6117, and .6853. Obviously, the math constructed-response items were measuring something quite different from the math Performance Event scores. This lack of compatibility made combining the math Performance Events and math constructed-response items into a single math score, as was being done, indefensible. It would have made more sense, from a measurement perspective, to combine the math constructed-response scores with the arts and humanity scores than with the math Performance Events.

In the early spring of 1996, it was decided that the 1995 Performance Events scores could not be reported because of questions about their legitimacy. Nevertheless, the KDE approved the administration of these tests for the spring of 1996. In August 1996, the Kentucky Department of Education promulgated an emergency regulation that not only eliminated the

Performance Events from future administration, but also removed their scores from the baselines and accountability scores for the current biennium. In order to comply with the legislative mandate that the assessment be primarily performance-based by 1996, the KDE insisted that constructed-response items were a form of performance assessment. The 1998 legislation that modified KIRIS into CATS eliminated any reference to performance assessment.

After the Performance Events were eliminated, there was concern in the legislature about the enormous expense incurred for the administration of an assessment that could not be used. The Office of Education Accountability hired the firm of Coopers and Lybrand to conduct an audit to determine whether Advanced Systems in Measurement and Evaluation should reimburse the state for test materials that were unusable. The auditors were unable to complete this task because the alterations in the contract surrounding the elimination of the Performance Events were based on verbal agreements, and there were few written records. Change orders could not be located, and there was no way to match contract deliverables with the amounts invoiced. The issue was eventually dropped.

10. Avoid matrix sampling.

Matrix sampling requires the assembly of a large pool of items that covers everything in the content standards. A number of different tests are created, with each made up of different subsets of questions. Across the sample, the breadth of the content is covered, but each student is assessed on only part of this content. The use of matrix sampling increases content validity, but it does so at the cost of reliability and the loss of information about individual student performance. The overall reliability of the assessment is lower than it would be for nonmatrix sample tests, and it is far too low to support reporting individual student scores. Furthermore, individual scores lack content validity.

When the National Assessment of Educational Progress was designed, it was intended to evaluate the American education system as a whole. Only later was it used to compare states, and it was never intended for use in making comparisons below the state level. The restrictions on the levels at which scores could be reported that characterize matrix sampling were useful in obtaining the cooperation of local school district officials. They were reassured because the use of matrix sampling meant that scores could be reported only at the state level. Schools and school districts could agree to participate without fear that the results would be used to hold them accountable.

When the KIRIS assessment was designed, Advanced Systems in Measurement and Evaluation, the original contractor, was told to make the design of the assessment similar to the NAEP tests. Using the NAEP as their model, ASME included matrix sampling in the design of KIRIS. An assessment can be constructed to have an acceptable level of content validity through a process of randomly sampling content. The use of matrix sampling with KIRIS precluded the use of individual student scores. When students realize that they are not to be held accountable for their individual performance, their motivation lags and the validity of all scores, including those for individual schools, is harmed.

Tests must be equated from year to year and the inputs from tests over different content areas and different formats must be equated in order to make meaningful comparisons. Under the best of circumstances, when a large number of multiple-choice items are administered to a large sample of students, accurate equating is difficult to achieve. When constructed-response items are used with a standards-based system, equating becomes even more difficult. Adding the different forms that are required for matrix sampling makes the process nearly impossible.

For the above reasons, the use of matrix sampling is not recommended. The advantages of increased content validity are canceled by the loss in reliability. What is most surprising is that when Kentucky's assessment was revised in 1998, the matrix-sampling model was retained. This may have been the result of a misunderstanding of the nature and prerequisites of content validity or a commitment to the belief that individual scores should never be used.

11. Portfolios are inappropriate for large-scale assessments.

With KIRIS and now CATS, writing achievement is assessed using a writing portfolio and an on-demand writing task that is included with the constructed-response questions. Writing achievement is assessed at grades four, eight, and twelve. For the KIRIS portfolio assessment, students included five writing samples from their language arts class and a sixth selection from another class. In the interest of reducing the amount of class time devoted to assessment, CATS requires fourth-grade students to submit only four selections, and middle and high school students to submit five selections, which includes a selection from another class. Decisions about what is to be included in the portfolio are made by the student.

The writing portfolio is intended to serve two purposes: (1) to evaluate teachers, principals, and schools and (2) to improve student writing skills. Unfortunately, it is difficult to accomplish both purposes well. Advocates of the use of writing portfolios assert that their use increases the importance of writing and provides extensive practice for students. To do this effectively, teachers need to work closely with students. A good teacher will spend more time with weaker students and less with better students. If teachers extensively assist students in the preparation of their portfolios, the portfolios will no longer reflect student writing ability and will be an invalid measure of these skills. Extensive teacher assistance, particularly when it focuses on the lower-performing students, also suppresses variability and thereby lowers reliability. If policies are instituted that restrict the amount of assistance teachers are allowed to provide, the instructional value of portfolios will be diminished.

In Kentucky, teachers help students assemble their portfolios, which are graded at the student's school. Although some principals arrange the grading of portfolios in such a way that teachers do not grade their own student's portfolios, the ethical standards published by the KDE do not prohibit this practice. Giving teachers the responsibility for assisting in the assembly as well as the evaluation of portfolios, then using the results of this evaluation to measure teacher effectiveness creates a conflict of interest.

Portfolio scores have always been the most unreliable of any of the input data used for computing school accountability scores. Anomalies in the scoring of the portfolios become obvious when the breakdown of KIRIS scores across schools is examined. Many small schools have shown dramatic increases that are difficult to defend as reflecting legitimate increases in student writing performance. The average portfolio scores for some schools have made gains as great as 50 points, say from 20 to 70 (on the KIRIS/CATS 1 to 133 scale). It is possible for teachers to compromise the validity of the portfolio in two ways: (1) teachers can grade the portfolios of their own students too leniently, or (2) teachers can provide too much help to students in the writing of the selections included in the portfolio.

As the school administrator, the principal is responsible for both ensuring the integrity of the assessment and, at the same time, making sure that his or her school has adequate scores to obtain rewards and avoid punishment. Since KERA was implemented, principals have understood that the writing portfolios are the one aspect of the assessment that is completely controlled by teachers and the one that can be most easily manipulated. Rather than urging teachers to be objective in their evaluations, principals are more likely to pressure them to get higher scores. The more pressure that is placed on teachers to increase portfolio scores, the less effective portfolios will be as an assessment tool.

Reports from audits of portfolio scoring indicate the degree to which teachers are under pressure to be generous in their grading. Despite enormous efforts aimed at ensuring that teachers correctly grade portfolios, the audited results of randomly selected portfolios are startling. An examination of Table 8.5 reveals the percentage of scores assigned by auditors that differed from those assigned by teachers. Only at the Novice level did auditors grade the portfolio higher as often as lower. At the other three levels, the auditors almost always assigned lower scores than the teacher.

TABLE 8.5   Percentage of Auditor Scores That Differed from
Those Assigned by the Teacher

Category	4th Grade	8th Grade	12th Grade
Novice	22	4	10
Apprentice	10	25	22
Proficient	24	44	44
Distinguished	71	94	91

In response to concerns about the level of assistance students received in the creation of portfolios entries, the KDE published a set of ethical guidelines in 1996, which were approved as regulations. The 1996 guidelines included a blanket statement that teachers could not make corrections on student work. Because of controversies surrounding this regulation, the standards were rewritten in 1999. Instead of referring to student work in general, the new document focused on the entries that were to go into the writing portfolio. This is not as much of a change as it seems because almost anything a student writes can be included in his or her portfolio. From among all possible entries, the student chooses the four or five pieces that are to be included. Because one selection must come from outside of the language arts class, almost anything a student writes in any class is a candidate for inclusion in his or her portfolio. The 1999 rules allow a teacher to indicate the location of spelling, grammar, and punctuation errors, but prohibit any direct corrections. This means that a teacher can tell students that they have misspelled a word, they have made an error in grammar, or used inappropriate punctuation, but cannot provide the correct usage. Once a student is told that he or she has made an error, it is up to the student to figure out how to correct it. Furthermore, the ethical guidelines say that students are not supposed to obtain help from anyone else, including parents or peers.

These rules are intended to serve a purpose that goes beyond the protection of the integrity of the assessment system. They also make it unethical to teach writing using any approach other than the *writing process method,* an extension of the whole-language method of teaching reading. The director of the Kentucky Writing Program describes this policy as "best practice in writing." Advocates of these approaches believe that reading and writing are entirely natural processes and that students acquire these skills most easily with minimum interference from teachers. It is assumed that learning to read and learning to write are the same as learning to speak. Children learn to speak naturally, needing no prompting from parents. Correcting a young child's speech can interfere with this natural process and supposedly can cause speech defects. The writing process approach assumes the same for writing. It is asserted that correcting a child's writing will inhibit the child and prevent him or her from becoming a good writer.

Writing process is not so much a method of teaching writing as it is a philosophical justification for why students should learn to write on their own. There is also the belief among advocates of the writing process method that the most important outcome of writing activities by students in school is the opportunity for them to express their feelings; that is, advocates of the writing process method believe all writing is personal. The role of writing as a means of communication is deemphasized. Avoiding criticisms of student writing is believed to encourage the expression of feelings by students.

One of the strongest recommendations of the OEA panel[29] was that the portfolio scores be removed from the accountability index. The OEA report states, "Evidence about the adequacy of the measurement provided by the portfolios is limited but sufficiently negative to indicate that the portfolio scores are not at this time appropriate for use in the KIRIS high-stakes accountability system." That suggestion has been rejected by the KDE because of their purported value for instruction. Again according to the OEA report, "Evidence about the impact of the program [portfolios] on instruction is limited, largely anecdotal, and inconsistent."

The use of writing portfolios as a way to assess writing ability should be strongly discouraged. The experience in Kentucky provides evidence that they cannot be scored reliably and that the rules that must be implemented to protect their integrity end up having a strongly negative effect on the teaching of writing. It is not too much of an exaggeration to say that Kentucky's students are poorer writers as a result of the inclusion of writing portfolio scores in school indexes.

Concluding Comments About Lessons from Kentucky

The Kentucky accountability system has been in existence since 1992 and cost almost a billion dollars in its first eight years.[30] Despite the enormous commitment of resources, there is scant evidence supporting the success of Kentucky's educational reform. The only indicators of improvement in student achievement are KIRIS/CATS accountability scores, and these seem to be the result of changes in the scaling of the test.

One reason for the failure of the Kentucky accountability system is the confused and contradictory theoretical basis for the assessment. The KERA legislation and KIRIS itself were based on a traditionalist approach to education. Traditionalists believe that all students should be taught a standard liberal arts curriculum and that all students can learn this material at a high level or at least should be given the opportunity to do so. Associated with traditionalism is a commitment to conventional instructional methods, the recognition that students must be required to learn some content, the value of hard work, and commitment to high standards. It also places teachers in a central role in the education process. First and most fundamentally, traditionalists are committed to the belief that the level of academic achievement as determined by academic achievement tests can be used to judge the effectiveness of a school.

The KDE, which is charged with the implementation of the assessment system, has adopted a progressive education philosophy.

Progressive educators advocate the adoption of a student-centered classroom in which students choose their own school activities. They also believe that the proper role of the teacher is that of a guide or consultant who can help students reach their own goals. Most significantly, they believe that students differ in academic ability and that not all students can succeed at the same level. They oppose the assessment of academic achievement associated with standards-based reform because they believe it is unfair to students with low ability. Even more important, they do not believe that the assessment of academic achievement is a legitimate way to evaluate the quality of schools and teachers.

The adoption of a progressive education policy by the KDE has led to the paradox of a system in which schools are required to improve their student's academic achievement as measured by KIRIS or CATS or face unpleasant consequences of the CATS accountability system while being required by the KDE to adopt progressive instructional strategies. The mandated strategies were never intended to increase academic achievement. At the same time, low-performing schools are discouraged from adopting instructional methods that have been shown to be effective in improving academic achievement.

Because of these conflicts in educational philosophies, Kentucky is squandering the most important benefit of standards-based reform, its capacity to pressure educators into adopting effective instructional strategies. If there are meaningful consequences attached to performance, it might be expected that teachers would seek the best ways to improve their student's performance. An examination of the instructional material used by the Distinguished Educators who are sent in to help low-performing schools is rife with references to cooperative learning, developmentally appropriate practices, self-directed learning, learning styles, and multiple intelligence—the language of progressive education.

The second reason that KERA, KIRIS, and CATS have failed to improve academic achievement in Kentucky is the structure of the assessment system itself. Too often, ideology was substituted for sound psychometric practice in the construction of the test.

The ultimate purpose of the test was to compare schools. The test was never intended to evaluate the performance of individual students. The best way of comparing schools is the tried and true multiple-choice, norm-referenced test. This is the way most states conduct their standards-based reform. The authors of the KIRIS/CATS assessment were too clever for this. They wanted to create an assessment that was like no other. They also wanted a test that included the project approach so beloved by progressive educators, that is, performance tasks and portfolios. As a result, on a per-pupil basis, Kentucky has the most expensive testing system of any state. At the same time, the system is characterized by poor reliability and validity.

After twelve years, despite constant vociferous criticism and a series of expensive, highly critical reports written by distinguished experts and after numerous panels and committees have cited a litany of shortcomings and suggested extensive changes that needed to be made, the system persists largely unchanged. There were great expectations for change and seeming agreement between the legislative branches and the governor's office in the spring of 1998. After the dust cleared and the laws were passed, the essential elements remained in place. Bureaucracies are characterized by inertia, and changes come slowly if at all. Many Kentucky citizens, all over the state, in and out of education, are convinced that this system is not working. They also believe that it is having a deleterious impact on education in their state. The system's supporters have been able to fend off their critics for twelve years, and by manipulating the scaling so that schools appear to be doing better, they have prevented meaningful changes in the system.

Notes

1. *Rose v. Council for Better Education, Inc.* 790 S.W. 2d 186 (Ky. 1989).
2. Lawrence Picus, "Estimating Costs of Alternative Assessment Programs: Case Studies in Kentucky and Vermont" (paper delivered at the annual meeting of the American Educational Research Association, Chicago, March 1997).
3. Bert Combs, *Creative Constitutional Law: The Kentucky School Reform Law* (Lexington, Ky.: Pritchard Committee for Academic Excellence).

4. The Evaluation Center, Western Michigan University, *Evaluation of the Development and Implementation of KIRIS Through December 1994 (KIER Report)* (Frankfort, Ky.: The Kentucky Institute for Educational Research, January 1995).

5. Ronald K. Hambleton, Richard M. Jaeger, Daniel Koretz, Robert Linn, Jason Millman, and Susan E. Phillips, *Review of the Measurement Quality of the Kentucky Instructional Results Information System, 1991–1994* (OEA Report) (Frankfort, Ky.: Office of Educational Accountability, 1995).

6. James Catterall, William Mehrens, J. M. Ryan, E. J. Flores, and P. M. Rubin, *Kentucky Instructional Results Information System: A Technical Review* (Frankfort, Ky.: Kentucky Legislative Research Commision, 1998).

7. Daniel Koretz and Sheila I. Barron, *The Validity of Gains in Scores on the Kentucky Instructional Results Information System* (Santa Monica, Calif.: RAND, 1998).

8. Western Michigan University Evaluation Center, *KIER Report.*

9. Office of Educational Accountability, *OEA Report.*

10. American Psychological Association, American Educational Research Association, and National Council on Measurement in Education, *Standards for Educational and Psychological Testing* (Washington, D.C.: American Psychological Association, 1985).

11. Office of Educational Accountability, *OEA Report.*

12. Koretz and Barron, "The Validity of Gains in Scores on the Kentucky Instructional Results Information System."

13. Wilmer W. Cody, "Commissioner Cody Comments on Education," *Louisville Courier Journal,* 13 December 1998, A10.

14. Robert Guitterez and Robert E. Slavin, "Achievment Effects of the Nongraded Elementary School: A Best Evidence Synthesis," *Review of Educational Research* 62, no. 4 (1992): 333–76.

15. Robert Glaser, "Instructional Technology and the Measurement of Learning Outcomes: Some Questions," *American Psychologist* 18 (1963) 519–21.

16. American Psychological Association, American Educational Research Association, and National Council on Measurement in Education, *Standards for Educational and Psychological Testing* (Washington, D.C.: American Psychological Association, 1999).

17. Richard M. Jaeger, "Certification of Student Competence," in *Educational Measurement: Third Edition*, ed. R. L. Linn (New York: MacMillan, 1989), 485–514.

18. John P. Poggio, D. R. Glassnapp, and D. S. Eros, "An Empirical Investigation of the Angoff, Ebel, and Nedelsky Standard-Setting Methods" (paper delivered at the meeting of the American Educational Research Association, Los Angeles, April 1981).

19. Richard M. Jaeger, D. Irwin, and D. Pratto, *An Iterative Structured Judgment Process for Setting Passing Scores on Competency Tests: Applied to the North Carolina High School Competency Test in Reading and Mathematics* (Greensboro, N.C.: University of North Carolina at Greensboro, Center for Educational Research and Evaluation, 1980).

20. R. L. Linn, George Madaus, and J. Pedulla, "Minimum Competency Testing: Cautions on the State of the Art," *American Journal of Education*, 91 (1982): 1–35.

21. Gene V. Glass "Standards and Criteria" *Journal of Educational Measurement* 15 (1978): 237–61.

22. Lorrie A. Shepard, "Setting Standards," in *Practices and Problems in Competency-Based Instruction*, ed. M. A. Bunda and J. R. Sanders (Washington, D.C.: National Council on Measurement in Education, 1979).

23. National Research Council, *Grading the Nation's Report Card: Evaluating NAEP and Transforming the Assessment of Educational Progress* (Academic Press, 1999).

24. Robert L. Linn, Daniel M. Koretz, Eva L. Bake, and Leigh Burstein, *The Validity and Credibility of the Achievement Levels for the National Assessment of Educational Progress in Mathematics* (Los Angeles: Center for the Study of Evaluation, University of California, 1999).

25. James Pellegrino, Lauress Wise, and Nambury Raju, "Guest Editors' Note," *Applied Measurement in Education*, 11, no. 1 (1998): 1–7.

26. Gene V. Glass, "Standards and Criteria."

27. George K. Cunningham, *Assessment in the Classroom* (London: Falmer Press, 1998).

28. R. Lukhele, David Thissen, and Howard Wainer, "On the Relative Value of Multiple-Choice, Constructed-Response, and Examinee-Selected Items on Two Achievement Tests," *Journal of Educational Measurement* 31, no. 3 (1994): 234–50.

29. Office of Educational Accountability, *OEA Report*. 4-3, 4-38.

30. Lawrence Picus, "Estimating Costs of Alternative Assessment Programs: Case Studies in Kentucky and Vermont."

Chapter 9

Accountability
Works in Texas

Darvin M. Winick
and Sandy Kress

Scores on national tests suggest that Texas public school students perform at higher levels than students from most other states, and many people are surprised with the results. Students from southern states with large minority populations are not supposed to lead the nation in academics, but in some categories Texas students outscore all others. Among the major, large industrial states, Texas has a claim on first place in elementary education. Scores for all student groups are going up.

There are many reasons why results are improving, but four factors are most important: leadership, accountability, decentralization, and sustained external pressure for results. There is a clear focus on student performance. The question is not whether schools are as good now as they used to be. They probably are. The real question is, how good do schools need to be? Standards that were appropriate when unskilled jobs were easy to find and many students were not expected to finish high school are now inadequate, so results must improve.

This paper is a slightly revised version of an October 19, 1998, presentation.

Texas School Reform

Education reform in Texas starts with the belief that better management of the public schools will bring improved results. Two simple premises are critical: Public schools can be effective and student performance can be improved. School improvement in Texas has been an important issue for almost two decades, and piece by piece essential changes have been introduced. An integrated, results-based accountability system is in place that includes curriculum standards, campus performance objectives, annual measurement, public reporting, rewards for success, and consequences for failure. Educators on each campus in the state choose instructional programs to fit the needs of their students. Public attention to academic results is keen.

Everyone is expected to pitch in. Students and parents have the major burden, but teachers and administrators are obligated to see that students do as well as possible and the larger community is responsible for seeing that the public system is well run and academically effective.

The recent history of Texas school reform began in the early 1980s. Ross Perot was appointed by Governor Mark White to head a panel of citizens to study public education and develop recommendations for improvement. Guided for the most part by educator recommendations, funding was increased, teacher pay levels were raised, and elementary class sizes were reduced. In order to maintain certification, teachers were required to pass a basic skills test. Perhaps the best-known reform was the highly publicized "no pass, no play" requirement for students. Although these reforms did not lead to noticeable improvement in student results, the effort began a shift of resources to the early grades and opened up the system to outside scrutiny. A select group of citizens, including several important members of the business community, was appointed to the Texas State Board of Education. Lasting attention to the academic performance of the public schools by the business community followed. Charles Duncan, former U.S. Secretary of Energy and an appointed state board member, kept the focus by continuing to ask publicly, "Are the kids learning?" Duncan helped organize the Texas Business and Education Coalition and served as its first business chair.

Reform activities sprouted in different parts of Texas during the remainder of the 1980s. Under pressure from the business community, school boards and administrators in Dallas and Houston began to explore means to increase system accountability. Local citizens' groups began to study school performance. A systematic "shining of the light" on academics was under way. Coincident with local experiments in the use of improved management techniques, elected officials were encouraged to take an interest in public school reform. A series of special commissions and blue ribbon panels studied and reported on school management, usually in conjunction with court-directed review of the state school finance system. Charles Miller, a Houston businessman, chaired a 1989 task force that successfully tied organizational and financial reform together. As one result, the legislature in 1991 appropriated funds for the Educational Economic Policy Center to study accountability in public education and to make recommendations to the legislature. This public research center, with Charles Miller as board chair, produced a three-part report, "A New Accountability System for Texas Public Schools," which proposed what it claimed would be the strongest public school accountability system in the country. With active business community support over formidable resistance of many special interest groups, the legislature adopted the bulk of the center's recommendations in 1993.

It is important to note that although Texas today has a fully integrated accountability system, the pieces of the system were not implemented in a particularly orderly manner. The reforms were promoted essentially when political and other considerations permitted. For example, the core of the accountability system was adopted before the state's content standards were made rigorous. There were standards at the time, so student progress on them could be measured. The goal simply was that improvement in student achievement must occur over time. As student performance has improved, at administratively and politically propitious times, standards and expectations have been raised. Revised state assessments are being placed into alignment with the more rigorous standards. Teacher training, textbooks, and other vital educational inputs are being improved to respond to both the revised assessments and the higher standards.

Leadership

Effective leadership is important. Longtime Lieutenant Governor Bill Hobby did much to keep attention on the performance of the schools. Governor Bill Clements helped create the Policy Center. The late Lieutenant Governor Bob Bullock and his education committee chair, Senator Bill Ratliff, insisted on legislative passage of the accountability system. Many business leaders helped drive reform. In addition to the contribution of Charles Duncan and Charles Miller, Paul Roth of Southwestern Bell helped organize the first major statewide, business-supported reform group, and Jim Kettlesen of Tenneco played a central role in organizing Texans for Education.

While governor of Texas, George W. Bush actively developed and promoted policies and legislation that created opportunities for education reform. His focus on early childhood education and the development of reading and comprehension skills was important, and his reading initiative became a major statewide movement. During Governor Bush's administration, a complete rewrite of the state education code was enacted, a new discipline management system was installed, and new, more rigorous curriculum standards were completed. Under the new code and accountability system, school administrators and teachers know what is expected and have great latitude to organize, program, and manage their schools to meet the standards. State-required reports and bureaucratic procedures are minimized. Governor Bush chose a commissioner of education, Mike Moses, who actively supported decentralization and cooperated in transferring authority from the state to the teachers and administration. The new code requires that poorly performing schools and districts be put on notice that they face "receivership" if results do not improve.

In January 1998, Governor Bush emphasized his interest in academic results by calling for an end to the practice of promoting students who are not ready for success in the next grade. As a rational progression to his call for reading proficiency by the end of third grade, he helped pass legislation that requires intensive attention to all third-grade students who do not pass the state's third-grade reading test before they enter fourth grade. Special funds are allocated for intensive reading programs. Legislation passed that requires all schools to assess reading readiness, beginning in kindergarten. Over time, passing requirements are scheduled to be put in place for reading and mathematics for promotion at the end of grades five and eight.

Governor Rick Perry, Bush's successor, continues the Texas push for performance. With the encouragement of Mike Moses's successor, Jim Nelson, and Governor Perry, the legislature recently passed a major mathematics initiative that parallels the earlier reading program. Special attention to reading and mathematics are part of the ongoing effort of the business community to maintain the pressure for improved results.

Accountability

Most people quickly agree that public schools should be held accountable for results, but as the history of school reform shows it is hard to obtain agreement on specifics. As hard as it is for business executives to understand, educators are not used to being held responsible for academic results. Like many "good" concepts, accountability is easier to talk about than implement. A set of commonsense steps is required for accountability for results to became a routine part of school system management:

- Clear curriculum standards describing what students should know and be able to do must be defined.

- Annual objectives must be set for the part of the curriculum to be covered in each grade on each campus.

- Assessment must be made of how well students in each grade on each campus are meeting established annual objectives.

- Reports of student achievement at each campus for each grade must be widely distributed.

- Recognition for educators on campuses meeting or exceeding standards must be available.

- Consequences for repeated failure must be genuine and important.

As sensible as the accountability steps seem, many educators have difficulty actually aligning their practices with them. Accepting responsibility for results is threatening in a culture where quantitative results have not traditionally been available to measure success. However, the idea that academic results must be used to judge the effectiveness of individual schools is gradually becoming accepted. Fortunately, Texas moved early to establish clear organizational goals for its public schools, and standards and annual objectives are no longer unusual. Accountability for results is a fact of life in Texas. Once involved, many teachers and administrators appreciate the recognition they receive for good student performance.

Reliable, objective, and standardized assessment of achievement is integral to accountability. However, opposition to consistent measurement runs deep among educators who fear the community reaction to "below average" results. Although technical problems exist, the opposition to standardized measurement is primarily political. Naturally, local district trustees, administrators and local realtors prefer laudatory reports and worry that test scores, which will be compared across schools, may show weaknesses in their school programs. Poor public school ratings may cause a drop in real estate values. Nevertheless, accountability is a hollow concept without clear standards and reliable measurement of results.

In Texas, annual standardized reading and mathematics tests are given to all eligible students in grades three through eight. Writing proficiency is tested in grades four, eight and ten, and high school students must pass an exit examination to graduate. Science and social science tests are given in grade eight. These criterion-referenced tests have made up the Texas Assessment of Academic Skills (TAAS), and all sample the state curriculum. Scores are not forced into a grading curve; all students are expected to pass. Tests are released to the public after each administration. The state is currently developing a new series of criterion-referenced assessments to match more stringent standards. The state's new test is called the Texas Assessment of Knowledge and Skills (TAKS). Students in grades three through eleven will participate in the new regime.

To obtain good measures of Texas student performance, policy makers chose to develop and use criterion-referenced instruments— that is, tests that directly sample the curriculum. All students are expected to pass. State educators participate in test development to assure that the assessments are aligned with content objectives. Texas tests are constructed by National Computer Systems and Harcourt Brace Educational Measurement, a prominent, national testing service. Their involvement provides all stakeholders with a degree of confidence in the validity and reliability of the assessment instruments. And finally, to make parents and citizens aware of the relationship that the state tests bear to national norm-referenced tests, state law requires periodic sampling of student performance by a reputable national test.

Strong legislation is in place to allow for a variety of responses to the results that students and schools achieve. Each campus in the state is rated annually as "exemplary," "recognized," "acceptable," or "low performing." Annual campus report cards that show grade-by-grade results are sent to all parents and released to the media. Results are reported by ethnic group. Measures of improvement and comparisons between schools with similar student demographics are available to the managers of the system and to the public. Detailed reports for each campus and district in the state are available in print and online. Individual sanctions are applied by the state for poor performance, up to and including closing or taking over a school or a district.

Perhaps the most fascinating feature of the accountability system is the actual impact on behavior in the field. Observations suggest that the "bright light" focus on low-performing schools is playing a major part in improving results in ineffective schools, particularly elementary schools, that previously seemed impervious to reform efforts. Reports from large school districts are that the replacement of mediocre principals, infusion of directed, additional resources, and the modification of practices are pervasive. For the first time, in many cases, parents are able to use facts to express concern. Faced with public reports of poor results, bureaucrats and politicians who previously had protected the status quo are permitting and sometimes supporting substantial change. As a result, even with rising standards, the number of low-performing schools in Texas was reduced from 257 in 1995 to 145 by 2000.

In addition, the accountability system has encouraged improvements in the better performing schools. Now, parents and teachers, confronted with higher ratings in similarly situated schools down the road or in a neighboring town, are forced to ask whether their students should do better. From 1995 to the 1999–2000 school year, the number of recognized schools increased from 1,004 to 2,009, and the number of exemplary campuses is up from 255 to 1,296.

Because of a system that now holds them accountable for results, district and campus leaders are more eager to find and deploy more effective instructional strategies. Administrators, principals, and teachers are more open to research-based techniques and materials, for instance, in early reading instruction. Math instruction, which was frequently delivered badly in elementary grades, seems to be improving. Different school configurations and more options for students are being considered.

Decentralization

A good accountability system both permits and requires decentralization. True results-based accountability requires the delegation of adequate authority to those who are held accountable. In other words, if a campus faculty is to be responsible for results, it is necessary to give them considerable control over the "how" of instruction. Historically, when frustrated by lack of achievement, legislators and "central" bureaucrats mandate solutions. Yet when the state maintains control of how instruction is delivered, it takes on much of the responsibility for student results. Local educators get a free ride when they can say, "The state made me do it." Merely suggesting that accountability is a good idea does not cause anything to happen. Publishing standards and assessing results are important steps, but the understanding that community-level program and administrative decisions have consequences is basic to allowing local control.

Educators are accustomed to defining their responsibilities in terms of what they do, not by the results of their efforts. Then, if they "do right" based on what their peers accept, they are not accountable for what happens to students. This odd attitude suggests that poor student performance is caused only by factors beyond the control of educators. Poor results can be conveniently blamed on heedless students, uncaring parents, miserly taxpayers, and timid legislators. The fact that this "no effect" argument is insulting to teachers, out of step with reality, and fatal for accountability has to be clearly understood. Good teachers and well-managed schools do make a difference in student performance. Decentralized decision making makes sense, and public recognition for local successes is fundamental to accountability. Consequences for lack of success are just as fundamental.

It is strange to see the confusion in many communities over decentralization. Many individuals who demand that the state mandate the adoption of their pet ideologies, textbooks, or programs ask at the same time for "local control." Some educators complain about state rules while asking the state for explicit directions so that difficult local decisions can be avoided. The inconsistency of both demanding mandates from a central authority and demanding local control is obvious, confusing, and contrary to good management.

In Texas, the necessary tie between authority and responsibility is clear, and substantial decentralization is in place. Local educators and elected school board members are expected to set local programs and reap rewards or sanctions for the results. Parents who are dissatisfied with academic results can take their concerns to locally elected or appointed officials.

External Pressure

Attempts to change public education are neither new, unusual, nor very successful. Over the years, educators have received many valuable suggestions from outsiders. The most common response to calls for improved results is to hold a conference and propose further study. Because "reformers" have little staying power, the key for an existing system in handling calls for change is to study and stall. The study-report-hold-a-conference-and-go-home strategy produces headlines, but little real change. Clearly, an effort beyond issuing reports is required.

In reality, causing change to happen is tough work. Special interest groups in education are large, well organized, and effective in protecting the status quo. Education school faculties join with public school interest groups to form a powerful lobby. Protection of existing jobs, programs, and vendor relationships is often the first priority of school officials. As the major employer and purchaser of goods and services in many communities, school board members and administrators have considerable patronage potential. Many individuals, including some educators, have a large economic stake in existing programs, textbooks, and services.

In addition, and of great importance in understanding the school improvement process, many citizens are reluctant to criticize local public schools. It is easy to accept the fact that students in other communities are not receiving an adequate education, but it is tough to accept deficiencies in one's own neighborhood school. Denial is a real and powerful emotion. Parents want to believe that their children's schools are good. Publicly complaining about the system and its powerful vested interests can be very unpopular. Parents fear that their complaints may cause their children to be unfairly treated. At the local level, it's far easier to organize a booster club than a reform movement.

In Texas, a well-organized, permanent force from outside the system is in place to combat the reluctance of parents and the organized resistance of special interests that are built into the system. Four fundamental principles are widely promoted:

- Educating children is more important than protecting jobs and vendors.

- Excellence must be publicly rewarded and poor performance censured.

- School administrators and teachers are accountable for the parts of public education that they control.

- Support for new funding is contingent on the accomplishment of agreed-upon reforms.

An active, full-time effort is ongoing to exert external pressure for accountability and decentralization. The effort goes beyond organizing business partnerships, local parent groups, neighborhood initiatives, and educator-controlled, site-based management committees. The effort includes determining what policies are needed to force constructive change, organizing a base of political support, setting up and funding permanent organizations around which this support can rally, and building an experienced, professional governmental affairs operation to contribute to the development of sound public policy and legislation. Three groups have provided persistent pressure.

Established in 1989, the Texas Business and Education Coalition (TBEC) exists to gain public acceptance and provide a permanent support base for public school accountability. Organized and supported by the business community, TBEC is a permanent force for change. Its board includes business executives and educators, but not elected officials. Educators are asked to join if they agree with TBEC positions. TBEC is considered a major voice for educational quality and high standards. Its representatives deal actively with state leaders, elected officials, legislative committees, and educational interest groups. A full-time, paid executive director and staff help develop and support local groups and community leaders who are interested in school reform.

Texas corporate members of the Business Roundtable and other large companies fund Texans for Education (TFE), an active lobbying group. This organization provides year-round contact with gubernatorial and legislative staff, legislative committees and the State Board of Education. During legislative sessions, TFE representatives actively participate in the evaluation, development, and support of legislative proposals that have an impact on public education. To gain leverage, TFE maintains close contact with the governmental affairs representatives of major corporations that are active in Texas. When critical issues arise, TFE works to develop a unified "business" approach in support of standards and accountability.

In addition, the Governor's Business Council (GBC) provides strong support for specific education initiatives. Made up of some 100 senior executives of Texas employers, the GBC actively supports public policies important to the economic health of the state and is a strong supporter of efforts to improve education. During the administration of Governor Bush, the GBC had a premier role in change issues, including:

- Protection and enhancement of the state public school accountability system.

- Support for the governor's initiative to improve preschool and elementary school reading instruction and to develop alternatives to social promotion for children who do not read well.

- Development of start-up and continuing technical and financial support for public charter schools.

- Introduction of technology innovation into the public school system.

- Improvement of teacher preparation and training programs.

GBC, TFE, and TBEC representatives work together on the development of legislative, regulatory, and policy positions. Paid professionals and many volunteers are involved in each group. Efforts are continuous.

Individual educators and community leaders also help maintain and protect accountability and decentralization in Texas.

High-quality teachers were among the first educators to see the value of stressing results and rewarding academic improvement, and many educators are now supporters. Backing from legislative leadership is essential as well. However, the major thrust and financial support comes from representatives of the business community. Though many business people have little taste for the controversy that school reform involves, enough understand the importance of public education to create a powerful interest group. There probably is no other organized force with the ability to challenge the status quo. Those who attempt to cause significant, systemic change in public education with less focus, organization, and effort will likely be disappointed.

Systemic Change

Fundamental, systemic change is the true reform goal. To force change, test results for individual campuses and districts are reported to the parents and the public and are widely covered by the media. In Texas, a focus on academic results becomes the rule rather than the exception. Decentralization and results-based accountability cause as well as allow fundamental changes in behavior among students, teachers, and administrators.

- Students and parents understand that individual effort is important and a requirement for promotion through the grades.

- Teachers have a greater opportunity to demonstrate good instruction, be sensitive to student needs, manage their classrooms, and remove disruptive youngsters.

- Principals have a better chance to show their communities that schools are effective and they can shape their schools' policies, budgets, and practices.

- School districts are freed from burdensome state control and regulation and are largely deregulated.

- The commissioner of education can focus on the measurement and evaluation of local school performance.

316   Testing Student Learning, Evaluating Teaching Effectiveness

Deregulation also opens up opportunity for innovation through charters and alternative programs. In Texas, parents and students have choices. Students attending poorly performing schools may be eligible for a public education grant to transfer to a better school, and parents may join together to seek an open enrollment or local charter to establish a new school that will better suit their children's needs. With encouragement from Governor Bush, a privately funded resource center and a financial foundation were established to assist innovative charter schools.

As surprising as this news may be, experts around the country commonly regard education policies in Texas to be among the best in the nation. *Education Week* gave Texas a solid "A" for its accountability system. Other national groups also have been complimentary.

Results Are Encouraging

In 1996, many people, including most Texans, were surprised when white fourth-graders in Texas ranked first among their peers in the nation in math on the respected National Assessment of Education Progress (NAEP). And so did African-American fourth-graders. Hispanic fourth-graders came in sixth, well ahead of other states with large Hispanic populations. A higher portion of Texas white fourth-graders scored at or above the proficient level than those in any other participating state. Recently released NAEP results from the 2000 mathematics assessment validate the strong performance of Texas students.

Outcomes on the 1998 NAEP writing assessments are also impressive. Texas student performance ranked among the best in the nation. In reading, 1998 NAEP results showed Texas white student performance second only to Connecticut. Hispanic and African-American students placed ninth and tenth.

Texas was one of thirteen states that participated in the most recent international benchmarking study (Third International Mathematics and Science Study, 1999). Texas, with the highest portion of low-income students of the participating states, had the second-highest scores. Texas students scored above the international average in mathematics.

Perhaps more telling is the fact that Texas student performance results are consistently strong when compared with the results in other large, high-minority-population states. On a cost/benefit basis, Texas public schools do very well. Although recently increased, Texas per-pupil expenditures for public education have historically been below the national average. Yet Texas academic results are consistently above average, sometimes well above average. Relatively speaking, on average, Texas citizens get a "good buy" from their public schools.

Texas's state academic performance measures consistently show steady, strong improvement. The percentage passing all TAAS tests in all grades has risen from 55 percent in 1994 to 80 percent in 2000. Improvements in mathematics are especially pleasing. Minority students have improved at a faster rate than white students. The shrinking gap between African-American and Hispanic student scores and white student scores is important as a policy matter and as a community concern. Expectations are for all students to pass the state test.

Inevitably with a high-stakes accountability system, concerns arise that some of the players may encourage inappropriate exemptions from testing or actually engage in cheating and other fraudulent activity. Although there have been examples of such behavior and the state education agency has stepped up monitoring, these abuses do not seem to be widespread. Indeed, exemptions are being reduced. In 2000, Texas tested almost 2 million students—more than 90 percent of all the children in grades three through eight and grade ten. From 1996 to 2000, limited English proficiency exemptions fell from 62,000 to under 30,000. Special education exemptions fell by more than 3,000 students.

During the same four-year period, the number of high school students taking advanced placement exams increased by more than 50 percent. A record number of students, more than 100,000, took the SAT in 1998—Texas reported the largest increase in participants of any state in the country. Now more than half of all Texas high school graduates take the SAT. Even with the dramatic increase in the number of students taking the test, average scores have not declined.

Challenges Remain

In Texas, test scores are up for every grade and, indeed, every ethnic group. Building on this progress is now possible. Having a strong performance measurement process, robust accountability system, and organized public support network in place, Texas can now consider further reform. Being the most improved in the country does not mean that results are good enough for the challenges of the times. Constant improvement is occurring and additional challenges remain.

- Measurement of schooling results must begin earlier. Assessment of program success prior to the end of third grade is necessary if critical, early instruction is to be evaluated. The number of students who are excluded from accountability ratings must be systematically reduced. Only those who are incapable of participating should be left out. The results from Spanish versions of the TAAS and the results for many special-needs students have recently been included, and eventually all students will participate in the accountability system from the beginning to the completion of their public school career.

- Beginning in 2003, a revised, more rigorous assessment system (TAKS) was activated. Schools now need to meet new passing standards. Still, most schools should expect that most students will pass. Objectives, as a matter of policy, ought increasingly to focus on high levels of proficiency. The bar must be raised for all schools, whether merely acceptable or exemplary. The new test regime must garner public support as standards are raised.

- The plan to eliminate the causes for social promotion is an important policy advancement. Individual school administrators and faculty need to share responsibility with students and parents on this issue. A student ought not to be promoted until he or she has a reasonable opportunity to succeed in more advanced work. Social promotion is common, and it does no one, least of all the artificially promoted youngster, any good. A clear incentive to educate

students effectively in the first place must be in place, and
if extra intervention is needed to get a student to the proficiency level required in the next grade, success of such an
intervention must become a regular part of campus
accountability.

- Increased attention to high school performance is needed.
  Currently, the state requires for graduation that high school
  students pass a fundamental reading, writing, and mathematics achievement assessment. But it is wrong to pretend
  that good jobs and/or college success await graduates who
  accomplish only the fundamentals. Additional knowledge
  and skills, particularly in mathematics and the sciences, are
  needed if the high school diploma is to signify readiness for
  higher education or the world of work.

- And finally, although the number of high school dropouts
  is decreasing, concern exists for these students who do not
  complete high school.

- Statutorily required alternative programs for below-grade-
  level students need further development.

The accountability system in Texas has brought about significant improvement in the elementary schools and discernible
progress in the middle schools. Improvement in the performance
of high school students is more difficult to verify. With better-
prepared youngsters now entering high school, more should be
expected. Additional attention to the effectiveness of high school
programs is now appropriate.

The Task Ahead

The challenges ahead for public education in Texas are complex
and varied, but there are ongoing initiatives that will likely continue improvement trends. Performance gains are expected.

Former Commissioner Moses, with the support of Governor
Bush and the approval of the State Board of Education, developed a new curriculum that is clear, rigorous, and based on more
specific standards than the one it replaces. New educational

expectations, based on the new curriculum, will yield better courses, textbooks, and instruction in the years to come. Governor Perry is actively continuing the effort to improve instruction.

Texas is moving toward the goal of a first-class education for its young citizens. Progress accelerated during the Bush administration. Support continues. Yet, there is more to do. It is a fact that academic performance in Texas began its rise as the accountability system was put in place and the public became more aware of actual results. Cause and effect can be debated, of course. It is possible that schools just got better. However, most observers are convinced that leadership, accountability, and decentralization are the cause, and better academic results are the effect. External pressure for good performance must continue.

Sustaining progress is a constant challenge. Rewards and sanctions are valuable to the extent that they are fairly and wisely used, but a reluctance remains within public education to make difficult personnel decisions. Teacher preparation programs simply do not prepare professionals to teach effectively in modern, accountability-driven schools. Teacher certification requirements are inadequate. It is always easier to go public with excuses than attack the status quo. Parents are too often satisfied if their children receive good grades and a diploma, even if academic quality is missing. Grade inflation is a pernicious problem. Low college entrance requirements put little pressure on the public school system. A long history of shifting blame for poor results to parents for lack of support and to the legislature for not providing adequate funds is not easily overcome.

Better evaluation of instructional programs is a management task. Individual program evaluation must be accomplished at the local level for accountability to have meaning. But comfortable ("sound good, feel good") ideas are too easily accepted. Some local educators look for easy ways to raise test scores, preferably a way that will not change the existing organization or upset teacher education programs, entrenched interests, or important vendors. Too many program selection decisions are not based on qualified research.

As long as any students achieve below their ability level, school reformers have work to do. Academic success varies widely at the individual school level. Students on some supposedly good suburban campuses score well below average when compared with students on similarly situated campuses. Many schools with supposedly hard-to-educate students have embarrassingly low test score averages while other schools in the same neighborhood with similar students have high scores. The excuses for poor performance are common, but hard to accept when evaluated at the individual campus level. It is hard to understand the patience some school districts have for low-performing schools.

Evidently, gains in student performance occur when gains are expected and rewarded. Business and community groups must help by keeping the pressure on the system for graduates who can read, write, and compute. Support from political leaders is important. Public attention and support is vital. Texas's experience shows that good educators and community leaders can be recruited as partners for change. Some teacher organizations have been strong allies. Many individual educators have become strong supporters of a well-administered reward system. There is ample work for everyone. A fully informed public must continue to back results-driven accountability, for no single accomplishment will have greater impact on our society's future than establishing excellence in our public schools.

In an age of cynicism about government, it is easy to focus only on the difficulties that remain in public education and thus be pessimistic. More appropriately, the journey ahead should be acknowledged and the progress to-date recognized. The work ahead requires both a celebration of the vast dedication and effort of the many who have produced the gains to date and an understanding that future commitments of effort and support are critical.

We have only one next generation to educate. For its sake, then, we bear a great responsibility to get it right.

Conference Agenda

HOOVER INSTITUTION SYMPOSIUM
Testing America's Schoolchildren

Lou Henry Hoover Building, Room 102
Hoover Institution
Stanford University
October 19, 1998

Agenda

10:00 AM   **Discussion with California Policy Makers**
             MODERATOR:
                      Williamson M. Evers,
                      Hoover Institution
             Informal discussion with members of the
             California Board of Education, board staff,
             California legislative staff, and other state and
             local policy makers.

NOON   LUNCH, Stanford Faculty Club

1:30 PM   **Symposium with Invited Members of the
             General Public**
             WELCOME
                      John Raisian, *Director*,
                      Hoover Institution
             INTRODUCTION
                      Williamson M. Evers,
                      Hoover Institution

SPEAKERS:
Barbara Foorman,
University of Texas, Houston Medical Center:
"Early Reading Assessment"

Stan Metzenberg,
California State University, Northridge; California Academic Standards Commission:
"What Do National and International Assessments Tell Us About Math and Science Reform?"

George Cunningham,
University of Louisville:
"Lessons to Be Learned from Kentucky's Accountability System"

Brian Stecher,
RAND:
"Portfolio Assessment"

Sandy Kress,
Aken, Gump, Strauss, Hauer & Feld, Austin, Texas:
"Assessment and Accountability: The Texas Case"

Herbert Walberg,
University of Illinois:
"Examinations to Improve Educational Productivity"

Contributors

GEORGE K. CUNNINGHAM is a professor in the department of educational and counseling psychology at the University of Louisville. He is the author or coauthor of three textbooks on psychological and educational measurement: *Educational and Psychological Measurement* (1986), *Measurement and Evaluation in Psychology and Education*, fifth edition (1991), and *Assessment in the Classroom: Constructing and Interpreting Tests* (1998). He frequently consults with state government agencies regarding the design of testing programs.

WILLIAMSON M. EVERS is a research fellow at the Hoover Institution, serves on the White House Commission on Presidential Scholars, and served during 2001–2002 on the National Educational Research Policy and Priorities Board. During 2003, he served as a senior adviser for education to Administrator L. Paul Bremer of the Coalition Provisional Authority in Iraq. He also is a member of the panels that write mathematics and history questions for California's statewide testing system and served as a commissioner of the California State Commission for the Establishment of Academic Content and Performance. He is editor of and contributor to *What's Gone Wrong in America's Classrooms* (1998); coeditor of and cocontributor to *School Accountability* (2002); contributor to *A Primer on America's Schools* (2001); cocontributor to *Our Schools and Our Future* (2003); and coeditor of *Teacher Quality* (2002) and *School Reform: The Critical Issues* (2001).

JACK M. FLETCHER is a professor in the department of pediatrics at the University of Texas–Houston Health Science Center, and associate director of the Center for Academic and Reading Skills. For the past 20 years, he has done research on many aspects of the development of reading, language, and other cognitive skills in children. Recently, he served on the RAND Reading Study Group, the National Research Council Committee on Scientific Principles in Education Research, and the President's Commission on Excellence in Special Education.

BARBARA R. FOORMAN is professor of pediatrics and director of the Center for Academic and Reading Skills at the University of Texas–Houston Health Science Center. She is widely published in the area of reading and language development. She serves on the editorial boards of several journals and national consensus committees on reading and is principal investigator of several federally funded grants. She was the chairwoman of the Houston Independent School District's Committee on a Balanced Approach to Reading and worked on the revision of the Texas Primary Reading Inventory, a diagnostic test used in 95 percent of the school districts in Texas and in several other states.

DAVID J. FRANCIS is professor and chair of psychology at the University of Houston and director of the Texas Institute for Measurement, Evaluation, and Statistics. He has conducted research on normative and disordered development of cognitive and educational skills in children, particularly in the areas of reading and language, with special emphasis on the statistical and psychometric aspects of these developmental processes. Dr. Francis recently served as chair of the Advisory Council on Education Statistics and as an advisor to the Department of Education during Negotiated Rule-Making for the No Child Left Behind Act of 2002 and is currently serving on the Independent Review Panel for the National Assessment of Title I.

SANDY KRESS is a partner in the law firm Akin, Gump, Strauss, Hauer & Feld. He served as senior advisor to President George W. Bush on education-policy aspects of the No Child Left Behind Act of 2002. Kress previously served as president of the board of trustees of the Dallas Public Schools. He serves on the Education Commission of the States as an appointee of then Texas governor George W. Bush. He has also served as counsel to the Governor's Business Council and Texans for Education and as a member of the Texas Business and Education Coalition. Kress was appointed by Texas lieutenant governor Bob Bullock to the Educational Economic Policy Center. He was later asked to chair the center's Accountability Committee. This committee produced the public school accountability system that was later adopted into Texas state law.

WILLIAM A. MEHRENS is a private consultant and a professor emeritus of measurement at Michigan State University. He has held office in several professional organizations, including serving as president of the National Council on Measurement in Education (NCME), president of the Association for Measurement and Evaluation in Guidance, and vice president of Division D of the American Educational Research Association. He is a coauthor of *Measurement and Evaluation in Education and Psychology,* currently in its fourth edition.

STAN METZENBERG is an associate professor of biology at California State University–Northridge. He is a member of the California State Curriculum Development and Supplemental Materials Commission. He has served on the Science Content Review Panel for the California Standardized Testing and Reporting examinations and was a science consultant to the California State Commission for the Establishment of Academic Content and Performance Standards. His research is focused on the molecular biology of infectious disease agents, specifically HIV and Taenia solium.

RICHARD P. PHELPS taught secondary school mathematics and science in the village of Baskouré, Burkina Faso, in West Africa. He has held research positions at the Organisation for Economic Co-operation and Development, the U.S. General Accounting Office, Westat, and Indiana's Education Department. He wrote *Kill the Messenger: The War on Standardized Testing* (Transaction Books, 2003) and edited *Defending Standardized Testing* (Lawrence Erlbaum, 2004). He also edits a weekly column, "In Defense of Testing," for the EducationNews.org Web site and serves in the Consultants Network of the Education Consumers Clearinghouse.

ALAN R. SIEGEL is a professor of computer science in the Courant Institute of Mathematical Sciences at New York University. In the mid-1970s, as part of a program run by the City University of New York system, he taught inner-city teenagers remedial mathematics—beginning with the addition of one-digit numbers and ending with basic algebra.

At NYU, he has taught graduate courses in such topics as the design of integrated circuits and the mathematical analysis of algorithms. He has published numerous research papers in theoretical computer science as well as fundamental results in probability and geometry. He has served as director of the doctoral program, director of industrial relations, and deputy chairman for the department of computer science at NYU.

BRIAN STECHER is a senior social scientist in the education program at RAND. His research emphasis is applied educational measurement, including the implementation, quality, and impact of state assessment and accountability systems; the cost, quality, and feasibility of performance-based assessments in mathematics and science; and the development and validation of licensing and certification examinations. He is also a program evaluator, and he recently directed the statewide evaluation of the California Class Size Reduction initiative. Stecher is a member of the Technical Design Group, advising the California Department of Education on the development of that state's accountability system. He has published widely in professional journals, and he is currently a member of the editorial board of the *Educational Assessment Journal.*

HERBERT J. WALBERG is university scholar and emeritus research professor of education and psychology at the University of Illinois at Chicago. He has written and edited more than fifty-five books, including the *International Encyclopedia of Educational Evaluation* and *Psychology and Educational Practice.* He is a fellow of the Advancement of Science, the American Psychological Association, and the Royal Statistical Society. Walberg also is a founding fellow and vice president of the International Academy of Education, headquartered in Brussels, for which he edits a booklet series on effective educational practices that is distributed by UNESCO.

DARVIN M. WINICK is an organizational psychologist and a retired management consultant. He is a senior research fellow in the college of education at the University of Texas–Austin. He is chairman of the National Assessment Governing Board and a member of NAGB's committee on standards, design, and methodology. Winick has been working on public school reform since 1983.

Index